A FORTY-DAY
STUDY
of the BIBLICAL
STORY

The Story of Christ

• VOLUME ONE: PREPARING THE WAY •

RICK JORY

WESTBOW
PRESS®
A DIVISION OF THOMAS NELSON
& ZONDERVAN

WestBow Press books may be ordered through booksellers or by contacting:

WestBow Press
A Division of Thomas Nelson & Zondervan
1663 Liberty Drive
Bloomington, IN 47403
www.westbowpress.com
1 (866) 928-1240

ISBN: 978-1-9736-9471-7 (sc)
ISBN: 978-1-9736-9472-4 (hc)
ISBN: 978-1-9736-9470-0 (e)

Library of Congress Control Number: 2020911449

Print information available on the last page.

WestBow Press rev. date: 07/01/2020

To my grandson, Chase David Blissett

Sola Scriptura

CONTENTS

AUTHOR'S FOREWORD

I must admit, I wasn't displaying much love, joy, peace, patience, gentleness, kindness, or self-control. I had just discovered that the coursework for my second doctorate required the completion of a residency course titled *The Biblical Story.*

They had to be kidding!

For my theological education, I had spent five years on my masters—centered on the Bible.

This was followed by another five years as I worked on my first doctorate—centered on the Bible.

And I was now pursuing a second doctorate—centered on the Bible.

But apparently this wasn't enough. The degree requirements mandated one additional course that would be centered on the Bible.

This meant joining other doctoral students at Dallas Theological Seminary listening to a week of lectures—centered on the Bible.

Did I really have to do this?

Attending the on-campus course meant a repeat of the long drive from Denver to Dallas. I would be staying in student housing for the week—decent and functional, but the creature comforts are well hidden. McDonald's and Schlotzsky's would replace my wife's cooking.

Not good.

And daily, I would have to sit in a class and hear some professor tell me about the Bible.

Don't get me wrong. Studying the Bible is my passion. It is a gratifying, on-going journey of wonderful surprises. There is always more to learn and new and fascinating connections to make.

I am not sure why I'm wired this way, but I find enjoyment in digging deeply into each book of the Bible, pouring through commentaries, and referring to the original languages when and where necessary. The more I explore the Bible, the more I recognize these writings are truly God-breathed. And when the God of all of creation has taken the time to speak to us, I am interested in what He has to say.

Back to Dallas though, what could a simple, one-semester overview of the Bible add to what I already knew? Wouldn't this be a waste of time?

Early Monday, when the day for the first class arrived, I found myself sitting in a classroom, joined by eleven or so other students. Before the professor walked in, several of us shared our moderate disenchantment in having to take the course.

Things quickly changed.

Dr. Charles Bayliss entered the room, said an opening prayer, and then began his lecture. By first break, I was hooked. I don't remember whether it was the first day of class or the second, but I stayed after class for almost two hours asking Dr. Bayliss question after question and listening intently as he provided gracious and thought-provoking answers.

Dr. Bayliss has changed the way I read and study the Bible. I have not taught the Bible the same way since taking his course. Nor have I preached or listened to a sermon in the same way. Actually, after taking that one course, I haven't lived my life as a Christian in the same way either.

So, what happened? What changed?

As you continue reading, you'll find out. But perhaps, for now, I can share four observations specific to this volume and our study of the Old Testament:

1. We learn the Old Testament as a jumble of separate, and in most cases, unrelated stories. Nothing promotes seeing these as an integrated message from God—*the* Biblical Story. Many of the Old Testament's connections to the New Testament remain obscure.
2. We avoid spending time in the Old Testament. Afterall, we're Christians—and we learn about Christ in the New Testament.
3. Even when we do take time to read from the Old Testament, much of it is hard to understand and is confusing. To a large extent, this is due to the material not being organized chronologically.
4. Regardless of whether we are studying the Old Testament or the New Testament, we go about it from an entirely incorrect perspective. The Bible is not our story. It is God's story. But we do our best to make it about us.

A Forty-Day Study of the Biblical Story addresses each of these observations. Let's look at these in more detail.

1. We learn the Old Testament as a jumble of separate, and in most cases, unrelated stories.

    To understand this first point, allow a rough analogy. There is not much enjoyment in contemplating a single piece from a jigsaw puzzle. It may create some level of interest—but not much. Even looking at three pieces, or even ten pieces, isn't that interesting.

    What makes a jigsaw puzzle attention-grabbing is the process of figuring out how the pieces fit together. Slowly, a pleasant, unified, comprehensible picture begins to appear. The more complete that image becomes, the more anxious we are to grab another piece and see where and how it fits.

    In some ways, the books and stories of the Old Testament are like the pieces to a jigsaw puzzle. In and of themselves they create some level of interest—but they don't become attention-grabbing until we begin to see how the individual pieces relate to the whole. And the whole includes all of the Bible—both the Old Testament and the New Testament.

    Unfortunately, our study of the Old Testament may never reach beyond looking at the individual pieces. And perhaps there is a reason for this. Whether you are new to the church, or a life-long churchgoer, your exposure to the Bible has probably been much like mine. Portions of the Bible are discussed piecemeal. Each week we are given a new sliver of the biblical text. All of this is informative, and we walk away with a greater understanding of the revelation that God has given us.

    But nothing fits the pieces together. How is the book of Leviticus connected to the book of Hebrews? How is John's reason for writing his Gospel related to Psalm 2? How do we connect the covenant ceremony of Genesis 15 with the cross—much less understand that ceremony to begin with? Why is the book of Ruth included as part of the Bible? What does it have to do with anything? Or better yet, why do we have the book of Esther—where God is not mentioned at all? What makes each of these important? How are they related, or are they?

In short, how is God's story—God's revelation—unified?

And that's where *A Forty-Day Study of the Biblical Story* comes in. We will journey through scripture in a way that brings all of the bits and pieces into a unified whole—because almost all of our focus is going to be on what makes the Biblical Story whole: Jesus Christ. We examine the Old Testament through the lens of what we learn about Jesus.

And as we put these seemingly unrelated pieces together, we begin to see a picture emerge. Everything starts to make sense. Everything fits. Every component is exactly what it needs to be such that we end up with a perfect design and an integrated whole.

2. The second observation is that we avoid spending time in the Old Testament.

    This is somewhat related to the first observation. Because Christianity centers on Christ, many of us focus most of our time with the writings contained in the New Testament.

    This makes sense. Here, we find the accounts of Jesus of Nazareth—the Christ. We read about his words and his works. We learn about his birth and his life, and his death and resurrection. As followers of Christ, all of this is relevant and rewarding.

What would happen, though, if we looked at the Old Testament specifically to find out what it teaches us about this same Jesus of Nazareth? Wouldn't this change not only how we study the Bible, but also what portions of the Bible we decide to study?

Let's use the book of Leviticus as an example. It offers some tough reading. Not many of us will accelerate our cars on the drive home in order to skip dinner and dig into the text of Leviticus.

But what happens if we connect Leviticus to the book of Hebrews, and to portions of Jesus' teachings that we call the Sermon on the Mount, and add to this what the feasts of Israel have to do with the Messiah? Going through the relevant portions of Leviticus this way allows the text to make sense and builds upon our knowledge of who Jesus is.

Using our jigsaw puzzle analogy, we begin to see that Leviticus has many, many pieces that are part of the overall puzzle (which is true of every book of the Old Testament). We can't complete the picture without these pieces. Our study of Leviticus becomes meaningful and enjoyable—we'd be missing something if we hadn't taken the time to go through this portion of God's Word.

Studying the Bible this way—focusing on how all of the biblical text points to Jesus—lets us see that Christ is as much a part of the Old Testament as he is the New Testament. And that's the approach we take in this volume. We go through the Old Testament focusing on how it points to Jesus.

Even though this first volume is on the Old Testament, it contains close to 300 verses and passages of scripture from the New Testament. This wasn't by design. It came about because the New Testament sheds light on the Old Testament (and in volume 2, we'll see how the Old Testament sheds light on the New Testament).

The Bible is an integrated message—a unified story. And making these connections not only adds to our interest in the Old Testament, it gives us a deeper, broader view of who Jesus is and why he came to earth.

And that's also where *A Forty-Day Study of the Biblical Story* comes in. It shows the importance of every element of the Old Testament because each of these points to Christ, leading us to a more correct and complete understanding of who Jesus is and, as importantly, why we need him.

3. The third observation relates to how the Bible is organized— or perhaps, disorganized. This makes reading the Bible, particularly major portions of the Old Testament, confusing.

   Normally we are exposed to portions of the Old Testament piecemeal—but when we do get serious about Bible study, sooner or later we go about reading the Bible cover-to-cover. There is nothing wrong with this approach. But the books of the Bible are not organized chronologically. Unless someone has provided us with a history of Israel alongside of what we are reading, and organizes what we study along a timeline that parallels that history, we are in a fog of confusion.

   Let's take the writing of the prophet Hosea, for example. Here is the first sentence of his text:

   > This is the word of the LORD that came to Hosea son of Beeri in the days of Uzziah, Jotham, Ahaz, and Hezekiah, kings of Judah,

and of Jeroboam son of Jehoash, king of Israel.
(Hosea 1:1)

How many of these people do we know at first glance? Are any of them important? What or who is Judah? Is that important to know? What is Israel? When did Hosea write this? He tells us God spoke to him in the days of Uzziah, but when did Uzziah live? What was happening? Why did this writing make it into the Bible?

The second verse reads:

> When the LORD first spoke to Hosea, He told him, "Go, take a prostitute as your wife and have children of adultery, because this land is flagrantly prostituting itself by departing from the LORD."

What on earth is going on, literally? Is this true, what God is commanding Hosea to do? Why would He want Hosea to marry a prostitute? This must have been important to God, and He must have wanted His people to understand its importance. Did they?

Do we?

Reading Hosea won't give us the answer. But knowing the history of Israel will. And as we learn about this history and study the prophets along this timeline, we recognize that we don't need to understand all there is to know about people like Uzziah, or Jotham, or Ahaz. We just need to know about the failure of Israel's leaders and how God calls a specific prophet, at a specific time, to deliver a specific message, for a specific reason. We see that everything God has done is perfectly orchestrated and we understand the reasons behind His actions.

And that's also where *A Forty-Day Study of the Biblical Story* comes in. Much of our discussion in this first volume will follow Israel's history. We will study portions of the biblical text not as they have been arranged in the Bible, but chronologically, as each writing or story becomes relevant to what is happening with God's chosen people.

4.   The fourth, and perhaps most important observation, is that we approach the Bible with an entirely incorrect perspective.

This item centers on perspective. Today's preacher has the task of making the Bible relevant. This includes teaching on how to we are to apply the text to our lives as followers of Christ. But this means that the Bible is often presented to make each of the stories *about us.* "How do *I* apply this story to *me* and *my* circumstances in *my* world for *my* benefit?"

The Bible is God's story. God's story is *for* us—but very little of it is *about* us. In this study, we are going to focus on God. Yes, all that God has done—everything—is for us. But before we bring ourselves into the picture, we need to focus on what God is telling us about Himself. It is His story.

And this, too, helps us see that the story is about Jesus. *All* of scripture is about Jesus. Throughout our journey of the Biblical Story, we are going to find why this is the case. We'll learn why an obscure Galilean carpenter has become the center of all of history.

So that's what this two-volume work is about.

-   We will be able to see how each element of the Bible contributes to an integrated whole.

- In this volume, we will see how the entire Old Testament points to Christ, prepares the world for Christ, and shows why a Savior is needed.
- We will place the Biblical Story in parallel with the history of God's chosen people. The biblical text will be reviewed chronologically.
- We will pursue an overriding perspective that recognizes that the Bible is *not* about us. It is God's Story and we're going to read it from the perspective of it being God's Story.

Hopefully, after completing this, you too will never read, teach, or preach the Bible in the same way. Each time you turn to a page of scripture, you'll be asking, "How does this fit into *the* Story?" "What does this teach about God?"

And, as you find answers, you will be overjoyed at what God has done in the past, what He is doing today, and what God's plans are for our future. We serve an awesome God.

As to the structure of these two volumes, when I began working on this, I naively thought I could handle the material in forty relatively short lessons. I was at page 187 of the first draft and was only up to lesson 25—the post-exilic minor prophets (this has now become lessons 29 and 30). After a bit of head-scratching and soul-searching, I concluded it was best to break the material down into two volumes. This first volume devotes forty lessons to the Old Testament. Volume 2 includes forty lessons covering what we learn about Jesus from the New Testament.

Taking this approach means that, in general, each lesson is of a reasonable length, allowing this to be used as a daily devotional or for personal Bible study. This can also facilitate group Bible study. Appendix A provides suggestions and discussion questions if the book is used for that purpose.

My goal is simple: I want us to never open a page of the Bible again without seeing Jesus. The aim is not just head knowledge, but heart transformation.

Let's enjoy this journey together, as we begin volume 1, *A Forty-Day Study of The Biblical Story: The Story of Christ.* In this first volume we see how God has prepared the way for the arrival of His son.

ABOUT THE SERIES

Plans are to include the following in this series:

A Forty-Day Study of THE BIBLICAL STORY: *The Story of Christ*
(*Volume One: Preparing the Way*)*
(*Volume Two: The Arrival of the Christ*)*

A Forty-Day Study of THE BOOK OF JOHN: *Who is Christ?*

A Forty-Day Study of THE BOOK OF HEBREWS: *The Supremacy of Christ**

A Forty-Day Study of THE BOOK OF ROMANS: *What is a Christian?*

A Forty-Day Study of SALVATION AND SANCTIFICATION – *Our Journey in Christ**

---

* Available online and through various booksellers.

1

It's Not About Us

A restaurant located just outside of Denver, Colorado, excels in offering New Orleans cuisine. Even though it's in the heart of Bronco-land—as in the Denver Bronco's football team—the walls of the restaurant are covered with banners, signed jerseys, and photographs of star players from the New Orleans Saints. One can also see an occasional customer proudly wearing a Saints' jersey. *Who dat!*

But that's probably not the first thing one notices when entering the restaurant. Deeply etched into the concrete steps leading to the front door, one sees: "JER. 29:11."

If this seems a bit cryptic, Google it.

And then select "shopping."

You will find wall art, tee shirts, bracelets, coffee mugs, writing pens—all referencing the biblical verse Jeremiah 29:11. Some of the merchandised items contain the verse in its entirety. Others don't quote the verse, but only show the book-chapter-verse reference: "Jeremiah 29:11." Still others don't reference the Bible at all but simply repeat the first nine words: *"For I know the plans I have for you…".* The astute Bible student knows where the verse comes from and can fill in the rest from memory.

What is Jeremiah 29:11?

Let's look.

> For I know the plans I have for you, declares the LORD, plans to prosper you and not to harm you, to give you a future and a hope.

I find this verse very uplifting. If I wore bracelets, perhaps I would have one with the "JER. 29:11" engraving. I'm not too sure about the tee shirt. But a coffee mug would certainly be nice.

But there is a problem.

While Jeremiah 29:11 is God speaking, He is not speaking to me—or to you. He is not making a promise to me—or to you. He's not even making a promise to an individual.

He is making a firm, unchangeable promise and commitment to a specific group of people, at a specific time, and for a specific reason.

Sorry folks, we are not in that picture.

And while 29:11 must have offered these people wonderful comfort, they heard God's *entire message*—not just this verse. The complete message for them had to have been unsettling.

Let's hear what they heard.

Just a few verses prior to Jeremiah 29:11, God tells these people:

> Seek the prosperity of the city to which I have sent you as exiles. Pray to the LORD on its behalf, for if it prospers, you too will prosper. (Jeremiah 29:7)

What?

Is God serious?

The people being addressed are the Israelites—those that once lived in Judah (Judea). They are now held captive by the Babylonians. They have seen their nation destroyed by the Babylonians. Jerusalem, the center of their identity, life, and culture lay in ruins due to the Babylonians. The temple has been ravaged by the Babylonians. The wealth of the nation has been boxed up and carted off by the Babylonians. The people are now some seven hundred miles from their homeland and live in bondage to the Babylonians.

And God is telling the Israelites they have to *pray for the Babylonians* if they, themselves, want to prosper. God wants them to pray for their destroyers and captors! He commands them to seek the prosperity of those who demolished their homes and homeland and murdered their friends and relatives!

Now do you want to wear that "Jer. 29:11" bracelet? Do you want to pray for the prosperity and success of your enemies and adversaries?

To make matters worse—immediately before our verse of hope, God tells the Israelites they will remain in Babylon *for seventy years* (Jeremiah 29:10).

Seventy years!

Virtually everyone hearing these comforting words from God will never live to see their homeland restored to anywhere near its former glory. In fact, most will never live to see their homeland at all. They will die in Babylonia.

Now, what about Jeremiah 29:11?

Think about this if you are one of the thousands that have the "JER. 29:11" hooded sweatshirt. Are you willing to pray for the prosperity of your enemies? Are you willing to wait upon God's will—even though it may be your children or your children's children that receive the promised blessing? And keep in mind, Jeremiah's prophecy was not meant for you anyway!

This is just one example of how we take the biblical text out of context—*and try to make the story about us.*

On any given Sunday, it is easy to hear a sermon that goes down this path. Look at 1st Samuel 17—the story of David and Goliath, for example. This is familiar to just about everyone. We have all heard lessons on the young boy, David, going up against the uncouth Philistine giant, Goliath. Perhaps we have heard a sermon climaxed with the deep, James Earl Jones voice of the preacher declaring, "With enough faith, you, too can conquer the giants you are facing."

Really?

I know people of great faith that weren't able to conquer cancer. Or depression. Or patch up a broken marriage. Or defeat their dependence on alcohol.

And if the lesson is to teach us to be more like David, are we to commit adultery? David did. Are we to promote murder? David did. Should we raise a dysfunctional family? David did—with a daughter that gets raped by her half-brother, who in turn is killed by another of David's sons, who himself ultimately becomes bent on killing David. The drama found in each episode of *As the World Turns* can't compete with the stories surrounding Israel's greatest king.

We are not David. David is David. God chose David to be King of Israel—and told David that the Messiah, the Son of God would be a descendant of David. Yes, the Bible teaches us a good bit about David. But the important lesson centers on *God's story—God's plan—God's promises—God's provisions—God's power*—and mostly about *this Messiah and Son of God.*

The story about David is not about us. Oh, it impacts us—there is no question about that. But we need to see the life of David in the context of the Biblical Story first—and not as our story.

Let's look at another example. It comes from Mark 4:35–41. Jesus is crossing the Sea of Galilee with his disciples, only to face a violent storm. Jesus calmly quietens the storm and asks those with him,

> "Why are you so afraid? Do you still have no faith?" (Mark 4:40)

This seems to be another teachable, preach-able story out of the Bible. With enough faith, we can calm the storms in our life.

But can we?

Is that what Jesus is teaching?

Is he talking about the disciples' faith in *their* abilities—or having faith in *Jesus'* abilities? Is the lesson about the storm? Or the disciples? Or is it about Jesus?

Look at the lesson learned by the disciples. What do the disciples tell us about their experience?

The disciples don't puff out their chests and say, "Wow—now look at what we can do. Bring on a storm and we'll handle it."

No.

Seeing what Jesus did actually *scares them*—perhaps more so than the storm itself! The text describes them as being overwhelmed with fear. This fear comes *after* the storm has been calmed:

> Overwhelmed with fear they asked one another, "<u>Who is this</u>, that even the wind and the sea obey Him?" (Mark 4:41)

This story is recorded by all four Gospel writers—and it is not about us. It is not even about the disciples. It is about Jesus. *Who is this, that even the wind and the sea obey Him?*

We are no different than the disciples. God draws us to Jesus where we are to ask, *"Who is this?"*

And that's what the biblical text is about: Jesus. It answers the question, *"Who is Jesus?"*

After his resurrection, Jesus came alongside two disciples headed away from Jerusalem and toward the small village of Emmaus. He overhears their conversation and asks what the two are talking about.

The events surrounding the crucifixion of Jesus were on everybody's mind, so the two ask Jesus,

> "Are You the only visitor to Jerusalem who does not know the things that have happened there in recent days?" (Luke 24:18)

And then Jesus, unrecognized by the two, begins sharing with them. The historian Luke tells us,

> And beginning with Moses and all the Prophets, He explained to them what was written in all the Scriptures about Himself. (Luke 24:27)

Can you imagine what a Bible lesson that must have been? Notice the focus: Jesus teaches all that scripture has to say *about himself*.

The Bible is about Jesus.

What specific part of scripture was Jesus referring to?

All of it.

A follower of Jesus, John, records an event early in Jesus' ministry. Jesus had performed a miracle but did this work on the Sabbath—God's ordained day of rest. The religious Jews were offended by this. John writes,

> Because of this, the Jews tried all the harder to kill Him. Not only was He breaking the Sabbath, but He was even calling God His own Father, making Himself equal with God. (John 5:18)

Jesus then carefully and clearly authenticates who he is. He is God.

Jesus tells them, referencing John the Baptist:

> "But I have testimony more substantial than that of John. For the works that the Father has given Me to accomplish—the very works I am doing—testify about Me that the Father has sent Me. And the Father who sent Me has Himself testified about Me. You have never heard His voice nor seen His form, nor does His word abide in you, because you do not believe the One He sent." (John 5:36–38)

How has God testified about Jesus?

Jesus answers this for us:

"You pore over the Scriptures because you presume that by them you possess eternal life. <u>These are the very words that testify about Me.</u>" (John 5:39)

Hopefully we are beginning to see that not only is the **Bible** *not* about us—**it is about Jesus**; the Son of God and God incarnate (items shown in bold are addressed in more detail at the end of each lesson). The entire Bible is God's revelation and testimony concerning Jesus.

Let's remember what the disciples asked after Jesus calmed the storm: "*Who is this?*"

We are to ask that same question. And the Bible will give us a thousand and one answers. All correct and all for our benefit.

And that's what makes studying the Bible both informative, and enjoyable.

From lesson 1: What do we learn about God?

- God has revealed Himself to us in a number of ways.
- The Bible is God's revealed word to us.
- The Bible is mostly God's story—not ours.

Bible: It is hard for us to not talk about the things we love. Whether it be grandchildren, our latest round of golf, or the love-hate relationship with our local football team, we tend to dwell on where we center our passion.

In my case, conversations often steer toward a discussion of God and the Bible.

Occasionally, though, the person I'm talking with will interrupt the conversation and interject, "I don't believe in the Bible."

This doesn't catch me off guard or upset me. Unfortunately, I hear this often—often enough to have developed a standard response. I simply ask, "Really? Which book? Which author?"

Nine times out of ten—no—make that ten times out of ten, the individual can't answer me. They respond with a confused look, as if to say, "What do you mean 'which book or which author'? We're talking about the Bible, aren't we?"

It is obvious that the individual has never understood what the Bible is. The Bible is not one book—it is a collection of sixty-six different writings from forty different authors, written over a period of around 1500 years. And yet, there is an integrated message that runs throughout the Bible. Our study focuses on this integrated message.

it is about Jesus: If you go to church on Sunday and hear preaching or teaching, ask yourself, "What did I learn about God? What did I learn about Jesus?" If an answer doesn't readily come to mind, it may be time to look for a new church home.

2

The Apostolic Witness

In lesson 1, we looked at how the Biblical Story is God's revelation. It is His Story—and it centers on Jesus.

In this lesson, we will look at one more example showing how we have to be careful when we treat scripture as it being about us. It focuses on some of the last words Jesus spoke before his ascension: Acts 1:8. Jesus is talking to the disciples, now called **apostles** ("sent ones"):

> "But you will receive power when the Holy Spirit comes upon you, and you will be My witnesses in Jerusalem, and in all Judea and Samaria, and to the ends of the earth."

If we make this text about us, we may miss the significance of what is happening. If you are a Christian, you *have* received the Holy Spirit—the same Spirit Jesus is describing in Acts 1:8. And you and I *are* called to be witnesses of Christ.

But this text is not addressed to us. Jesus is about to ascend to the Father and is giving his last words specifically to the apostles. He is telling *them* exactly what *they* are to do.

They will receive power. This word "power" in the Greek is the same word Matthew, Mark, and Luke use when they are talking about miracles. These are "mighty acts." Jesus is telling the apostles they will receive this power—they will be able to perform mighty acts— when the Holy Spirit comes to them.

We are not the apostles.

Can we raise the dead?

Peter did (Acts 9:40).

Paul did (Acts 20:10).

Look at the power Paul was given:

> God did extraordinary miracles through Paul, so that even handkerchiefs and aprons that had touched him were taken to the sick, and their illnesses were cured, and the evil spirits left them. (Acts 19:11, 12)

How many of your ailing friends have you cured with your hanky?

And let's look at Peter:

> As a result, people brought the sick into the streets and laid them on cots and mats, so that at least Peter's shadow might fall on some of them as he passed by. Crowds also gathered from the towns around Jerusalem, bringing the sick and those tormented by unclean spirits, and all of them were healed. (Acts 5:15, 16)

That is power—power from God—power given to a specific group of men for a specific purpose.

And what is that purpose? Again, look at Acts 1:8,

> "But you will receive power when the Holy Spirit comes upon you, and you will be My witnesses in Jerusalem, and in all Judea and Samaria, and to the ends of the earth."

The power is given to the apostles to enable them to be witnesses to who Jesus is. They have one mission: to tell the world about Jesus. And their mighty acts help authenticate who they are as witnesses concerning Jesus. Their mighty acts display God's power within them, and these acts validate the source and truth of their message. These were the same men on the boat in the storm that asked, *"Who is this?"* Now they know who Jesus is. They will proclaim this to the world—even if it means torture and their eventual executions in pursuing this mission and ministry.

And these apostles are continuing to perform this ministry today. Their witness became the written word of the New Testament.

Since we are learning about the Biblical Story, let's provide a brief background of what the Bible is.

The Bible is God's written revelation to man. The term "written" is used because God reveals Himself to us in a number of ways. He reveals Himself through His creation. The psalmist writes, "The heavens declare the glory of God; the skies proclaim the work of his hands" (Psalm 19:1).

God reveals Himself through history. I can share a very simple example. I've traveled to some thirty-seven different countries. I have never met a Macedonian, or a Roman, or a Jebusite, or even a Canaanite. But I have met many Jews. As we will learn shortly, the Jews are God's chosen people—central to the Biblical Story and God's plan of redemption. Despite centuries of persecution and removal from their homeland, they are still an identifiable people and will remain so—because they remain central to God's acts in history.

God also reveals Himself, and authenticates His message, by explaining the meaning behind historical events and telling His people—and us—about events before they occur. These are the writings of the prophets, also found in the Bible. We'll be looking at some of the prophetic writings throughout these lessons.

Most importantly, God reveals Himself not just through His creation, history, and His Word. His clearest and most complete revelation is through His word becoming flesh—Jesus. We will have much to say about Jesus as our lessons continue.

The Bible is God's written word. Throughout ancient history, God set aside a chosen people, the Jewish people, through which to reveal Himself and His plans to humankind. God selected individuals within this group to record His message and His dealings with these chosen people of God. Their writings were assembled and **accurately transmitted** throughout the centuries. They refer to these as the Hebrew Scriptures. For non-Jewish Christians, we call these the Old Testament—which this volume will focus on.

The zenith of this history occurred with the birth of "Immanuel" (also spelled "Emmanuel")—God with us. This happened slightly over 2000 years ago when Jesus of Nazareth was born. Jesus is also referred to as **the Messiah and the Christ**. The author of the book of Hebrews helps explain who Jesus is:

> On many past occasions and in many different ways,
> God spoke to our fathers through the prophets. But in
> these last days He has spoken to us by His Son, whom

He appointed heir of all things, and through whom He made the universe. (Hebrews 1:1, 2)

A close follower of Jesus tells us even more:

In the beginning was the Word, and the Word was with God, and the Word was God. He was with God in the beginning. Through Him all things were made, and without Him nothing was made that has been made. In Him was life, and that life was the light of men. The Light shines in the darkness, and the darkness has not overcome.

The Word became flesh and made His dwelling among us. We have seen His glory, the glory of the one and only Son from the Father, full of grace and truth. (John 1:1–5, 14)

This was written by John. He closes his historical account of Jesus with the words:

There are many more things that Jesus did. If all of them were written down, I suppose that not even the world itself would have space for the books that would be written. (John 21:25)

That's probably an understatement. In the Biblical Story, we learn that Jesus is God. If we're curious as to who God is, we look at Jesus.

In Acts 1:8, Jesus commands the apostles to be his witnesses—and the New Testament is written by people like John and the other Apostolic witnesses to let us know what Jesus said and did, and most importantly, to teach us who Jesus is.

The first writing found in the New Testament is that of Matthew. Matthew was a tax collector that became one of Jesus' disciples. He recorded Jesus' life in the book given his name—the book, or **Gospel** of Matthew. The book of Matthew is an Apostolic witness of who Jesus is.

Mark knew the Apostle Paul and was also a close friend of the Apostle Peter. He wrote the book of Mark. Early writers associated with the Church tell us the book of Mark is actually Peter's recollections of Jesus, as **Peter told these to Mark**. So, in the book of Mark we also have a witness of who Jesus is.

Luke was a traveling companion of the Apostle Paul and collected information on Jesus. He documented this in the book called by his name ("Luke"). He also wrote about the early church and the "acts" of the Apostles and the Holy Spirit—the book we refer to as "Acts." Again, we have another historical account of who Jesus is.

John, who we referred to above, was one of the closest disciples of Jesus and recorded Jesus' life in the book of John. We also have three of his letters (epistles) that became part of the New Testament and the Christian Bible. John's writings, too, witness the historical Jesus.

Paul began as rabbi Saul, a Jewish zealot on a mission to exterminate the movement associated with the followers of Jesus. He encounters Jesus and becomes Christianity's greatest missionary. Most of the writings in the New Testament come from Paul—and these, too, are part of the Apostolic witness. Paul wrote both to churches (such as his letters to the Romans, Corinthians, Galatians, and Ephesians) and also to individuals (such as his letters to Timothy, Titus, and Philemon).

Who did we leave out?

We have two letters from the Apostle Peter. Like the Apostle John, Peter is another very close disciple of Jesus. Peter also became a companion of Paul's.

We also have writings from two of Jesus' half-brothers, James and Jude.

Included in the New Testament is a writing specifically to Jewish believers, called "Hebrews." Its authorship is uncertain.

Lastly, God revealed future events to the Apostle John, and the New Testament closes with this revelation from God—the book of Revelation.

Acts 1:8 isn't about us. It is about those closest to Jesus, called to a special mission and given special powers, so that they could be special witnesses to who Jesus is. And their mission **isn't about themselves**—it is about Jesus. It is about God.

The Bible is God's story—who He is and what His plans are—past, present, and future.

There is no other writing in existence like it.

Again, let's remember what the disciples asked after Jesus calmed the storm: *"Who is this?"*

As we said in lesson 1, we are to ask that same question.

And the Bible will give us the answers.

Let's begin.

From lesson 2: What do we learn about God?

- God gave special powers and a special assignment to the Apostles of Jesus.
- God's revelation includes the Apostolic witness of who Jesus is. This is the Christian New Testament.

apostles: The word "apostle" means "one who is sent out." In the Bible these are messengers, or ambassadors, on mission for Jesus. These were extraordinary men called by God.

Actually, that's not true.

They were ordinary men.

Through the power of God's Spirit, they became extraordinary.

Ephesians 2:20 tells us that the foundation of the Church are the twelve Apostles—with Jesus being the cornerstone. These were witnesses to the resurrected Jesus (1st Corinthians 9:1) and explicitly chosen by the Holy Spirit to be special instruments of God (Acts 9:15). As we have seen, they were also given the ability to perform miracles, signs, and wonders (Acts 1:8; Acts 2:43; 2nd Corinthians 12:12).

While the word "apostle" in the biblical text can refer to the disciples who were commissioned by Jesus, it can also refer to others who were on mission for Jesus. Barnabas is referred to as an apostle (Acts 13:2; 14:4), as is Titus (2nd Corinthians 8:23). Andronicus and Junias might have been referred to, or identified, as apostles (Romans 16:7). Epaphroditus is referred to as a "messenger" (Philippians 2:25)—however the word translated here as messenger is the same term for "apostle."

If you are a believer in Jesus, you, too, are a "sent one." You are his ambassador. You are to be a messenger and minister of reconciliation (2nd Corinthians 5:18–20), teaching others about Jesus (Matthew 28:18–20). We are sent to bring God's Word to the world (Romans 10:15).

accurately transmitted: No other ancient writing has been transmitted as accurately as the biblical text. I know of no scholar— even secular scholars—that would disagree with that statement. Time does not permit a detailed discussion on this topic. However, a relatively recent confirmation of biblical accuracy came about through the discovery of the Dead Sea Scrolls. Found among these ancient writings was a full copy of the "book" written by the prophet Isaiah—a prophet who lived and wrote seven hundred years before the birth of Christ. The Isaiah Scroll, found relatively intact, is a thousand years older than any previously known copy of Isaiah's writing to which we have access. And yet, a comparison of this ancient document with our later texts show an amazing accuracy in the transmission of the text.

the Messiah and the Christ: The term "Christ" is not a name; it is a title. This is also true for the word "Messiah." "Christ" comes from the Greek word *"Christos"* which is a translation of the Hebrew word, "Messiah", or "Anointed." Throughout our study of the Bible, the term "Christ" and "Messiah" will be used interchangeably.

Gospel: The word "gospel" is used for the Greek word *evangelion* and means "good news." We call the first four books of the New Testament—Matthew, Mark, Luke and John—the "Gospels" because they announce the good news concerning Emmanuel, God with us (Jesus' presence on earth). In that Matthew, Mark, and Luke write very similar accounts, these are further designated as the "synoptic Gospels"— "synoptic" roughly meaning "same *(syn)* viewpoint *(optic)*."

John's Gospel is quite different from those of the other Gospel writers. While Matthew, Mark, and Luke focus on what Jesus said and did, John focuses on who Jesus is.

We get the concept of "gospel" from the prophet Isaiah. He writes,

> "Comfort, comfort My people,"
>   says your God.
> "Speak tenderly to Jerusalem,
>   and proclaim to her
> that her forced labor has been completed,
>   her iniquity has been pardoned." (Isaiah 40:1, 2)

The term "forced labor" refers to warfare. Israel has suffered in warfare, but the prophet sees a time when the Deliverer—the Messiah—will appear. This person will ultimately bring to the people the rule (reign) of God. Isaiah's writing continues:

> Go up on a high mountain, O Zion, herald of good news. Raise your voice loudly, O Jerusalem, herald of good news. Lift it up, do not be afraid! Say to the cities of Judah, 'Here is your God!' (Isaiah 40:9)

What is this good news? The prophet then declares,

> Behold, the Lord GOD comes with might, and His arm establishes His rule. His reward is with Him, and His recompense accompanies Him. (Isaiah 40:10)

The Good News is the appearance of the Messiah and the deliverance of the people of God. If you are a Christian, you are included in this deliverance—and are called to proclaim the Good News to others.

Peter told these to Mark: As you read Mark's gospel, look for what is said about Peter. You will find very little. Compare this to the Peter we find in the historical accounts written by Matthew or Luke or John. Peter's role as a disciple and apostle, and many of the significant events between Jesus and Peter, are left out of Mark's writing. This is understandable if Peter, in proper and commendable humility, is the one relating the life of Jesus to Mark, who is recording the information being shared.

This leads to our next comment . . .

isn't about themselves: Who is the "hero" or central character in the book of Matthew? Or Mark? Or Luke or John, or any of the other writings found in the New Testament? It is amazing how the authors remain in the background—their total focus is on Jesus. The Biblical Story is all about Jesus.

3

Why Jesus?

In our previous two lessons, we said the Bible is all about Jesus.

Why is this the case?

Why is it so important for us to know about this Galilean carpenter who walked the earth two thousand years ago? After all, here was a man born of a peasant woman in an obscure village. He never wrote a book. He never held a political position or commanded an army. He never obtained great wealth. He died virtually alone, put to death as a common thief by Roman crucifixion.

Why does the world remember him?

Why has so much of history been changed because of him?

James Allen **Francis** (1864-1928) wrote:

> I am far within the mark when I say that all the armies that ever marched, and all the navies that ever were built, and all the parliaments that ever sat, all the kings that ever reigned, put together have not affected

the life of man upon this earth as powerfully as has
that One Solitary Life.

The "One Solitary Life" James Allen Francis is talking about is the
life of Jesus of Nazareth.

Why are these words so true to the mark?

We've mentioned the Apostle John before, a follower of Jesus. He
took Jesus' post-resurrection command recorded as Acts 1:8 seriously
(as discussed in our previous lesson). You will recall, prior to his
ascension to heaven, Jesus gathered the disciples—the closest of his
followers—and told them they would be his witnesses in Jerusalem,
and in all Judea and Samaria, and to the ends of the earth. John's
testimony concerning Jesus included documenting Jesus' life. His
writing shares many of the things that Jesus did while he was on
earth. But more importantly, John writes his historical account of
Jesus to tell us who Jesus *is*. John tells us:

> Jesus performed many other signs in the presence of
> His disciples, which are not written in this book. But
> these are written so that you may believe that Jesus is
> the Christ, the Son of God, and that by believing you
> may have life in His name. (John 20:30, 31)

John has written his message so that we might believe Jesus is the
Christ, the Son of God.

What do these terms mean? What does it mean when we hear that
Jesus is the Christ? What is implied when John tells us Jesus is the
Son of God? As we go through the Biblical Story, we will learn quite
a bit about Jesus. But where do we get these terms "Christ" and "Son
of God" from the Bible? What makes them important? And we know
they are important because Jesus was put to death when he claimed
that these terms applied to himself.

We also know, from history, that the grave could not hold Jesus. No one of history disputes whether or not his tomb was empty. The tomb was empty, and a body was never found. Some suggest his body was stolen, but the close followers of Jesus had the audacity to claim Jesus rose from the dead and they were willing to die for this conviction.

Jesus rose from the dead? Why? We know what the words mean, but what is the significance of this event?

Of course, the resurrection of Jesus was miraculous—but why is it so central to the course of human history? Why does so much revolve around Jesus? Why are the world's calendars calibrated to the time of his birth? Why do even non-believers celebrate in joy each year when Christmas comes around—the day honoring the birth of Jesus?

In this lesson series, we begin to answer these, and other questions. And as we get into the very opening chapters of the Bible, we will begin to see why the Bible is all about Jesus. We will also see why the grave could not hold Jesus. And we will explore why the resurrection of Jesus is foundational to all that the Bible has to say.

Note that John writes, "that by believing you may have life in His name." Before our lessons conclude, we are going to know what "life in his name" means. But we are getting ahead of the story.

John tells us he wrote down the events in Jesus' life "so that you may believe that Jesus is the Christ, the Son of God." Why does John emphasize the titles "Christ" and "Son of God?"

Actually, John is not the only one with an interest in these titles. Jesus is arrested and brought before the Jewish high priest Caiaphas. Here, Jesus is asked a question, as recorded by another disciple of Jesus, Matthew:

> The high priest said to Him, "I charge You under oath
> by the living God: Tell us if You are the <u>Christ</u>, the
> <u>Son of God.</u>" (Matthew 26:63)

Here are those two words: <u>Christ</u> and <u>Son of God</u>. Why is this central to the high priest's questioning of Jesus? Why does Caiaphas focus on this?

And, again, it is because of these two terms that Jesus is executed. Why?

There is another nuance to explore. The Jews did not have the authority to carry out capital punishment. They must send Jesus to the Roman leader, Pilate if their desire to have Jesus executed is to be fulfilled.

Pilate, being a Roman citizen and not a Jew, is not concerned with concepts or titles like "Christ" or "Son of God." The Jews can worry about those types of issues.

But in Pilate's world, there is only one king—the Roman emperor. Pilate asks Jesus if he considers himself to be king (John 18:33–40). Jesus' affirmation is rebellion. Rome will put Jesus to death.

Christ.

Son of God.

King.

The religious and secular leaders send Jesus to his death because he claims ownership of these titles. What do these titles imply? What makes them important?

All three designations come to us from something written a thousand years before Jesus walked on his earth. They come from Psalm 2. We will begin our biblical journey looking at this Psalm—and then we will proceed from there to the first book of the Bible and its opening words.

The key to understanding this Psalm is to recognize that there are three "voices" speaking to the reader: that of the narrator, that of God the Father, and that of Jesus the Son.

Let's examine Psalm 2 verse by verse. Throughout this lesson series we'll be using the **Berean Study Bible** translation:

Psalm 2:1, 2 – [Narrator]:

> Why do the nations rage
>   and the peoples plot in vain?
> The kings of the earth take their stand
>   and the rulers gather together,
> against the LORD
>   and against His Anointed One.

The nations and their leaders are conspiring and plotting—but this is in vain. What they are trying to do is both futile and fruitless. Despite this, they join together to go against God and against someone anointed by God. When we see the term "**LORD**" in all capitals, this is referring to God.

The word translated "His Anointed One" in the above is where we get the word "Messiah" from the Hebrew, and "Christ" from the Greek. The Psalmist is depicting an event where all of the world opposes God and His Anointed, the Christ. The Biblical Story is the story about this on-going opposition—and how the conflict ends.

So Caiaphas, the high priest when Jesus is on trial, is really asking if this man Jesus is the Psalm 2 Christ. And John writes his Gospel hoping that his readers will truly know that Jesus *is* the Christ.

Psalm 2:3 – The narrator continues, telling us what these earthly kings are saying:

> "Let us break Their chains
> and cast away Their cords."

The earthly rulers want nothing to do with God's rule or Christ's rule. They view this as being placed into chains and cords (the word "cords" can also be translated "shackles"—the equivalent of modern-day leg chains or handcuffs). This, too, is an on-going theme of the Biblical Story. Humankind has rebelled against God's rule and God's order. God's requirements and desires seem too restrictive. We don't want subservience to the God of creation. We want to be our own God. For those who don't know God in a personal way, they perceive the God of Christianity as a God that places people in chains and "cords"—they don't want this.

No one would want this.

Of course, for the Christian, God does not offer bondage—he offers freedom. But let's continue.

Psalm 2:4 –

> The One enthroned in the heavens laughs;
> the Lord taunts them.

In verse 4, the narrator tells us that God ("the One enthroned") laughs at these earthly kings and their peoples, as does the Lord (here the Hebrew word is "Adonai"—not YHWH—see the notes on "LORD" below).

Psalm 2:5 – But the laughter turns to anger. Describing God, the narrator continues,

> Then He rebukes them in His anger,
> and terrifies them in His fury…

The patience of God has run out. He is no longer laughing at the futility of the earth's rulers. God now rebukes them in anger. Their rebellion provokes the wrath of God. Yes, within the Biblical Story, we learn that God is a God of unfathomable love. And, although we don't like to focus on this, we also learn that God's justice demands that sin and rebellion be punished. Our God is a God of wrath. God's wrath is His righteous punishment of sin.

And now God speaks.

Psalm 2:6 –

> "I have installed My King on Zion,
>> upon My holy hill."

We get a second term for God's Anointed (God's Christ or Messiah). He will also be *King*, and he will rule "on Zion."

Zion is Jerusalem. This is not a figure of speech. This depicts a reign of Jesus on this earth and from this earth's Jerusalem. This has not yet occurred—but it will occur. All of this is spelled out in the Biblical Story. God has clearly revealed what His plans are, and here I could add, "and how the story ends." However, the story does not end. There is an eternity that every human being will experience. Again, this, too, is spelled out in the Biblical Story.

Psalm 2:7 – We now hear words from this Messiah as he quotes what has been spoken to him by the Father:

> I will proclaim the decree
>> spoken to Me by the LORD:
> "You are My Son;
>> today I have become Your Father."

We are now introduced to the third term: Son of God. When God says, "You are My Son; today I have become Your Father," we can now connect the three titles "Christ," "King," and "Son of God"—and they all refer to the Galilean carpenter, Jesus.

In the Biblical Story, God promises an heir to Israel's king David—an heir who will sit on David's throne and rule a kingdom that is everlasting. This is revealed in 2nd Samuel 7:11–14:

> The LORD declares to you that He Himself will establish a house for you. And when your days are fulfilled and you rest with your fathers, I will raise up your offspring after you, who will come from your own body, and I will establish his kingdom. He will build a house for My name, and I will establish the throne of his kingdom forever. I will be his Father, and he will be My son.

Note, this king is also the Son of God, as we see in Psalm 2. We also see both of these terms confirmed by the angel Gabriel when he announces that Mary will deliver a child:

> "Behold, you will conceive and give birth to a son, and you are to give Him the name Jesus. He will be great and will be called the Son of the Most High. The Lord God will give Him the throne of His father David, and He will reign over the house of Jacob forever. His kingdom will never end!" (Luke 1:31–33)

Seven hundred years before Jesus was even born, God's spokesman (prophet) Isaiah foretold of this event, also recognizing the Messiah as King:

> For unto us a child is born,
> unto us a son is given,
> and the government will be upon His shoulders.
> And He will be called

Wonderful Counselor, Mighty God,
Everlasting Father, Prince of Peace.
Of the increase of His government and peace
there will be no end.
<u>He will reign on the throne of David</u>
and over his kingdom,
to establish and sustain it
with justice and righteousness
from that time and forevermore.

The zeal of the LORD of Hosts will accomplish this.
(Isaiah 9:6, 7)

Earlier we saw that during Jesus' trial, the high priest wanted to know if Jesus was the Christ and Son of God, and the Roman official, Pilate, asked if Jesus considered himself to be a king. The high priest (Caiaphas) was interested in the religious implications because of fear and doubt. Were the Jewish religious leaders condemning God's Anointed? Pilate, on the other hand, was making sure no one would challenge the authority of the Roman Emperor by claiming to be a king.

Jesus is the Christ, the Son of God, and King—resulting in his condemnation and execution by both the religious and secular leaders of his day.

Look closely at the text of Psalm 2:7 –

I will proclaim the decree
spoken to Me by the LORD:
"You are My Son;
today I have become Your Father."

God declares this Christ-King to be His son.

This can be confusing. Jesus is not the son in the context of how we view a human father and a male offspring. Jesus is God's Son in the sense that he is God made manifest in human form (John 1:1, 14). He is God's son in that, even though his incarnation (becoming "flesh") was done through the "seed of woman" (Genesis 3:15, a key term that we will learn about shortly), this was not through an earthly father but through God, the Holy Spirit (Luke 1:35). He is also designated God's son from the earthly perspective of inheritance. All that the Father has belongs to the Son.

From the perspective of God's chosen people, though, there is the additional nuance. The Jewish leaders knew full well what "Son of God" meant in the context of Hebrew Scriptures and Psalm 2. To be the Son of God meant equality with God. To be God's son was to be God. To make this claim amounted to blasphemy, and the person making this claim was to be put to death.

While on his earth, Jesus repeatedly made this claim and did so in both word and deed. The Jewish form of execution was stoning, but the Jews did not have the authority to carry out capital punishment— so Jesus was put to death under Roman rule and through the Roman method of capital punishment: crucifixion.

All of this might sound confusing right now, but as we go through the Biblical Story it becomes clear.

Psalm 2:8 – Jesus continues reciting what God the Father has said to him:

> "Ask Me, and I will make the nations Your inheritance,
> the ends of the earth Your possession."

The Son is to ask the Father and he will be given possession (ownership and rule) over all the nations of the earth. It is interesting to put this into the context of Satan's **temptations** toward Jesus. The historian, Luke, records the following:

> Then the devil led Him up to a high place and showed Him in an instant all the kingdoms of the world. 'I will give You authority over all these kingdoms and all their glory,' he said. 'For it has been relinquished to me, and I can give it to anyone I wish. So if You worship me, it will all be Yours.' (Luke 4:5–7)

Satan offers Jesus all the kingdoms of the world, but God, says, "Ask Me, and I will make the nations Your inheritance."

Jesus refuses Satan's offer—and continues in total obedience to God the Father, knowing that this would mean the cross. Consequently, Jesus "has been appointed heir of all things" (Hebrews 1:2).

Psalm 2:9 – This Christ, Son of God, and King continues to quote the Father:

> "You will break them with an iron scepter;
>   You will shatter them like pottery."

Jesus' first recorded teaching occurs at the synagogue in Nazareth. He begins by reading from the book of Isaiah, starting with the sixty-first chapter (Isaiah 61:1 and part of verse 2, as told to us by Luke in Luke 4:16–21):

> "The Spirit of the Lord GOD is on Me,
>   because the LORD has anointed Me
>   to preach good news to the poor.
> He has sent Me to bind up the brokenhearted,
>   to proclaim liberty to the captives
>   and release from darkness to the prisoners,
> to proclaim the year of the LORD's favor..."

The sentence from Isaiah does not end here—but Jesus stops his reading. He tells those gathered, "Today, this Scripture is fulfilled in your hearing" (Luke 4:21).

The actual Isaiah text continues, "and the day of our God's vengeance." But Jesus does not read this portion of Isaiah's prophecy. He stops mid-sentence because the vengeance of God, the wrath of God—that which is mentioned in Psalm 2—would not and does not happen at Jesus' first appearance on earth. There will be a time, though, when this sentence is completed—when Jesus returns to earth and the world will see and experience "the day of our God's vengeance."

John quotes this verse from Psalm 2 in Revelation 2:27. He describes a male child that will "rule the nations with an iron scepter" (Revelation 12:5; 19:15). When Jesus returns, he will not be as a "Lamb, looking as it had been slain" (Revelation 5:6) but as the "Lion of the tribe of Judah" (Revelation 5:5). He will return as "King of Kings and Lord of Lords" (Revelation 19:16). That's the "back half" of Isaiah 61:2. It is what Jesus did not read in the Synagogue, because his fulfillment of this text is yet to come.

But it most certainly will come.

Let's continue. The narrator will now return and end the Psalm:

Psalm 2:10, 11 –

> Therefore, be wise, O kings;
>> be admonished, O judges of the earth.

The rulers on earth are told to be wise.

And what is this wisdom?

> Serve the LORD with fear,
>> and rejoice with trembling.

Wisdom is found in serving God and rejoicing in God. The warning is clear. Instead of conspiring and plotting, and rising up against God and His Anointed, the peoples of the earth should serve God and celebrate His rule.

But how do we do this? How do we serve God?

The narrator answers this.

Psalm 2:12a –

> Kiss the Son, lest He be angry
>> and you perish in your rebellion,
>> when His wrath ignites in an instant.

Kings and rulers of the earth need to submit to God's anointed son with the kiss of homage *before* he comes with his might and wrath to put down those who rebel against him. "Kiss the son" is a Hebraic phrase that reminds us of a lowly servant kissing the feet of a Lord or King. We worship God when we bow down before Christ and worship him. Studying the Bible and learning about Jesus is part of our worship.

We honor God, we serve God, we celebrate God by honoring His son—by honoring Jesus. And Jesus is what the Bible is all about.

Psalm 2:12b: The narrator will now end this Psalm:

> Blessed are all who take refuge in Him.

This one sentence sums up all of history.

To escape God's wrath, to escape the Isaiah 61 "day of vengeance of our God"—requires that we take refuge in Jesus. To be blessed by God Himself requires that we take refuge in Jesus. And as we study God's Word, we learn of these unfathomable blessings.

<u>This is why the Bible is all about Jesus</u>. The *only* way we can escape God's wrath, and the *only* way we can receive God's blessings, is through the man who told us clearly, "I am the way, and the truth, and the life, no one comes to the Father except through Me" (John 14:2).

James Allen Francis was absolutely correct. All the armies that ever marched, and all the navies that ever were built, and all the parliaments that ever sat, all the kings that ever reigned, put together have not affected the life of man upon this earth as powerfully as has that One Solitary Life. That life is the life of the Galilean carpenter, Jesus—the Messiah, Son of God, and King.

Since the Bible is God's revelation, and since the only way to God is through Jesus, God has purposefully made His Word to us all about Jesus.

We'll see this is true from the Bible's very opening pages, to the promise found in the Bible's very last words:

> He who testifies to these things says, "Yes, I am coming soon." Amen. Come, Lord Jesus! (Revelation 22:20)

So, in this journey, from the opening pages of the Bible, throughout the biblical text, and to the Bible's very end, we are going to focus on Jesus—the Christ, the Son of God, the King. *Blessed are all who take refuge in Him.*

From lesson 3: What do we learn about God?

- God's creation is in rebellion against God. But God will provide to His Creation, His Anointed (the Messiah or Christ), one who will be referred to as the Son of God, and one who will be established upon a throne and whose kingdom will last forever.
- We find out from the New Testament that this Christ, Son of God, and King is Jesus.
- God is honored when we honor Jesus and seek refuge in him. Failure to do so results in God's wrath.

Psalm 2 gives us the titles Messiah (Anointed), the Son of God, and King. We also learn the following:

- Political and religious leaders will conspire against him (2:1–3).
- He will seek God for his inheritance (2:8).
- He will have authority over all things (2:8, 9).
- He will destroy those who do not honor him (2:12).
- We are to seek refuge in him (2:12).

Francis: This quote is available at https://www.bartleby.com/73/916.html, (accessed June 26, 2019).

Berean Study Bible: Unless otherwise noted, all scripture quotations in these lessons use the Berean Study Bible. This is done due to copyrights and copyright approvals. To access this translation, see www.biblehub.com.

Students often ask what Bible translation I recommend. There are three major types of biblical translations that are readily available in

English: word-for-word translations, thought-for-thought translations, and paraphrases of the biblical text.

A "word-for-word" translation tries to match the original text as closely as possible. The English Standard Version (ESV) is a good example. Other translations are more interested in conveying the meaning behind the original words, and these are known as "thought-for-thought" translations. The New International Version is along the lines of a "thought-for-thought" translation. Paraphrases are not direct translations but discuss the text using everyday English. Eugene Peterson's *The Message* is a good example.

Which is better? Each has value and I use all three.

To provide an example of the difference, many of us here in the U.S. know how to translate: ¿Como se llamó usted? This is Spanish for "What is your name?" By translating it this way we are creating a thought-for-thought translation. This would also apply to a paraphrase in this case because the sentence is quite simple.

But "como" means "how." "Se llamó" means "it was called." "Usted" means "you." So, a word-for-word translation would run more along the lines of "How you call yourself?"

"What is your name" and "how you call yourself" mean the same thing. But one sounds more pleasing to our ears in our culture and language, and may be more readily understood. This is why many prefer using a thought-for-thought translation, or even a paraphrase of the biblical text.

By the way, if you type in "What is your name?" in English and ask for the Spanish translation, Google Translate does not return "¿Como se llamó usted?" It returns ¿Cuál es tu nombre?—a word-for-word translation.

Is one translation better than another? For general purposes, not really. Actually, I prefer if my students bring several different translations to class so we can discuss any nuances between specific words or concepts in any given translation. Of course, should we need additional clarity as to what the text is saying, we should always refer to the original Hebrew or Greek.

LORD: In the Hebrew Scriptures, God is referred to as "YHWH" (sometimes pronounced by non-Jews as "Yahweh"—sometimes "Jehovah"). "YHWH" is also known as the "tetragrammatron," that is, the "four letters."

To the Jew, the name "YHWH" is sacred—so much so that it should never be pronounced by the lips of sinful man. In reading Hebrew Scriptures, when "YHWH" appears in the text, the Jewish reader utters the word "Adonai," which means "Lord."

Because of this, our English Bible translations do not write "YHWH" into the text. Instead, when it appears in the Hebrew, the English word "LORD" is substituted and is written in all capitals—the translation of "Adonai." So, when we see LORD (all capitals) it refers to God the Father.

Of course, scripture also contains the word "lord", that is, "Adonai" separate from "YHWH." To differentiate, when scripture uses Adonai ("lord") it is typed using upper- and lower-case letters, and not in all capitals. Normally, but not in all cases, "Lord" (upper- and lower-case) is referring to Jesus.

Whose Value System?

We are now ready to start our journey. The Bible begins with the book of Genesis, and opens with a central, foundational truth:

> In the beginning God created the heavens and the earth. (Genesis 1:1)

This is a simple sentence—just seven words in the original **Hebrew** language. But the theological implications are staggering. Since God is the Creator:

- He has ownership of His creation. *It is His—not ours.*
- He has *the* say in His creation. He can do with His creation, and to His creation, whatever He desires.
- In that God created this, it is reasonable to expect Him to have a purpose for His creation. If so, it probably behooves us to find out what that purpose is.
- How can we learn what that purpose is *unless God reveals this to us?*
- Lastly, but perhaps most importantly, we, the created, are not God.

There is something else that is startling. Later in the Biblical Story, we will find out that Jesus is also the Creator—and Jesus is also God.

We've seen this before, but let's look at it again. In his account of Jesus, John introduces Jesus and writes:

> In the beginning was the Word, and the Word was with God, and the Word was God. He was with God in the beginning. Through Him all things were made, and without Him nothing was made that has been made. In Him was life, and that life was the light of men. The Light shines in the darkness, and the darkness has not overcome it. (John 1:1–5)

There is more we could say, but for now let's continue.

In the creation story, we hear a term repeated several times: "God saw . . . it was good." We begin to learn about God's character and His creation:

> Genesis 1:4 – "And God saw...was good."
> Genesis 1:10 – "And God saw that it was good."
> Genesis 1:12 – "And God saw that it was good."
> Genesis 1:18 – "And God saw that it was good."
> Genesis 1:21 – "And God saw that it was good."
> Genesis 1:25 – "And God saw that it was good."

And then we get to Genesis 1:31. Creation has been completed, and we read, "...it was very good."

The repeated phrases, "God saw... it was good," show God evaluating what He has created. God assesses His creation and sees that it is good. It is God that establishes the value system. It is God that determines what is good. And what He created was a perfect reflection of who God is and what God desires. It is His world—not ours. He is God, and we are not.

Then God said, "Let Us make man in Our image, after Our likeness, to rule over the fish of the sea and the birds of the air, over the livestock, and over all the earth itself and every creature that crawls upon it."

So, God created man in His own image;
   in the image of God, He created him;
      male and female He created them. (Genesis 1:26, 27)

Now we enter the picture. We are created in God's image, and we are created to rule over God's created order. To be created in God's image means we are to represent God—we are to reflect who God is. This also places a special value on humankind. According to God's Word, no other created entity has been created in the image of God.

Look at the following verses:

Genesis 1:11 – Then God said, "Let the earth bring forth vegetation: seed-bearing plants and fruit trees, each bearing fruit with seed according to its kind." And it was so.

Genesis 1:12 – The earth produced vegetation: seed-bearing plants according to their kinds and trees bearing fruit with seed according to their kinds. And God saw that it was good.

God's plan is for oak trees to bring forth oak trees—and for apple trees to bring forth apple trees.

Genesis 1:21 – So God created the great sea creatures and every living thing that moves, with which the waters teemed according to their kinds, and every bird of flight after its kind. And God saw that it was good.

Genesis 1:24 – And God said, "Let the earth bring forth living creatures according to their kinds: livestock, land crawlers, and wild animals according to their kinds." And it was so.

Genesis 1:25 – God made the beasts of the earth according to their kinds, the livestock according to their kinds, and everything that crawls upon the earth according to its kind. And God saw that it was good.

We see the word "kind" or "kinds" ten times. A rose bush is to produce a rose bush. An elephant is to produce an elephant.

Everything creates and reproduces an image of itself.

But look what happens at the creation of humankind (Genesis 1:26).

Then God said, "Let Us make man in Our image, after Our likeness..."

We expect the phrase "after their kind." Instead there is an unanticipated change. We see: "in Our image."

This is an abrupt and startling difference in God's order of things. Humankind is not going to reproduce "after their kind"—humankind is going to reproduce God's image! Man is to produce that which reflects the image of God. We are to mirror who God is as His representatives on earth.

This places a different value on human life. All human life. This has nothing to do with Jew or Gentile, believer or non-believer, Asian or African. It has to do with who we are—made special in that we are created in God's image.

Here you might be saying, "Wait a minute. Humans produce humans, and my son looks just like me."

There are two kinds of images. One is a physical image, what we see with plants and animals reproducing "after their kind." We also see this physical image in children who have a physical resemblance to their biological parents.

But there is also another kind of image—the "obedient" image. While we don't raise our children to physically *look* like us (this either happens, or it doesn't), we do try to teach them to *act* like us (or even to act better than we do). We want them to maintain proper behaviors and values, reflecting who we would like them to be. This is their *obedient* image. We want them to obey our desires and we want this for *their* well-being.

This is true of God's desires for us and is part of what it means for us to be created in the image of God. We are not the physical image of God, of course, but we are to be an obedient image of God. We are not only to represent God; we are to obey God's desires for us. And God wants this for *our* well-being.

This also means, unlike plants and animals, we have been given the ability to respond to God. We have an awareness of God and an understanding of what God wants. Animals do not have this ability. They have no longing for God, nor the desire to know God. In this terminology, animals have no "image." They were not created in the image of God.

Note what is being said. We are given the capacity and desire to think about God and have a relationship with God.

Is that true?

You might be thinking that atheists fall outside of this—that they don't have the capacity or desire to think about God. But even atheists (those that don't believe in a god or gods) and agnostics (those that are "not knowing," that is, those not sure whether or not God exists) still think about God. In fact, some atheists spend a considerable amount of time and energy thinking about something that, to them, **doesn't exist**! They do their best to convince those around them there is no God. And some even seem to hate God.

This makes no sense. How can you hate something that doesn't exist? If there is no God, why bother? Why are they so upset and angry? If He doesn't exist, they should move on and let us be. But this, in and of itself, is part and parcel of what it means to be made in the image of God and have an awareness of God. Our being made in God's image is independent of whether one believes in God or not.

As image-bearers there is something innate within each one of us that connects us to God. Only in the case of the atheist, energy is spent trying to create distance from God. It's just one facet of the Psalm 2 rebellion.

Let's continue.

The first man's awareness of God allowed him to respond to God and act out the desires of God. And God stated his desires. Plants and animals are to multiply and fill the earth (see Genesis 1:22, for example). Fish are to make fish and birds are to make birds. They are to multiply. God's desire is for humankind to also multiply, but look what is added:

> God blessed them and said to them, 'Be fruitful and multiply, and fill the earth and subdue it; <u>rule over</u> the fish of the sea and the birds of the air and every creature that crawls upon the earth.' (Genesis 1:28)

While the animal kingdom is to produce their physical image, mankind is to reproduce an obedient image—to respond to God and to reflect his desires. In this capacity, we are to rule over God's creation.

And God provides a further instruction.

> And the LORD God commanded him, 'You may eat freely from every tree of the garden, but you must not eat from the tree of the knowledge of good and evil; for in the day that you eat of it, you will surely die.' (Genesis 2:16, 17)

We'll get back to this shortly.

Reading the first two chapters of the book of Genesis, one notices that both contain the creation story (although the original Hebrew had no chapter divisions, or verse designations). Chapter 1 ends, "And God looked upon all that He had made, and indeed, it was very good. And there was evening, and there was morning—the sixth day" (Genesis 1:31). Chapter 2 begins by announcing God's "rest" on the seventh day and then recites the creation in more detail.

God rested? God did not rest because he was tired. His "rest" represents his completed work. It is God's expression of satisfaction with what He has done as he evaluates His creation and sees that His creation is good.

As chapter 2 continues, man is formed first—out of the dust of the ground. He is given life through the "breath" of God (Genesis 2:7). In Chapter 1, we see the term "good" used seven times in God's assessment of what He has created. But in Genesis 2:18, we now see that something is *not* good:

> The LORD God also said, "It is <u>not good</u> for the man to be alone. I will make for him a suitable helper."

Hmmm. Something in God's good creation is not good? Does this mean God had erred in what He has done?

No.

God is saying that, up to this point, the creation process is not yet complete—that He has not yet finished His creation.

Notice what is happening:

> And out of the ground the LORD God formed every beast of the field and every bird of the air, and He brought them to the man to see what he would name each one ...

> But for Adam no suitable helper was found. (Genesis 2:19, 20)

Animals could not help Adam, or rule with Adam, because they do not have the image of God. So, in Genesis 2:22 we read,

> And from the rib that the LORD God had taken from the man, He made a woman and brought her to him.

Two things are important to notice. At this point in God's revelation, this first woman has not been given a name. When she is named—and what she is named—are important. But this comes later in the text.

Secondly, it appears God has designed **a certain order** in his creation: God—man—woman—animal world. We will see how this becomes important also.

But these must await the next lesson.

From lesson 4: What do we learn about God?

- God is the Creator. By implication:
    - God is all powerful
    - God is the Owner over His creation.
- God establishes the value system and makes the rules for His creation.
- What God has made is good. This places value in the world around us and in each one of us.
- God wants us to reflect who He is to each other and to the world around us.

---

doesn't exist: I find the thought patterns of many atheists, and their consequent behavior, amusing (and sad). I don't believe in the one-horn unicorn. But why on earth should I spend time and energy angry at the non-existent one-horn unicorn? And yet, the "religion" of the atheist is anger and warfare against, from their perspective, the non-existent God.

a certain order: That the first woman is made after man, and from man, has created discussion and debate throughout the Christian community for centuries. Much of this center on the role women can and can't have when it comes to the church. Are men and women "equals"—the egalitarian view? Or do women have different, but complementary roles and responsibilities—the complementarian view?

Books have been written on this, and the scholarly debate has been reasonable and rational, with both sides basing their conclusions on the biblical text. And yet, there remains no clear consensus.

As to their equality, there are many that can present a case that this first woman was made equal to Adam. After all, on three separate occasions the biblical text states they were both made in the image of God.

But if they are equal, why didn't God simply create both from dust— and do so at the same time? Why create Adam, and then at a later time create the first woman? For the ancient Jews accustomed to the laws of primogeniture, doesn't the creation order imply something about man versus woman, and doesn't this oppose egalitarianism — the concept that both are equal?

And why create the first woman out of Adam? Doesn't this suggest woman's existence required Adam? And why does it seem that Adam is held responsible when the first woman disobeyed? Why is God's command concerning the tree, which is given three times, only given directly to Adam and Adam alone?

And why, after they disobeyed, is "woman" finally given a name— and is named by Adam?

Scholarly discussions on both egalitarianism and complementarianism can be found in *Two Views on Women in Ministry* (Gundry, Stanley N. and James R. Beck, eds., Grand Rapids: Zondervan, 2005). Beck, one of the book's editors, writes, "We believe *one can build a credible case* within the bounds of orthodoxy and a commitment to inerrancy *for either one of the two major views* we address in this volume, although all of us view our own positions on the matter as stronger and more compelling" (emphasis added—in his introduction, page 15).

More in-depth discussions of the Genesis story and man-woman can be found in the following:

Alice Mathews, *Gender Roles and the People of God: Rethinking What We Were Taught about Men and Women in the Church* (Grand Rapids: Zondervan, 2017).

Michelle Lee-Barnewall, *Neither Complementarian nor Egalitarian: A Kingdom Corrective Evangelical Gender Debate* (Grand Rapids: Baker, 2016), 121-146.

Linda L. Belleville, "Women in Ministry: An Egalitarian Perspective" in *Two Views on Women in Ministry*, 25-35; and Craig L. Blomberg, "Women in Ministry: A Complementarian Perspective," in *Two Views on Women in Ministry*, 128-132.

Lee-Barnewall notes, "Genesis 2-3 consistently and strikingly portrays Adam and Eve's relationship in an asymmetrical way. Adam provides the source for Eve's creation, and he is the only one told to bring unity to the relationship" (p. 143). However, she also notes that the text "lacks any explicit commands for Adam to exercise authority over Eve" (p. 144).

Blomberg takes a countering view, describing how the Genesis text clearly shows Adam's special position due to such things as him being created first and him being the one who gives Eve her name. Belleville counters, "power in naming" is not supported by biblical scholarship (see p. 28).

My view is that God has clearly structured an order to His creation— and this will come into play in our next lesson. While this is separate from the discussion as to whether or not women should hold senior leadership positions within a church (senior pastor, as an example), I do want to stress that I see nothing in scripture that prevents women from preaching or teaching. I base this, in part, on Acts 18:24–26:

Meanwhile a Jew named Apollos, a native of Alexandria, came to Ephesus. He was an eloquent man, well versed in the Scriptures. He had been instructed in the way of the Lord and was fervent in spirit. He spoke and taught accurately about Jesus, though he knew only the baptism of John. And he began to speak boldly in the synagogue. When Priscilla and Aquila heard him, they took him in and explained to him the way of God more accurately.

As my former professor and New Testament scholar, Craig Blomberg writes, "At the very least we have a positive example of a Christian woman helping to teach an adult Christian man in the area of religious doctrine" (Craig L. Blomberg, "Women in Ministry: A Complementarian Perspective" in *Two Views on Women in Ministry*, 147).

For what it's worth, when I've discussed this specific passage from Acts with those opposed to my view, they often counter, "but nothing says this teaching by Priscilla was done in public—see, the text says they took him in, they took him to their home." How does one respond, "Whatever" in a way that expresses love, joy, and peace?

There are other biblical items that support the preaching of women to others. The very first person told to announce the news of the resurrection was a woman. It was Mary Magdalene whom Jesus tells, "go and tell My brothers, 'I am ascending to My Father and your Father, to My God and your God'" (John 20:17). Jesus has just left the tomb, and his profound announcement to the disciples will come from a woman. Has there ever been a more important theological event and profound statement to share with others? The news of this was entrusted to a woman, and it is Christ himself that tells her to take this message to the disciples.

Sent on another important errand was the Corinthian deacon Phoebe. She delivered a letter from the Apostle Paul to those in Rome (Romans 16). She was entrusted with the greatest theological treatise that became part of the New Testament (an argument can be made that the letter to the Romans and the book of John are the two most important books of the New Testament). It is reasonable to expect that when she delivered this letter, she was prepared to answer questions from the recipients—although this is conjecture. Regardless, this important document was entrusted to a woman— one who was also a church leader.

Lastly, John tells us clearly why he wrote his Gospel. He tells the reader:

> But these are written so that you may believe that Jesus is the Christ, the Son of God, and that by believing you may have life in His name. (John 20:31)

Throughout John's Gospel we see, on many occasions and in many ways, Jesus truly is the Christ (Messiah) and Son of God. But in John's writing, who is the first person to make the specific declaration "You are the Christ"? It was a woman (John 11:27).

Having said this, though, I understand reasons for disagreement. They are well-stated with support from the biblical text. As one example from the viewpoint of an opponent of women in preaching, see "Here's What You Need to Know About John MacArthur's Stance on Female Preachers" by Jessica Mouser, November 15, 2019, available at https://churchleaders.com/news/366146-john-macarthur-stance-female-preachers.html?utm_source=outreach-cl-daily-nl&utm_medium=email&utm_content=read-more&utm_campaign=cl-daily-nl&maropost_id=&mpweb=256-8398057-713055790 (accessed November 18, 2019).

I believe some of the confusion in this area has been due to taking the biblical text that applies to the household (for example, Ephesians 5:23, where Paul tells us the "husband is the head of the wife") and applying this to the church. Household codes, or *Haustafeln*, can be found in Ephesians 5:21–6:9; Colossians 3:12–4:6; and 1st Peter 2:11–3:22.

5

The Rebellion of Humankind

We need to put the Biblical Story into context at this point in history. God did not give man ten commandments. He gave him just one.

In effect, God is telling Adam that he has been given all of creation. Adam will have **dominion** over everything he sees. If he looks to the east, all that he sees is his. If he looks to the west, he can journey westward for a day, or a week, or even a month. Everything he sees on that journey is his, as well. Or he can turn and look to the north. He can travel as far as he can heading northward, and all that he sees is his also. Or he can turn to the south. He can travel for as long and as far as he would like towards the south. Everything he set his eyes upon, every square inch of land that he would put his foot upon—all of it is his. The plants, the animals—everything. It is all Adam's.

That's a generous and gracious God. He's created this earth and He has handed it over to His image-bearers.

God adds just one small instruction:

While everything created on this earth was Adam's, there was one tree, single tree that was not his. Adam was told that if he ate from the fruit of this tree, he would die.

Let's think about this.

Do you think Adam took that long hike to the west to see all that God had given him? Do you think he even glanced northward with curiosity? Or eastward? Or looked toward the south?

Or is Adam like we are: there was no way he could get his eyes—and his mind—off that one, single, isolated tree containing the forbidden fruit?

Genesis 3:1 begins our next chapter of the Bible. We know the story well.

> Now the serpent was more crafty than any beast of
> the field that the LORD God had made. And he said
> to the woman, "Did God really say, 'You must not eat
> of any tree in the garden?'"

From our previous lesson covering creation, this should raise our curiosity. Notice what the serpent is doing. He can communicate with man. That's odd.

And the serpent is contradicting God and thus knows something about God. That's odd, too. We have said animals have no image, no awareness, of God. But this one does have awareness.

Somehow this animal is either being instructed from outside the natural realm, or this animal, itself, is something outside the natural. Regardless, something unnatural is happening.

This serpent is Satan—a fallen angel appearing as a serpent.

How do we know this? Nowhere in the Genesis text is the serpent identified as such.

We learn this from the very last book in the Bible. Revelation 12:9 reads,

> And the great dragon was hurled down—that ancient serpent called the devil and Satan, the deceiver of the whole world. He was hurled to the earth, and his angels with him.

Revelation 20:2 echoes this description,

> He seized the dragon, that ancient serpent who is the devil and Satan, and bound him for a thousand years.

But why would Satan appear as a member of the animal kingdom?

Remember from our last lesson, God's plan is to have man rule over the animal world. If Satan were to show up as some demonic angel, which he is, Adam has no command concerning that situation. But Satan shows up as a member of the animal world. God's order is for man to have dominion over the animal kingdom. But now man is shown listening to this animal and ultimately trusting in this animal.

This goes against God's instructions and created order. I suggest that the first sin was not the eating of the forbidden fruit. It was Adam and the woman listening to Satan and believing what this deceiver says instead of what God had said.

And why did Satan approach and speak to the woman and not Adam? This, too, goes against God's created order. The order was to be: God, man, woman, animal kingdom. Satan will reverse this: Satan, animal, woman, man—and no God.

Satan always wants to reverse God's order of things and ultimately remove God from the picture. His goal is to be worshipped by humankind. He always and consistently wants us to rebel against God's instruction. Instead of mankind having dominion over the animal world, an animal will appear (the serpent, or snake) and woman will obey this animal. In turn, Adam will follow suit. Satan begins his mission to reverse God's plan. He continues in active pursuit of this mission today.

It is here that we should share several things concerning "evil."

- Walt Disney has it all wrong. Disney always shows the wicked witch as being scary and ugly. No one would want anything to do with her. For those of us who are males, one's worse day would be a blind date with the wicked witch. But that's not the way evil works. Evil is most often attractive. It doesn't repel, it attracts and entices.
- Why did God create evil? He didn't. Evil is the absence of good. Evil came about when fallen angels, given their free will, and fallen man, given our free will, decided against God's rule and order. Just like darkness being the absence of light, evil is the absence of good. We, ourselves, create evil.
- Lastly (for now), for those old enough to remember the great moral philosopher and spokesman, the comedian Flip Wilson, you'll recall his often-used phrase "The devil made me do it."

Yes, Satan can tempt us—he even tempted Jesus. But we should also remember that we have ownership over our sin and rebellion against God. These are our choices—our decisions. A teaching from James, the half-brother of Jesus, is instructive:

> When tempted, no one should say, "God is tempting me." For God cannot be tempted by evil, nor does He tempt anyone. But each one is tempted when by

his own evil desires, he is lured away and enticed. Then after desire has conceived, it gives birth to sin; and sin, when it is full-grown, gives birth to death. (James 1:13–15)

We also need to recognize how rebellion against God occurs. Genesis 3 provides two examples: God's words are changed and are also directly contradicted. We first see this with Satan:

Did God really say, 'You must not eat of <u>any tree</u> in the garden?'

God did *not* say this.

God gave *all* of the trees to Adam and the woman *except one*. Satan makes God out to be a stingy task master that makes life hard and unreasonable. Satan wants us to view God as being unfair. But a reminder, God gave Adam and the woman everything. Everything. It was just the fruit from that one single tree that was off limits.

And Satan directly contradicts God:

'You will <u>not</u> surely die,' the serpent told her. (Genesis 3:4)

This is also counter to what God said.

Satan is dealing in fake news. What God has said is clear and certain:

"…for in the day that you eat of it, you <u>will</u> surely die." (Genesis 2:17)

Satan wants us to change the words of God and to doubt God and His fairness. But we don't need Satan's encouragement to do this. Look at **the first woman**. We are told,

The woman answered the serpent, 'We may eat the fruit of the trees of the garden, but of the fruit of the tree in the middle of the garden, God has said, 'You must not eat of it <u>or touch it</u>, or you will die.' (Genesis 3:2, 3)

Where did God say not to touch this particular tree? He didn't. Adam was only told he could not eat of its fruit. Like we saw with Satan, woman, too, has changed the words of God. She has added to God's conditions. In this respect, Eve might have been the very first Pharisee—but we're getting ahead of ourselves.

In the previous lesson, we saw where God established his value system, creating an ordered world. Seven times we see the phrase, "God saw" coupled with "it was good." But now look what happens:

When the woman <u>saw</u> that the tree <u>was good</u> for food and pleasing to the eyes, and that it was desirable for obtaining wisdom, she **took the fruit and ate it.** (Genesis 3:6)

Now it is the woman that "saw." And she, herself, is deciding what "was good." She is replacing God's wisdom and His value system with her own. She knows better than God.

But let's not be too hard on this first woman, because we are no different. This is precisely what you and I do. Routinely. We replace God's wisdom and value system with our own. And then we wonder why things get so messed up.

Note also, Satan tells the woman,

For God knows that in the day you eat of it, your eyes will be opened, and <u>you will be like God</u>, knowing good and evil. (Genesis 3:5)

And there it is. Satan has offered the greatest of all enticements. Satan is telling the woman that if she disobeys and eats the forbidden fruit, she will be her own God. He has closed the deal and has sealed the deception.

Mankind wants to be like God. In fact, we want to be our own god. How could the woman hold back? How could she obey God and refrain from eating of the forbidden fruit, if she had a shot at being her own god? Nothing would prevent the woman from tasting of the fruit and disobeying God's one, single, simple, sole prohibition.

Before we come down too hard on our great, great, great...great grandmother, we need to read the second part of Genesis 3:6,

> She also gave some to her husband, who was with her, and he ate it.

Adam was a direct witness to what the woman was doing. In God's ordering of His creation, Adam should have instructed the woman, "No." After all, the command not to eat of this particular tree was given to Adam and not the woman.

Adam not only evades his responsibility, as he silently witnesses the disobedience and rebellion, he joins in. Adam does this without offering one single word of objection or showing any evidence of restraint.

Satan is victorious. God's image-bearers have obeyed an entity from the animal kingdom of which they were to rule over. Man has failed in his responsibility concerning his role and relationship with woman. And both have gone against God's desires.

The obedient image has been broken.

We call this first disobedience the "fall of man." When this happened, four relationships were broken. We'll look at these in our next lesson. But before we do, we should think about how this relates to Jesus.

In the garden, the first Adam failed in obedience to God. In his letter to the believers in Rome, Paul talks about Jesus as the "second Adam":

> Just as one trespass brought condemnation for all men, so also one act of righteousness brought justification and life for all men. For just as through the disobedience of the one man the many were made sinners, so also through the obedience of the one man the many will be made righteous. (Romans 5:18, 19)

Adam broke the obedient image that God desired. Jesus maintained obedience. So, through Adam, all men would be condemned. Through Jesus, men could be forgiven and pronounced "not guilty."

Adam brought death. All would die both spiritual death (separation from God) and physical death (separation from the body). Jesus brought life.

Because of Jesus, we can escape judgment and condemnation—and God's wrath. We saw this in our study of Psalm 2: "Blessed are all who take refuge in him" (Psalm 2:12).

The Biblical Story is all about Jesus.

From lesson 5: What do we learn about God?

- God gave Adam, and gives to us, instructions (commands).
- But God has also given us free will. Adam chose to disobey God and go against God's instructions.
- Our disobedience brings death.

We also learn that Satan is an antagonist against God's created order, and Adam and Eve both became obedient to Satan.

dominion: This implies the world was made for humankind. We have God-given (natural) rights to explore, subdue, and partake of that which is around us.

the first woman: Eve isn't given her name until Genesis 3:20—after she has disobeyed God. Up to this point in the text, she is simply referred to as "woman." Soon we will see when Eve is given her name and what this name means. This is important to the Biblical Story.

took the fruit and ate it: Note the verbs "take" and "eat." For those familiar with the Bible, these same two words appear at the Lord's Supper. The first sin involved disobeying God's command by the taking and the eating of that which was forbidden. We observe communion and our remembrance of Jesus through the taking and eating as well. But now the focus is on the body of Christ and the shedding of his blood which, for the Christian, removes forever the penalty of disobedience.

6

Sin

When Adam and the woman rebel against God, four relationships are broken.

- The human race and its relationship with the rest of creation is now corrupt and broken.

  > "Because you have listened to the voice of your wife
  >> and have eaten of the tree
  >> from which I commanded you not to eat,
  > cursed is the ground because of you;
  >> through toil you will eat of it
  >> all the days of your life.
  > Both thorns and thistles it will yield you,
  >> and you will eat the plants of the field.
  > By the sweat of your brow
  >> you will eat your bread." (Genesis 3:17–19)

- The interrelationships between humans is broken.

And the man answered, "The woman whom You gave me, she gave me fruit from the tree, and I ate it." (Genesis 3:12)

Adam blames Eve, and indirectly blames God.

- Man's inner peace (his relationship with himself) is broken.

    "I heard Your voice in the garden," he replied, "and I was afraid because I was naked; so I hid myself." (Genesis 3:10)

God's image-bearers now carry fear and experience guilt and shame.

- And most importantly, the relationship between God's image-bearers and God Himself is broken.

    "They hid themselves from the presence of the LORD God among the trees of the garden." (Genesis 3:8)

God clearly told Adam that to eat of the tree would bring death. Adam died. He died a spiritual death—separation from God. And he would eventually die a physical death—separation from the body. And the Biblical Story teaches this predicament befell all of humanity—all of the sons and daughters of Adam. This includes you and me.

The Apostle Paul teaches that no one is righteous:

    There is no one righteous, not even one. (Romans 3:10, quoting Psalm 14:3 and Psalm 51:3)

He tells us about the universal nature of sin:

    All have sinned and fall short of the glory of God. (Romans 3:23)

We are spiritually dead:

> As for you, you were dead in your trespasses and sins.
> (Ephesians 2:1)

And because all of humankind is spiritually dead, we alienate ourselves from God:

> There is no one who understands, no one who seeks
> God. (Romans 3:11)

And our rebellion has earned each one of us death:

> The wages of sin is death. (Romans 6:23)

There is nothing, nothing in heaven or on earth, that we can do to repair the damage of our disobedience and rebellion. We cannot force God to forgive us—nor can we set the terms for His forgiveness.

Oh, but we try.

We "do" religion. Religion is man reaching for God. "If I just read the Bible, God will love me. If I just go to church, and give to the church, God will love me."

Or perhaps our attempts are not that sophisticated. "If I just carve an image of God onto this piece of wood and worship it, God will love me."

And some don't even try to reach for God. Adam and the woman simply tried to run from God. And many attempt this as well.

But look what God does:

> So the LORD God called out to the man, "Where are
> you?" (Genesis 3:9)

Of course, God knows where Adam is. But God calls out to Adam. God searches for Adam.

Here we learn something important about God. God is a God who seeks us out. He does not abandon us. He loves us so much that He seeks to find each one of us. He loves us so much that He will even die for us.

This is a key truth concerning Christianity. Religion is man reaching for God. Christianity is God reaching for man—and loving humankind to the extent that He became man and suffered punishment and death in payment for our sin.

And it is this, the blood of Christ, that repairs the brokenness. The Good News of God's story is that He will seek out his fallen image-bearers, and He will provide the pathway that will repair the four broken relationships mentioned above. God provides the way that opens His kingdom plans for humankind—allowing each one of us to return into His presence, becoming participants in His kingdom, and allowing us to spend eternity with Him.

Even though we are only in the third *chapter* of the Bible (with 1186 chapters to go), we begin to learn about what that way to God is. It comes from one of the most profound verses in the Biblical Story. We must read it carefully.

God addresses Satan, who remains in the form of the serpent:

> ...I will put enmity between you and the woman,
>   and between your seed and her seed.
> He will crush your head,
>   and you will strike his heel. (Genesis 3:15)

God is going to solve the problem of sin and sinful humanity through *"her seed"*—the "seed of woman." God's solution to sin comes from an offspring of woman.

There will be continual enmity (hostility) between the seed of woman and, referencing Satan, *"your seed."* Who are the "seed of Satan"? Does Satan have offspring?

Satan is an angel—a fallen angel—and angels do not have offspring. But in context, the seed of Satan are all who follow Satan. These are the people that live in sin and can be considered the children of Satan. They are the ones that reject God's provision—the seed of woman. And there are quite a number who fall into this group. Afterall, Satan is the ruler of this world. Which brings up another point we should address before proceeding. Who says Satan rules the world?

- Jesus does:

> I will not speak with you much longer, for the prince of this world is coming, and he has no claim on Me. (John 14:30)

- Paul calls Satan the "god of this world":

> In their case the god of this world has blinded the minds of the unbelievers, to keep them from seeing the light of the gospel of the glory of Christ, who is the image of God. (2nd Corinthians 4:4—ESV)

- John tells us that the entire world is under the control of Satan:

> We know that we are of God, and that the whole world is under the power of the evil one. (1st John 5:19)

God tells Adam and Eve, and us, that it won't be some angelic being that will destroy Satan ("...will crush your head"). No, it will be <u>the</u>

offspring of a woman. Notice that nowhere does the text mention this destroyer of Satan will come from the seed of man.

Later in the Biblical Story, we learn that this offspring is Jesus—conceived by God through the Holy Spirit but born of the virgin Mary. The prophet Isaiah had it right when he predicted, "For unto us a child is born" (the seed of woman), "unto us a son is given" (the Son of God)—Isaiah 9:6.

But God reveals something else here in Genesis 3 that should cause us to pause. Yes, the seed of woman will defeat Satan—the serpent will be crushed by, let's use the term, the Redeemer, the One who will redeem humankind. But note how Genesis 3:15 continues: "and you will strike his heel."

A heel-strike from a serpent means death. The Redeemer will die! This seed of woman will suffer the punishment of sin: death.

All of scripture is about Jesus—and Genesis 3:15 is important in what God reveals about Jesus. He will be born of a woman. He will destroy Satan. But his victory only comes through his suffering and death.

Yes, at present, Satan is the prince of the world. But this is only temporary. Throughout the Biblical Story, we will learn that Jesus represents the crowning achievement of God's plan of reconciliation. The broken relationships will be restored. For those who accept God's plan of redemption, Jesus' death reconciles them to God. Only Jesus' death does this—and Jesus' resurrection assures this. We are saved from God's punishment and wrath by the blood of Christ and the victory of the resurrection.

We're getting ahead of ourselves, but I think it is beneficial to take an early glimpse at our reconciliation.

As God imparts new life to the believer through the Holy Spirit (John 3), we become a new creation. This allows us to be ministers (ambassadors) of reconciliation.

Paul writes:

> If anyone is in Christ, he is a new creation. The old has passed away. Behold, the new has come! (2nd Corinthians 5:17)

The "old" includes the broken relationships. Paul continues,

> All this is from God, who reconciled us to Himself through Christ and gave us the ministry of reconciliation: that God was reconciling the world to Himself in Christ, not counting men's trespasses against them. And He has committed to us the message of reconciliation. (2nd Corinthians 5:18, 19)

All of creation awaits this process of reconciliation:

> For the creation waits in eager expectation for the children of God to be revealed. For the creation was subjected to frustration, not by its own choice, but by the will of the one who subjected it, in hope that the creation itself will be liberated from its bondage to decay and brought into the freedom and glory of the children of God. (Romans 8:19–21, NIV)

And the cornerstone of our reconciliation is God bringing us back into relationship with Him:

> Since we have been justified through faith, we have peace with God through our Lord Jesus Christ. (Romans 5:1)

Therefore, there is now no condemnation for those who are in Christ Jesus. (Romans 8:1)

Nothing is going to separate the Christian from God's love:

For I am convinced that neither death nor life, neither angels nor principalities, neither the present nor the future, nor any powers, neither height nor depth, nor anything else in all creation, will be able to separate us from the love of God that is in Christ Jesus our Lord. (Romans 8:38, 39)

Paul calls each believer into a ministry of reconciliation:

He has committed to us the message of reconciliation. Therefore, we are ambassadors for Christ, as though God were making His appeal through us. We implore you on behalf of Christ: Be reconciled to God. (2nd Corinthians 5:19, 20)

We are reconciled to God and we are to be ministers of reconciliation to each other. This, of course, was one of the key teachings of Jesus:

By this all men will know that you are My disciples, if you love one another. (John 13:35)

Returning to the Genesis text, I find it fascinating that Moses recorded what we label as Genesis 3:15 thousands of years ago—long before anyone ever had a glimpse of who this seed of woman would be our how God's plan of redemption would be played out. But from here on, those chosen by God will be seeking the arrival of this Redeemer—the arrival of the Messiah, the Son of God, and King.

And it is here, after Genesis 3:15, that woman is finally given her name (Genesis 3:20). She is called "Eve"—a name meaning "life." She would become the mother of all of humankind and thus bring life into this world. All of us are sons and daughters of Eve.

But there is another way to view her name. Disobeying God brought spiritual death—separation from God. Adam and Eve—and you and me, their descendants—are spiritually dead. But eventually there will be an offspring, this seed of woman, who will bring life to God's people. He is the resurrection and the life (John 11:25) and the way and the truth and the life (John 14:6). He will bring spiritual life (a return to God) and physical life (bodily resurrection) to those who accept God's plan and have faith in God's promises. In this context, Eve's name is a reminder of the promised Redeemer and seed of woman—the one who brings life. I believe this is why Eve remains unnamed until after Genesis 3:15. And I believe this is why she is given a name that means "life."

We've only brushed through the Bible's first three chapters—less than three-tenths of a percent of the Bible's chapters. But the foundation has been laid. God's perfect, pristine creation has been marred. God didn't do this. We did.

We did this by sin.

But already the story is about Jesus. The ultimate destiny for Satan and death is defeat by the Redeemer.

There are those that don't like the exclusive claims of Christianity. We have the audacity to say that Jesus is the *only* way to God. How dare us.

But this is what God says. Remember, this is His world, not ours. Our Creator God sets the rules. Man has rebelled against God, and only God can establish the way for forgiveness. And the way God has established for our redemption is through Jesus.

The Bible, God's revelation to man, is about Jesus because it is only through Jesus that man can be given new life and reconciliation.

Let's continue, but before we do, there are two additional points we need to briefly cover. These are important because much of the Bible centers on what these imply.

Adam was told that disobeying God would bring death. But Adam's physical death does not come immediately. We see that, while God is a God of judgment, he is also a God of mercy. Mercy is when we are not given the punishment we deserve or when this rightful punishment is delayed. We see God's mercy continually throughout the biblical text.

Secondly, when Adam and Eve sinned, they felt themselves to be exposed (naked). They fashion a covering for themselves out of leaves (Genesis 3:7). This is religion—man trying to take control over his own fate and cover the results of his own sin.

But God covers the two with animal skin (Genesis 3:21).

We quickly see that God is a God who provides. We cannot rely upon ourselves or our own efforts to solve our brokenness —particularly our broken relationship with God. When we rely upon our own efforts, this is religion. We must rely upon God and His provisions—what He has done and continues to do. This is Christianity. Christianity is not "rules"—it is "relationship." We rely upon our new relationship with God because of what Jesus has done for us.

We often talk about "faith." Faith is another word for reliance. Faith is trust. As we are spiritually awakened, we place our trust in God and His promises, and rely upon God and His promises. Faith also includes the element of obedience. We begin to return to the obedient image that God intended. This allows us to reflect God's image—His original intent when He made us as His image-bearers.

There is another point concerning what God did. Much has been made of God having to sacrifice an animal in order to cover Adam and Eve's nakedness. Sin creates death, and the covering of sin requires the shedding of blood. Much of God's Story revolves around this truth, which we will address shortly.

From lesson 6: What do we learn about God?

- God affirms that Satan will be destroyed.
- God's plan of redemption and forgiveness will be through one born of a woman (the seed of woman of Genesis 3:15).
- Up to this point in the Story, though, we are told very little about him. We know Satan will be defeated, but the One who defeats Satan will suffer and die.
- God is a God of mercy. God is a God who provides.

7

Why Bother?

As the Bible continues, the story is one of intensifying sin and rebellion coupled with progressive revelations concerning the seed of woman. It took God six days to create the heavens and the earth, but the story of this Redeemer, this Anointed One from God, will take several thousand years to unfold. But even before he appears on earth—the Bible will reveal a great deal about him. And it will also reveal *why we need him!*

We begin, though, learning about the deepening level of man's sinfulness. Eve, the mother of life, gives birth to a son, Cain, and a second son, Abel. Cain murders his brother (Genesis 4).

There is a pause in the Story, and we are provided a listing of Adam's descendants connecting Noah to Adam. This should elicit a question: Why did God bother to provide us with this list? These are men long since gone and the Bible tells us very little about them. Why are we given their names?

Let's look at each name and what the Hebrew word implies. I am indebted to the work of Chuck **Missler** for these insights.

Adam simply means "man."

Seth is Adam's son. In Hebrew, this comes from the word transliterated *sith*, which means "appointed." The Bible tells us this name was chosen in that God had appointed to Eve another son after the death of Abel (Genesis 4:25).

Seth names his son Enosh, which means "mortal," "frail," or "miserable." It is from the root *anash*, "to be incurable," used of a wound, grief, woe, sickness, or wickedness.

Enosh has a son, Kenan, whose name means "sorrow," "dirge," or "elegy." Missler informs us that the precise denotation is somewhat elusive. Some study aids unfortunately, and incorrectly, presume that Kenan is synonymous with Canaan.

Why would someone name a child the equivalent of "sorrow"? Or for that matter, why would you choose a name meaning "to be incurable"? We can't be certain, but often names like these might have referred to difficult circumstances surrounding the birthing process.

Kenan's son is Mahalalel, from *mahalal* which means "blessed" or "praise." The *el* in Mahalalel references God. Thus, Mahalalel means the "Blessed God". **Hebrew names** often include the *"el,"* as in Daniel (God is my Judge), Ezekiel (God will strengthen), and Bethel (House of God).

Mahalalel's son is named Jared, from the verb *yaradh*, meaning "shall come down." There is a provocative suggestion as to why Jared would be named this—but we will save this for later.

Jared's son is named Enoch, which means "teaching" or "commencement." He was the first of four generations of preachers. It is surprising that the earliest recorded prophecy is by Enoch, which, amazingly enough, deals with the Second Coming of Christ (we learn this from the New Testament book of Jude).

Enoch is the father of Methuselah. Methuselah comes from *muth*, a root that means "death," and from *shalach*, which means "to bring" or "to send forth." The name Methuselah means "his death shall bring." Methuselah's father (**Enoch**) was given a prophecy of the coming worldwide flood and was told that as long as his son was alive, judgment (the flood) would be withheld. In other words, Methuselah's death would bring forth the flood. The year that Methuselah died, the great flood came.

Methuselah's son is named Lamech, a root still evident today in our English word "lament" or "lamentation." The word *lamech* suggests "despairing." This name is also linked to the Lamech in Cain's line who inadvertently kills his son, Tubal-Cain, in a hunting incident (Genesis 4:19–25).

Lamech is the father of Noah. Noah's name is derived from *nacham*, "to bring relief or comfort", as Lamech, himself, explains in Genesis 5:29.

So why did God bother to provide us with this list of names?

Let's string them together:

Adam	man
Seth	appointed
Enosh	mortal
Kenan	sorrow
Mahalalel	the blessed God
Kared	shall come down
Enoch	teaching
Methuselah	his death shall bring
Lamech	despairing
Noah	rest, comfort.

I'm not sure what was going through Moses' mind when he was recording God's Word. But here, in the fifth chapter of the very first book of the Bible, we have God's plan of redemption: "Man [is] appointed mortal, sorrowful, [but] the blessed God shall come down teaching [that] his death shall bring [the] despairing **rest**, comfort."

The blessed God who shall come down is Jesus. And it is his death that brings rest—peace with God. Again, we are reminded of the truth Jesus told the religious leaders:

> You pore over the Scriptures because you presume that by them you possess eternal life. These are the very words that testify about Me. (John 5:39)

From lesson 7: What do we learn about God?

- From the previous lesson, we saw that God would destroy Satan and Satan's "seed" through the offspring of woman.
- Now we see hints that man's predicament will be solved by God, Himself coming to earth—and it will be His death that provides us peace.

Missler: See Chuck Missler, "The Gospel in Genesis: A Hidden Message" published February 1, 1996 and available at www.khouse.org/articles/1996/44/
(Accessed June 28, 2019).

Hebrew names: It is often profitable to research what a Hebrew name means. The process has been greatly simplified and all of the hard work already completed. Refer to the website: www.behindthename.com.

Enoch: A caution: there are two Enoch's in the Bible. One is a son of Cain and is mentioned in Genesis 4:17. The Enoch in Genesis 5 is not the same Enoch. Jude will mention Enoch in his writing (the book of Jude in the New Testament) and goes the extra step of telling us which Enoch he is talking about: *"Enoch, the seventh from Adam"* (Jude 1:14).

rest: The Bible depicts several kinds of rest. The creation rest refers to the seventh day after creation. God did not rest because he was tired—his "rest" represents the completion and celebration of His work.

While "rest" can imply cessation from labor, it can also be an expression of satisfaction, or an expression of confidence and of comfort. God rested to express satisfaction with what He had done. He saw that His creation was good.

"Rest" is also used in the Old Testament as a reference to the defeat of one's enemies (for example, see Joshua 14:15; 21:44; 23:1; 2nd Samuel 7:1; 1st Kings 5:4).

Specific to the children of Israel, we see two of the concepts associated with "rest" in Deuteronomy 12:8–10, as the children of Israel are about to enter the Promised Land (we'll get to this in the Biblical Story shortly):

> You are not to do as we are doing here today, where everyone does what seems right in his own eyes. For you have not yet come to the resting place and the inheritance the LORD your God is giving you.

> When you cross the Jordan and live in the land that the LORD your God is giving you as an inheritance, and He gives you rest from all the enemies around you and you live in security.

The concept of "rest" referring to the defeat of one's enemies is also found in the New Testament—but we may not notice it without this Old Testament background. Jesus promises his followers:

> Come to me, all you who are weary and burdened,
> and <u>I will give you rest.</u> (Matthew 11:28)

This does not imply following Christ will be easy or some type of restful vacation—certainly not cessation from work. To ask Jesus for his rest means we are asking Jesus for his Kingship—and his protection (salvation) from our enemies. The rest Christ offers removes us from bondage to Satan so that we can live in safety. But we must come to Christ, and we must accept his rest.

For a more complete discussion, see lessons 12 and 14 in *A Forty-Day Study of the Book of Hebrews: The Superiority of Christ.*

8

Why Bother, Part 2

The sixth chapter of Genesis begins the story of Noah's flood—a world-wide event which swept away all of humankind with the exception of Noah and seven others.

Why would God do this?

The typical Sunday school lesson teaches that the world was destroyed because man's sins had become great.

Really?

You don't think the last century was sinful? Two world wars. Hitler. Stalin. Mao. Pol Pot.

Or even our present century, where Americans alone kill close to a **million babies** each year?

From Adam and Eve on, the earth has always been sinful. Has there ever been a time when man's sin was not great?

Perhaps there is something else driving God's wrath and the destruction of humanity. Let's look at this.

Something strange and unsettling appears as we get to the opening verses of Genesis 6:

> Now when men began to multiply on the face of the earth and daughters were born to them, the sons of God saw that the daughters of men were beautiful, and they took as wives whomever they chose. (Genesis 6:1, 2)

The text is clear—especially in the original Hebrew. Men begin to multiply, and the *"sons of God"* begin taking on the *"daughters of men"* as their wives. "Sons of God" refers to direct creations of God. Adam was a son of God (direct creation of God). Angels are "sons of God" and are direct creations of God. We see this term "sons of God" used in several places in the Old Testament where it references angels (see Job 1:6–12; 2:1; and 38:7).

We, though, are not direct creations of God, per se. We are descendants of Adam. Believers are referred to as the **children of God** because we have been adopted into God's family (Romans 8:16, for example).

In Genesis 6, we learn that "sons of God"—angels, specifically fallen angels—begin to marry women, the "daughters of men."

What on earth is happening?

God has already told Satan that his downfall would come through the "seed of woman" (offspring of woman). What better way to thwart God's plan than to corrupt this seed. And that's exactly what the fallen angels are doing.

The unnatural offspring of these unnatural unions are called the **Nephilim**:

> The Nephilim were on the earth in those days, and afterward as well, when the sons of God had relations

with the daughters of men. And they bore them children who became the mighty men of old, men of renown. (Genesis 6:4)

How does God respond?

He must destroy the corrupted seed:

So the LORD said, "My Spirit will not contend with man forever, for he is mortal; his days shall be 120 years." (Genesis 6:3)

Although subject to differing interpretations, God is saying that the lives of those at the time would be ended in 120 years—the time of the flood. It would be this event that would rid the earth of this corrupted seed.

So God destroys the world through a worldwide flood. **Only eight people will be saved**, Noah and his wife, and Noah's three sons and their wives. This represents a new beginning for humankind.

Why was Noah chosen for salvation? Genesis 6 tells us,

This is the account of Noah. Noah was a righteous man, blameless in his generation; Noah walked with God. (Genesis 6:9)

The Hebrew word translated "blameless" means "complete," or "sound." Perhaps this is saying that, among Noah's generation, Noah's seed had not been tainted by the appearance of the fallen angels and Nephilim. Unlike others from this generation, it was Noah who was "sound." His descendants could fill the earth with humans not corrupted as the result of the intermarrying of fallen angels with daughters of men.

Before we complete the story of the flood, we might ask: if fallen angels were on earth prior to the flood, where did they go? After all, angels cannot die—they were not part of the **curse**.

The Bible answers this. The fallen angels that took part in this atrocity against God are removed from earth and punished through imprisonment. They are placed in chains—a word that may be figurative. Passages that reflect the imprisonment of these "Genesis 6 fallen angels" include the following:

> And the angels who did not stay within their own domain but abandoned their proper dwelling—these He has kept in eternal chains under darkness, bound for judgment on that great day. (Jude 1:6)

> For if God did not spare the angels when they sinned, but cast them deep into hell, placing them in chains of darkness to be held for judgment; if He did not spare the ancient world when He brought the flood on its ungodly people, but preserved Noah, a preacher of righteousness, among the eight. (2nd Peter 2:4, 5)

> For Christ also suffered for sins once for all, the righteous for the unrighteous, to bring you to God. He was put to death in the body but made alive in the spirit, in which He also went and preached to the spirits in prison who disobeyed long ago when God waited patiently in the days of Noah, while the ark was being built. (1st Peter 3:18–20)

Fallen angels are imprisoned in something the Bible refers to as the "abyss." However, the Genesis 6 fallen angels are chained in a special place called "**Tartarus**" (2nd Peter 2:4, translated as "hell" in the above).

One of the above passages deserves a closer look. According to 1st Peter 3:18–20, after Jesus was put to death on the cross, he visited the imprisoned spirits. Unfortunately, some translations, such as the BSB and KJV, tell us Christ "preached" to these spirits. But the Greek word used here is different from the word normally translated "preached" and used elsewhere in the New Testament when describing the "preaching" of the word.

The Greek word here is more properly translated "proclamation," and implies that Christ "proclaimed" to these spirits. Accordingly, the text can read "made proclamation to the imprisoned spirits" (NIV, NASB), or "proclaimed to the spirits in prison" (ESV).

Is this distinction important?

Yes. Let's look at 1st Peter 3:18–20 in more detail.

> For Christ also suffered for sins once for all, the righteous for the unrighteous, to bring you to God.

As we know, Christ died for our sins—the righteous (Christ) for the unrighteous (you and me). He died once, because his death satisfied the rightful punishment of sin by God (his death was a propitiation—an atoning sacrifice—for sin).

> He was put to death in the body but made alive in the spirit...

He went through bodily death . . .

> ... in which He also went and preached to the spirits in prison ...

At that time, he went and proclaimed to "spirits" who were in prison. There was a period when it was taught that these were the spirits (souls) of humans that died.

... who disobeyed long ago when God waited patiently
in the days of Noah, while the ark was being built.

Specifically, those holding this view suggest these were the "spirit souls" of the humans that died at the time of the flood.

But for Christ to visit them, and for him to preach to them, would imply someone, or at least these people, had been given "second chances" to learn about Jesus and be saved after death—something not taught elsewhere in the Bible. But in context of 2nd Peter 2:4 and Jude 1:6, we know the "spirits" are not those of humans but are the imprisoned fallen angels—beings from the spirit world.

And, we know from the Greek, Christ was not "preaching" to them—he is proclaiming. Christ is proclaiming his victory over Satan. These rebellious angels are followers of Satan—and it was Christ's resurrection that conquered Satan. As to Satan, for now, Satan is alive and well—and is not imprisoned with the Genesis 6 fallen angels. This will occur, though, during Christ's millennial rule on earth when Satan is bound for a thousand years. Satan's ultimate fate is the lake of fire, which we will get to later.

Before we leave this subject, it might also be beneficial to think about "sons of God" marrying "daughters of men" in relation to the story of Sodom and Gomorrah. In our next lesson, we're going to learn about Abraham. But there is an event involving Abraham and his nephew, Lot, that we will mention here.

Lot leaves Abraham and takes residence near the ancient towns of Sodom and Gomorrah, and eventually lives within Sodom. These two cities are exceedingly sinful, and God announces to Abraham that He will destroy both.

Two angels, messengers from God, are sent to Sodom (Genesis 19:1). The earthly men of Sodom want to rape these angels (Genesis 19:5). With this as background, let's re-read Jude 1:6, but add verse 7:

> And the angels who did not stay <u>within their own domain</u> but abandoned their proper dwelling—these <u>He has kept in eternal chains under darkness</u>, <u>bound for judgment on that great day</u>. In like manner, Sodom and Gomorrah and the cities around them, who indulged in sexual immorality and <u>pursued strange flesh</u>, are on display as an example of those who sustain the punishment of eternal fire. (Jude 1:6, 7)

It is interesting that Jude mentions angels that did not stay "within their own domain." These are the fallen angels of Genesis 6. They have been imprisoned by God ("He has kept in eternal chains under darkness"). They will remain in this state until the end-times judgment ("bound for judgment on that great day").

But note, immediately Jude jumps to Sodom and Gomorrah and says the people there indulged in sexual immortality "and pursued strange flesh." This might echo the unnatural relationships between the angelic realm and the human realm of Genesis 6. We could say more—but let's continue our discussion of the flood of Noah's day.

In our previous lesson, we saw how God provides us with the names of the individuals associated with Adam's descendants up to Noah. In the flood story, God provides us with another detail that should also stir our interest.

> On the seventeenth day of the seventh month, the ark came to rest on the mountains of Ararat. (Genesis 8:4)

For some reason, God gives us the exact day the flood waters recede and is Noah brought to safety. It's the 17th day of the 7th month.

Why bother giving us this tidbit of **information**? Let's see if we might deduce an answer.

There are two Hebrew calendars (calendars used by the Jewish people). One is the civil calendar, and it begins with the Jewish month of Tishri. The second is the religious calendar. This calendar was established at the time of the exodus as the people of Israel prepare to leave their captivity in Egypt (immediately before the first Passover celebration—we'll get to that event shortly).

> Now the LORD said to Moses and Aaron in the land of Egypt, "This month is the beginning of months for you; it shall be the first month of your year." (Exodus 12:1, 2)

Here, God establishes the calendar for Jewish religious observances. Both the civil calendar and the religious calendar have the same number of days, weeks, and months, but they are a half-year apart. This "new" calendar, which starts in the spring, was not in effect at the time of the flood. Therefore, we are interested in determining the date the ark came to rest by looking at the Jewish civil calendar, which begins with the month of Tishri.

We are told the ark came to rest on the 17th day of the 7th month. The seventh month from Tishri happens to be Nissan, the first month of the religious calendar.

Passover (again, we'll learn about this shortly) is celebrated on the 14th day of Nissan. But the ark did not come to rest on the 14th—it came to rest three days later.

Are you making the connection?

Christ was crucified on Passover.

How long was Jesus in the grave?

Three days.

Christ left the tomb on the 17th day of the 7th month. The ark came to rest on the 17th day of the 7th month.

It seems God arranged His "new beginning" for the earth, with the flood waters having receded and the ark coming safely to rest, on the exact day several thousands of years later as Jesus would leave the tomb and provide a new beginning for those who seek refuge in him. Perhaps this is why God chose to give us this date in the flood story.

We've said this before—and you'll hear it a few more times. The Biblical Story is the story about Jesus. Even providing us with the day the ark came to rest has implications concerning the Messiah.

Before we leave this section of Genesis, there is one other nuance that deserves mentioning. When the Biblical Story began, Adam and Eve were in the garden. Upon sinning, they felt their nakedness and covered themselves. They were fallen image-bearers.

Perhaps Noah is different. Out of all of the people on earth, Noah has been chosen for **salvation**. Perhaps Noah is the Redeemer. After all, the biblical text refers to him as a righteous man (Genesis 6:9, that we looked at earlier) and the world is experiencing a "new beginning" after the flood waters had receded. Perhaps Noah is a perfect reflection of God. Maybe he is the seed of woman that will defeat Satan?

But note what happens. Noah, too, ends up in a garden—in this case, a vineyard. And Noah, too, ends up naked. And Noah, too, experiences shame (Genesis 8:18–29).

Noah is no different than Adam or Eve, or you or me.

There is no one righteous, not one (Romans 3:10). All have sinned (Romans 3:23). Noah is not the anticipated Messiah, Son of God, and King.

We'll have to continue reading more in the Biblical Story and God's acts in history to find out who the Redeemer is. It wasn't Noah.

From lesson 8: What do we learn about God?

- God is a God of judgment and wrath.
- But God is also a God of grace, giving us what we don't deserve—and a God of mercy, not giving us what we do deserve.

million babies: The Communicable Disease Center (CDC) reports 45.7 million legal abortions performed in the United States during the period from 1970 to 2015. Fortunately, the rate of known abortions in the U.S. has trended downward—but the slaughtering of the innocents continues.

children of God: Among various translations, you will find places in the New Testament where you will see "sons of God" as referencing Christians. Sometimes, use of the masculine gender is justified. For example, Paul talks about us being adopted into "sonship" (Romans 8:15). Here, he is using the term "son" in that, during Paul's day, adoption and Roman inheritance laws centered on the male and Paul has a specific point to make concerning the Christian's inheritance (see Romans 8:18).

But most often, terms formerly translated "son" or "sons" are now properly translated "children" (similarly, terms formerly translated "brothers" are now often translated "brothers and sisters").

As stated in this lesson, the term "sons of God" in the Old Testament refers to angels, and sons of God are direct creations of God (i.e. Adam and all of the angels). We are sons and daughters of Adam and become children of God when He invites us into His family.

Only eight people will be saved: Technically, it was not eight who were saved, but nine. The ninth was Enoch, who was removed in advance (raptured).

"Tartarus": The Greek word shown in 2nd Peter 2:4 is transliterated "Tartarus." Translations such as the one used here, the Berean Study Bible (BSB), the New International Version (NIV) and King James Version (KJV) change this word to "hell." But the word "Tartarus" in the Greek is different from that used elsewhere in the New Testament to designate hell (also, Tartarus is a proper name, like Jerusalem or Jacob—and should not be translated).

Nephilim: The Hebrew word "Nephilim" can mean "fallen ones"— which might refer to the fallen angels that parented them. It comes from the Hebrew verb *naphal* which means "to fall." They exist pre-flood, but they also seem to appear after the flood. When the Israelites send "spies" to scout out the Promised Land, they return and talk about "giants" in the land—Nephilim:

> Then Caleb quieted the people before Moses and said, "We must go up and take possession of the land, for we can certainly conquer it!"
>
> But the men who had gone up with him replied, "We cannot go up against the people, for they are stronger than we are!"
>
> So they gave the Israelites a bad report about the land they had spied out: "The land we explored devours its inhabitants, and all the people we saw there are great

in stature. We even saw the Nephilim there—the descendants of Anak that come from the Nephilim! We seemed like grasshoppers in our own sight, and we must have seemed the same to them!" (Numbers 13:30–33)

curse: We've stated this before. Death (physical death) is separation from the body. Our souls do not die; our souls live forever. This is true for everyone, whether one believes in Christ and has accepted his provisions for salvation or not. And eventually, both believers and non-believers are given resurrected bodies. Angels do not go through this separation from the body. That is, they do not experience physical death.

information: The connection between the resting of the ark and the resurrection of Jesus is explained by Chuck Missler, who also provides the insights concerning the Genesis 5 genealogy. This is found in Chuck Missler, *Cosmic Codes: Hidden Messages from the Edge of Eternity* (Coeur d'Alene: Koinonia House, 1999), 251-253.

salvation: The word "salvation" does not always refer to life with God in heaven (the new heaven and new earth that await those who have been "regenerated"—brought back to spiritual life and into a relationship with God). Salvation is deliverance from danger or suffering, and the Bible can use the word we translate "salvation" to refer to victory, being brought to safety, or preservation in the here and now.

Paul uses the word "salvation" in Philippians 1:19 talking about his imprisonment and not his eternal destiny:

> For I know that this shall turn to my salvation through your prayer, and the supply of the Spirit of Jesus Christ" (KJV).

When used in this context, the Berean Study Bible and New International Version translate the word "salvation" using the word "deliverance" to help differentiate this form of salvation from salvation in the context of participation in God's kingdom and eternity with God.

9

God's Covenant with Abraham

The Biblical Story continues. We are looking for the seed of woman that will redeem humanity from its fallen state. The earth experiences a new beginning after the flood. Population increases—but humankind continues in wickedness. And God's continues to orchestrate His plan to offer salvation and forgiveness.

We learn in Genesis 12 that God selects a man from **Mesopotamia** named Abram, later to be called Abraham, as a key part in His plan. He tells Abraham, and us, why He is doing this:

> Then the LORD said to Abram, "Leave your country, your kindred, and your father's household, and go to the land I will show you.
>
>> I will make you into a great nation,
>>> and I will bless you;
>> I will make your name great,
>>> so that you will be a blessing.
>> I will bless those who bless you
>>> and curse those who curse you;

and all the families of the earth
will be blessed through you." (Genesis
12:1–3)

A great nation will come from this man that God has chosen. His name will be great. All the families of the earth will be blessed because of what God will do through this man and his descendants. This will be the work of God (note the "I will" statements above).

We refer to God's statement and promises to Abraham as God's "covenant" with Abraham—also referred to as the "Abrahamic Covenant." God places no stipulations—no conditions—on Abraham. God is going to uphold His covenant promises no matter what. In other words, this is an unconditional covenant. It is not dependent upon Abraham for its fulfillment. And nothing suggests that the covenant is temporary. It is an everlasting promise God gives to Abraham.

Here we must briefly pause and assure ourselves we understand what God is saying.

- God will make Abraham into a great nation.
- God will bless Abraham.
- God will make Abraham's name great.
- God does this so that Abraham will be a blessing to others.
- God will bless those that bless Abraham.
- God will bring blessings to all the families of the earth through Abraham.

That's quite a list. What did I leave out?

Oh. God also says He will curse those that curse Abraham. In English, the verse sounds poetic:

I will bless those who bless you
and curse those who curse you.

But we lose quite a bit when we go from Hebrew to English. The first word for "curse" in this verse comes from a Hebrew root that means something along the lines of "utterly destroy" (*aor*). The second word for "curse" comes from a completely different Hebrew root which means "to make light of something heavy" (*mekalelcha*). In effect, the verse can be translated, "I'm going to bless those who bless you—but I am going to utterly destroy those who make light of you." "Making light" of someone means we disrespect them. We don't place value on them. A reminder—this covenant, these promises to Abraham—are everlasting. And these words are the words of God.

Why, out of all the people on earth, did God choose Abraham? Although there are writings outside the Bible that attempt to justify the selection (in this case, Jewish writings outside the Hebrew Scriptures), from the words of the Bible we can deduce God chooses Abraham simply *because He wanted to*. There was nothing about Abraham that is special. Look closely at the last few verses in Genesis 11 and the opening verses of Genesis 12. Abram (Abraham) does absolutely nothing to win God's favor. It is God who makes the choice; it is God who makes the selection. God is God, and we, including Abraham, are not.

When God says He will make Abraham into a great nation, this signifies Abraham will have numerous descendants. But we have a problem. Actually, it is Abraham that has the problem. When God speaks these words, Abraham is seventy-five years old and has remained childless (Genesis 12:4).

This should be placed into context. The name "Abram" can mean "exalted father" or "father of many." Of course, Abram was given this name at birth by parents who no doubt thought their son would father many children, as was the custom in that place and time period (a custom that continues today).

And God changes Abram's name to Abraham, which means "father of a multitude" (Genesis 17:5). Similarly, God changes the name of Abraham's wife, Sarai, which means "my princess," to "Sarah," meaning "mother of nations" (Genesis 17:15, 16). Here, we have this elderly, childless couple that have the God-given names "father of a multitude" and "mother of nations."

This had to be an on-going embarrassment. Abraham had gone through early adulthood, middle age, and into the twilight years of his life remaining childless. In a paternalistic culture that honored fatherhood (and women being esteemed by the number of children they had), anyone shouting out "exalted father" and looking at Abram must have been wearing a big grin. And now, according to God, this childless, elderly man would be called "father of a multitude."

Part of what we learn in the Biblical Story is the necessity of God's image-bearers to display **faith**. We briefly discussed this word in lesson 6. In both the Hebrew and the Greek, the words "faith," "obedience," "trust," and "belief" are all connected (you are going to hear this truth several times). God's people are to be a people of faith—a people obedient to God who place their trust in Him.

The author of Hebrews tells us, "without faith it is impossible to please God" (Hebrews 11:6). Faith is important. Our faith does not bring us into the family of God, though. The blood of Christ does that. But our faith does show that we belong to the family of God.

And it seems God often does things to help us **achieve greater faith**. We see this constantly throughout the Biblical Story. If you are familiar with some of the stories found in the Bible, perhaps you are familiar with what follows:

- It had never before rained on earth—and yet Noah is told to build a boat and prepare for a world-wide flood. Noah builds the biggest boat the world had ever seen. Noah had faith.

- Childless Abraham and his barren wife are approaching 100 years of age and are promised a great family. Abraham eventually trusts God to fulfill His promise. Abraham had faith.
- Moses had spent forty years in voluntary exile from Egypt—only to be told to return and confront the most powerful man on earth. And, he is to ask the Egyptian ruler to rid himself of Jewish slaves that were helping to build his empire. Moses goes to this ruler, the Egyptian Pharaoh, confronts him, and delivers the people. Moses had faith.
- In their journey to the Promised Land, the Israelites are threatened by poisonous snakes, and many people are dying. Moses is told to make a snake out of bronze and attach it to a pole. If a snake bites someone, all the person has to do is to look at the pole and they will live. What a strange way to cure a snake bite—but it worked. The people who raised their eyes to the lifted pole did not die from the poisonous snakes. They had faith (we'll talk about this specific example in lesson 16).
- Joshua was told to march around a fortified Canaanite city, blowing horns, and the walls would come tumbling down. Joshua follows God's instructions and defeats Jericho. Joshua had faith.
- God chooses a man threshing wheat near a winepress to eventually lead an army that began with 32,000 men (Judges 7:3). They would be going up against 135,000 Midianites (Judges 8:10). The man's name is Gideon. But before God would allow the armies to meet, He has Gideon reduce his army to just 300 men. Gideon and his 300 men go up against the 135,000—and this small group defeats the mighty Midianites. Gideon had faith.

And by the way, Gideon didn't choose the strongest or the bravest for his small army. God simply had him select the men based upon how they drank water from the spring of Harod ("Harod," not to be confused with "Herod"—Judges 7:5-7).

Was God serious? Select men for battle based on how they sip water? But Gideon followed these instructions. Gideon had faith.

Oh, and one other point. When Gideon and the three hundred confront the Midianites, read the story carefully (particularly Judges 7:20). The "swords of Gideon" were nothing more than torches and ram horns. There were no swords! Gideon had faith.

-   Young David goes up against Goliath with a sling and five stones (1ˢᵗ Samuel 17:40). David had faith.

The list could continue—but you get the point. Things that are unreasonable, or even ludicrous from our perspective, are all used by God to show how we can rely upon His promises, His providence, and His power. God is a faithful God.

In the Abrahamic Covenant, God promises Abraham he will be the father of many.

How faithful is God?

Today's Arabs are direct descendants of Abraham. The population of the Arab world is 420 million.

Today's Jews are direct descendants of Abraham. There are an estimated 20 million Jews.

God also promises that Abraham's name would be great.

How faithful is God?

The Muslims revere Abraham ("Ibrahim")—the father of all Arabs. The Jewish people revere Abraham—the father of all Jews. And yes, Christians revere Abraham as the "father of faith." There are 1.8 billion Muslims in the world, and another 2.2 billion Christians.

Abraham truly is the father of a multitude, and truly has a great name. God has been faithful to His covenant promise.

But let's not leave out a key portion of the promise:

"... and all the families of the earth
will be blessed through you." (Genesis 12:3)

We have said this before: the entire scripture is about Jesus. In that Jesus will be in the **lineage of Abraham**, through Christ all the nations on the earth will be blessed.

How faithful is God?

God will come to earth and die. The Abrahamic Covenant will be honored. We learn more about this from Genesis 15—the subject of our next lesson.

From lesson 9: What do we learn about God?

- God enacts an unconditional covenant with a man named Abraham.
- Abraham is chosen not because of anything Abraham does, or any merit on Abraham's part.
- Through Abraham, God will establish a nation and all the nations on earth will be blessed. We'll learn later that the Genesis 3:15 seed of woman will be a descendant of Abraham.

Mesopotamia: This was a region that was part of the "fertile crescent" of antiquity. It occupied today's region of Iraq and Kuwait, along with portions of Syria and southeastern Turkey.

lineage of Abraham: Matthew wrote his historic account of Jesus mainly to the Jews (for those new to the Bible, we call his writing "the Book of Matthew," and in that it proclaims the good news of the arrival of the Messiah, this is also referred to as the "Gospel of Matthew"—"Gospel" meaning "Good News"). We discussed where the term "Good News" comes from in lesson 2.

Matthew begins this writing with the genealogy of Jesus—starting with Abraham, the father of all Jews.

But when he gets to Jesus, he does not mention Jesus' "father." He writes:

> Eliud was the father of Eleazar,
> Eleazar the father of Matthan,
> Matthan the father of Jacob,
>   and Jacob the father of Joseph, the husband of Mary,
> of whom was born Jesus, who is called Christ.
> (Matthew 1:15, 16)

Joseph is not called the father of Jesus. Instead, he is referred to as the husband of Mary. The reasons for this should be obvious. Jesus was conceived by the Holy Spirit, and his incarnation was not due to an earthly father. In lesson 35, we'll learn more about Matthew's genealogy, why it goes through Joseph and not Mary, and why it significantly differs from the genealogy of Jesus found in Luke's account.

Another example concerning the lineage of Abraham is found in the discourse in John 8:33–41. To his Jewish audience, Jesus says,

> "I know that you are Abraham's seed." (John 8:37)

Later Jesus says,

> "Your father Abraham overjoyed to see My day. He saw it and was glad." (John 8:56)

Notice that Jesus, a Jew, does not say "I know that *we* are Abraham's descendants." Nor does he say, "*our* father Abraham."

Jesus specifically refers to those to whom he is talking as being the descendants of Abraham, and Abraham as being *their* father ("you are Abraham's seed … your father Abraham"). While in his humanity, Jesus is a descendant of Abraham (through Mary), he is, more importantly, the Son of God. Abraham is not the father of Jesus—Jesus is the Son of God.

faith: We'll get to this later, but it deserves being mentioned now. *We are not saved by faith*—and don't let anyone tell you otherwise. You could have all the faith on earth—but if there was no cross, there would have been no payment of sin, and no salvation.

We are saved by the blood of Christ.

achieve greater faith: Faith is nothing we possess—unless God gives it to us. We are spiritually dead. Our faith is given to us by God as part of being brought to spiritual life (Ephesians 2:8, 9).

For a complete treatment of the topic of "faith," see *A Forty-Day Study of Sin, Salvation, and Sanctification: Our Journey with Christ.*

10

God Confirms His Covenant

As we saw in the last lesson, God promises Abraham a great name and numerous descendants. He also promises a land for these descendants.

But Abraham wants assurance that he can trust God and His promises. After all, up to this point, Abraham still remains childless.

Abraham confronts God. He asks about the land God has promised as part of His covenant oath:

> "Lord GOD, how can I know that I will possess it?" (Genesis 15:8)

That's a reasonable question. And God responds to Abraham:

> And the LORD said to him, "Bring Me a heifer, a goat, and a ram, each three years old, along with a turtledove and a young pigeon."
>
> So Abram brought all these to Him, split each of them down the middle, and laid the halves opposite each other. The birds, however, he did not cut. And the

birds of prey descended on the carcasses, but Abram drove them away. (Genesis 15:9b–11)

This sounds relatively bloody, only because it is relatively bloody.

We are reading about an ancient ritual practiced in that part of the world during the time of Abraham. To seal and make certain that a covenant oath would be obeyed, animals would be cut into two, with half of each carcass placed along the ground forming a pathway. The individual agreeing to the covenant would walk between the animal parts.

This depicted the seriousness of the covenant oath. In effect, by walking between the gory pieces of slain animals, the person is declaring he knows that he, too, will be torn into two and his blood will be spilled if he breaks the agreement or doesn't fulfill the agreement.

Again, this was an ancient ritual. And the king or master of the covenant agreement *never* had to walk between the animal parts— only the one subservient to the master. In this case, it would be Abraham (Abram).

The text continues:

> As the sun was setting, <u>Abram fell into a deep sleep</u>, and suddenly great terror and darkness overwhelmed him.
>
> Then the LORD said to Abram, "Know for certain that your descendants will be strangers in a land that is not their own; they will be enslaved and mistreated four hundred years. But I will judge the nation they serve as slaves, and afterward they will depart with many possessions. You, however, will go to your fathers in peace and be buried at a ripe old age. In the fourth generation your descendants will return here,

for the iniquity of the Amorites is not yet complete."
(Genesis 15:12–16)

And an amazing thing happens:

> When the sun had set and darkness had fallen, behold,
> a smoking firepot and a flaming torch appeared <u>and</u>
> <u>passed between the halves of the carcasses</u>. <u>On that</u>
> <u>day the LORD made a covenant with Abram</u>. (Genesis
> 15:17, 18)

Abraham is never called to walk between the bloodied pieces of the
sacrificed animals. Instead, God, appearing as a smoking container
of fire and blazing torch, passes between them.

Because we are not familiar with this ancient practice, it is hard for
us to fathom what this meant. But Abraham knew—and I'm sure he
was astonished. What God did was unheard of. We, too, should be
in awe.

God was telling Abraham that he would be blessed no matter what.
God was going to be faithful to the covenant—even if God's people
did not live up to the covenant. And God's faithfulness to the covenant
would mean that He would allow Himself to make payment through
His shed blood and broken body.

And that is exactly what happened.

There came a time when darkness would once again come down. But
instead of a smoking firepot and blazing torch, it would be the darkness
surrounding the Son of God shedding his innocent blood on the cross.

God would pay the price for mankind's failure.

As we've said, the entire Biblical Story is about Jesus.

From lesson 10: What do we learn about God?

- God's oath to Abraham includes a covenant ceremony. It significantly differs from what was normally done by the ancients, in that God declares He will guarantee the covenant with His own blood.

11

A Foreshadowing of Jesus

God promises Abraham numerous descendants—but Abraham and Sarah remain childless. They decide to help God along in the process. The two agree to let Abraham father a child through Sarah's maidservant, Hagar. A son named Ishmael is born of this union, but he is not the child of promise—that is, the Redeemer will not be a descendant of Ishmael. Sarah remains barren.

But God displays His faithfulness. Abraham and Sarah are given a son that they name Isaac. The Redeemer will come through Isaac's descendants.

We know this because of what God says to Abraham. It will not be the son through Hagar that represents the promises of the Abrahamic Covenant. It will be the son that Sarah has:

> "As for Sarai your wife, do not call her Sarai, for her name is to be Sarah. And I will bless her and will surely give you a son by her. I will bless her, and she will be the mother of nations; kings of peoples will descend from her."

Abraham fell facedown. Then he laughed and said to himself, "Can a child be born to a man who is a hundred years old? Can Sarah give birth at the age of ninety?" And Abraham said to God, "O that Ishmael might live under Your blessing!"

But God replied, "Your wife Sarah will indeed bear you a son, and you are to name him Isaac. I will establish My covenant with him as an everlasting covenant for his descendants after him. As for Ishmael, I have heard you, and I will surely bless him; I will make him fruitful and multiply him greatly. He will become the father of twelve rulers, and I will make him into a great nation. But I will establish My covenant with Isaac, whom Sarah will bear to you at this time next year." (Genesis 17:15–21)

This is echoed again in Genesis 21, as son Ishmael is being sent away:

God said to Abraham, "Do not be distressed about the boy and your maidservant. Listen to everything that Sarah tells you, for through Isaac your offspring will be reckoned." (Genesis 21:12)

God's plan of redemption—and the blessing of all the families on earth—will come through Isaac, the son of the union between Abraham and Sarah.

All is right with the world.

Until we get to Genesis 22. Abraham hears the voice of God:

"Take your son, your only son Isaac, whom you love, and go to the land of Moriah. Offer him there as a burnt offering on one of the mountains, which I will show you." (Genesis 22:2)

There is much here in these two sentences. In addressing Abraham, God calls Abraham's son Isaac, "your <u>only</u> son." What are we to make of this? What about Ishmael? Also, this is the **first time** in the Bible where we see the word "love." We don't see this word when the Bible talks about God's creation, or Adam and Eve, or the institution of marriage, or the birth of a son, Seth, after Cain had murdered brother Abel. But we see it here.

The reference to "your only son" may be equivalent to the title "beloved son" or "one and only son," as we see in John 1:18 and John 3:16 —

> No one has ever seen God, but the one and only Son, who is Himself God and is at the Father's side, has made Him known. (John 1:18)

> For God so loved the world that He gave His one and only Son, that everyone who believes in Him shall not perish but have eternal life. (John 3:16)

And adding the phrase "whom you love" is understandable in that Abraham had longed for the birth of a son through Sarah and God's fulfillment of His promise—creating Abraham's special love toward this son, Isaac, and a special bond between the two of them.

As importantly, the words foreshadow John 3:16 shown above: "For God so loved the world . . . He gave His one and only Son."

Abraham truly loves this "only son," Isaac.

But look at what is happening. God tells Abraham,

> "Go to the land of Moriah. <u>Offer him there as a burnt offering</u> on one of the mountains, which I will show you"

What?

After all of the wait for this special son, God is now telling Abraham to offer him as a sacrifice! What about God's promise to Abraham? God had told Abraham,

> "Your wife Sarah will indeed bear you a son, and you are to name him Isaac. <u>I will establish My covenant with him as an everlasting covenant for his descendants after him.</u>" (Genesis 17:19b)

God's covenant promises will come through Isaac—and yet Isaac is to be put to death. Again, we have to ask, quite literally, what on earth is going on?

There is another nuance in the text. Why does God tell Abraham to go to the land of Moriah—requiring a three-day journey to get there? Why this three-day delay? And why Moriah? Is the *place* of sacrifice important to God?

We're getting ahead of ourselves, but let's answer these questions now.

There is not a piece of real estate anywhere on earth that is more significant than Moriah. It is at Moriah where Abraham is willing to offer his beloved son to God. About a thousand years after this, it is at Moriah that Abraham's descendant, David, purchases a small parcel of land as he establishes his headquarters for ruling all of Israel. And it is at Moriah that David builds an altar to God (2nd Samuel 24:18–25). Shortly afterwards, it is at Moriah where David's son Solomon builds the temple to God:

> Then Solomon began to build the house of the LORD in Jerusalem on Mount Moriah, where the LORD had appeared to his father David. This was the place that David had prepared on the threshing floor of Ornan the Jebusite. (2nd Chronicles 3:1)

The temple will contain a special room separated from the people—and even the priests. It is called the Holy of Holies and could only be entered on one day of the year, the Day of Atonement, and only by one individual, the high priest. Traditionally, the exact spot where Abraham was willing to offer Isaac became the location of the Holy of Holies of Solomon's temple.

Abraham is called to go to Moriah because this is God's Story, God's plan. And it will be at Moriah, centuries later, that the Son of God accepts death on the cross for the sins of humanity.

Moriah, of course, encompasses the city of Jerusalem. This area is also referred to as Zion. It is foundational to the three major **monotheistic** religions: Judaism, Christianity, and Islam. While "Jerusalem" means "city of peace"—its history is anything but one of peace.

Even today there is considerable friction in that the Muslim "Dome of the Rock" shrine is believed to be located on the spot where the Holy of Holies of the temple once stood. This is also the flat area David purchased and built an altar, and the rock where Abraham was willing to sacrifice Isaac. There are Jewish writings outside the Bible that even suggest this stone outcropping is where civilization itself began. These writings suggest Adam, Cain, Abel, and Noah all offered sacrifices to God on this rock. Being outside of the Bible and not inspired scripture, we must consider this as conjecture—but interesting conjecture, nonetheless.

God commands Abraham to journey to Moriah, because God knows of His great plans for this specific location on His earth. Jerusalem is where God connects with humanity.

And these plans for Jerusalem are not finished. When Christ returns, he returns to Jerusalem. When he undertakes his thousand-year reign, he rules from Jerusalem.

Abraham is commanded to go to Moriah because it is here that God will sacrifice His Son. And it is here that His son will reign in glory.

The Biblical Story is all about Jesus.

The Genesis 22 text continues:

> So Abraham got up early the next morning, saddled his donkey, and took along two of his servants and his son Isaac. He split wood for a burnt offering and set out for the place God had designated. (Genesis 22:3)

It would be a three-day journey to get to Moriah (Genesis 22:4).

As they see the place God designates, Abraham and Isaac leave the servants, and walk to the place of sacrifice.

> Isaac said to his father Abraham, "My father!"
>
> "Here I am, my son," he replied.
>
> "The fire and the wood are here," said Isaac, "but where is the lamb for the burnt offering?" (Genesis 22:7)

Abraham responds:

> "God Himself will provide the lamb for the burnt offering, my son." And the two walked on together. (Genesis 22:8)

Have you ever contemplated what Abraham must be thinking? It has taken him three days to get to this site. He has had those three days to contemplate the loss of his son—a death to be carried out by his own hand. Now he and Isaac, the son whom he loves, will gather the wood for the fire—and Abraham will pick up the knife. In a few short minutes, Isaac will be dead.

The text continues:

> When they arrived at the place God had designated, Abraham built the altar there and arranged the wood. He bound his son Isaac and placed him on the altar, atop the wood. Then Abraham reached out his hand and took the knife to slaughter his son. (Genesis 22:9, 10)

Abraham has completed all of the preparations. All that is left is the piercing of Isaac's flesh and watching his son die.

But the process is stopped.

The "angel of the LORD" calls out to Abraham:

> "Do not lay a hand on the boy or do anything to him . . . for now I know that you fear God, since you have not withheld your only son from Me." (Genesis 22:12)

The text continues:

> Then Abraham looked up and saw behind him a ram in a thicket, caught by its horns. So he went and took the ram and offered it as a burnt offering in place of his son. And Abraham called that place The LORD Will Provide. So to this day it is said, "On the mountain of the LORD it will be provided."

> And the Angel of the LORD called to Abraham from heaven a second time, saying, "By Myself I have sworn, declares the LORD, that because you have done this and have not withheld your only son, I will surely bless you, and I will multiply your descendants like the stars in the sky and the sand on the seashore. Your descendants will possess the gates of their enemies.

And through your offspring all nations of the earth will be blessed, because you have obeyed My voice." (Genesis 22:13–18)

The process is halted. Abraham is not required to sacrifice his son. God intervenes, and God provides the sacrifice. Abraham will call this location "Jehovah Jireh"— "The LORD Will Provide." And this is exactly what God will do some two thousand years later, as Jesus becomes the sacrifice—the Lamb of God that takes away the sins of the world. God will provide what is required to reconcile us to Himself.

God restates his promise to Abraham: "And through your offspring all nations of the earth will be blessed" (Genesis 22:18). The LORD will provide—all nations of the earth will be blessed. But this will require Calvary's cross. The seed of woman *will* crush the serpent's head. But the serpent *will* strike his heel.

There are other facets of this story that can relate to the cross and the New Testament. Right after this event, and in the next verse, we read:

Abraham went back to his servants, and they got up and set out together for Beersheba. And Abraham settled in Beersheba. (Genesis 22:19)

The text tells us that Abraham returned to his servants, but it does not mention Isaac. Where is Isaac?

If you follow the text, you'll observe that Isaac does not reappear until two chapters later, when Abraham's chief servant brings Isaac a bride (this story begins in Genesis 24).

We get hints of Christ when we see Isaac bound and offered as a sacrifice at Mt. Moriah—a sacrifice, though, that is stopped. And in that Isaac leaves after this and we don't see him until later, this, too reminds us of Christ, where Jesus also leaves from view by way of his ascension to the Father.

Isaac reappears when he is being brought a wife. Christ, too, will reappear when he meets his bride, the Church.

And perhaps there is another nuance. Who is this servant of Abraham sent to find a bride for Isaac? We have to go back earlier in the text to find his identity:

> "O Lord GOD, what can You give me, since I remain childless, and the heir of my house is <u>Eliezer</u> of Damascus?" (Genesis 15:2)

It is reasonable to assume that the chief servant of Genesis 26, the individual sent to obtain a bride for Isaac, is Eliezer. This doesn't mean much, until we recognize that the name "Eliezer" means "helper" or "God is my helper."

The Holy Spirit is also known as "God as our helper"—God as our comforter. So, as Eliezer goes to a distant land to find a bride for Isaac, the Holy Spirit is at work today gathering a bride for Jesus (Jesus' Church),

Of course, we may be reading too much into the text, but all of this seems to fit as a foretelling of events surrounding Moriah and the Messiah. All of this tends to point toward Jesus. The Biblical Story is all about Jesus.

We will leave this portion of the Biblical Story, but before we do, we should look at how the book of Hebrews sheds light on the "binding of Isaac" and Abraham's willingness to obey God through the sacrifice of his son. The author of Hebrews writes:

> By faith Abraham, when he was tested, offered up Isaac on the altar. He who had received the promises

was ready to offer his one and only son, even though God had said to him, "Through Isaac your offspring will be reckoned." <u>Abraham reasoned that God could raise the dead, and in a sense, he did receive Isaac back from death.</u> (Hebrews 11:17–19)

In a sense, Isaac was returned from death. One can imagine that the minute God had commanded Abraham to go to Moriah, Isaac was basically dead—at least as far as Abraham was concerned.

Earlier we asked why Abraham was sent on a three-day journey to a special place to sacrifice Isaac. We know why Moriah was special and how it relates to events surrounding God's plan of redemption and Jesus.

And here, the three-day journey also echoes something about Jesus.

Where do we hear about a death for three days—and then a resurrection back to life?

The Biblical Story is all about Jesus.

From lesson 11: What do we learn about God?

- In lesson 3, our study of Psalm 2, we learn that God will provide the Messiah, Son of God, and King.
- In lesson 6, we said our God is a God who provides. This was in the context of God providing the covering for Adam and Eve's nakedness. But we also stated that the Good News of God's story is that He will seek out his fallen image-bearers, and He will provide the pathway that will repair the four broken relationships that resulted from humanity's disobedience. God provides the way that opens His kingdom plans for

humankind and allows us to return into His presence and to spend eternity with Him.

- And here, we learn of "Jehovah Jireh"—the LORD will provide. Throughout the Biblical Story, we will see a God of grace and mercy—One who continually provides for His creation. Of course, the pinnacle of His provision is the cross: God taking on the penalty we deserve to allow forgiveness and reconciliation.

---

first time: For those that use the New International Version translation of the Bible, you might take exception to my statement that Genesis 22:2 is the first place where we find the word "love" in the Bible. You might point to Genesis 20:13 (NIV):

> And when God had me wander from my father's household, I said to her, "This is how you can show your <u>love</u> to me: Everywhere we go, say of me, 'He is my brother.'"

However, the word shown as "love" in the NIV translation of Genesis 20:13 is a different Hebrew word than that of Genesis 22:2 and is often translated "kindness" (for example, in the King James Version and the New American Standard) or "loyalty" (for example, in the Berean Study Bible and Christian Standard Bible). The word "love" that first appears in Genesis 22:2 is a translation of the Hebrew word normally used in the biblical text that we translate as "love." This word is found 310 times in the King James translation.

monotheistic: There was a time when the ancient world believed in many gods. Usually, these gods were embodiments of natural forces. When God began His divine work through Abraham, He reveals a foundational truth: there is only one God. The three major religions, Judaism, Christianity, and Islam recognize one (mono) God (theism). These are "monotheistic" religions.

There are those, though, that suggest there are many gods (polytheism).

Others hold a "pantheistic" view—that God is within the universe and is a manifestation of the universe itself. Genesis 1:1 makes it clear that God is set apart from the universe in that He existed before the universe was created (although He can appear within the universe).

12

The Children of Promise

It may seem like we have spent an excessive amount of time on the first book of the Bible. We have sixty-five books to go, and we are not even halfway through Genesis, this first book!

But Genesis lays important foundations—and once we have reviewed these, we can spend much less time as we continue through the Bible's other books.

Let's do a recap, or inventory of where we are:

- God created all that there is.
- God creates humankind in His image, unlike the rest of His creation.
- But humankind is separated from God because of sin.
- There is no one righteous. All have sinned and all are subject to God's judgment, condemnation, and wrath.
- We can do nothing whatsoever to resolve this problem.
- God shows His grace and mercy by taking it upon Himself to deal with humankind's sin problem. Up to this point in the story, God has promised that Satan and Satan's followers

(the "seed of Satan") will ultimately be destroyed through an offspring of woman (the "seed of woman").

- God selects a man from Mesopotamia, Abraham, as he initiates His plan to redeem fallen humanity. Abraham does nothing to merit his selection by God.
- Abraham is promised numerous descendants, a land for these descendants, and most importantly, that the Redeemer will be a descendant of Abraham. Through this descendant, all nations will be blessed.

The rest of Genesis describes events associated with Abraham's descendants. As we saw earlier, we learn that God's blessing goes through Abraham's son, Isaac—not Abraham's son Ishmael:

> After Abraham's death, God blessed his son Isaac, who lived near Beer-lahai-roi. (Genesis 25:11)

> The LORD appeared to Isaac and said, "Do not go down to Egypt. Settle in the land where I tell you. Stay in this land as a foreigner, and I will be with you and bless you. For I will give all these lands to you and your offspring, and I will confirm the oath that I swore to your father Abraham. I will make your descendants as numerous as the stars in the sky, and I will give them all these lands, and through your offspring all nations of the earth will be blessed." (Genesis 26:2–4, see also Genesis 26:24)

Isaac will have two sons, Jacob and Esau. It will be through Jacob that the promise continues, as God tells Jacob:

> Your descendants will be like the dust of the earth, and you will spread out to the west and east and north and south. All the families of the earth will be blessed through you and your offspring. Look, I am with you,

and I will watch over you wherever you go, and I will bring you back to this land. For I will not leave you until I have done what I have promised you." (Genesis 28:14, 15)

Jacob will have twelve sons through his two wives and their respective handmaidens. He is also given a new name. We see this in Genesis 32, involving an unusual event where Jacob struggles with a heavenly stranger. The stranger announces:

> "Your name will no longer be Jacob, but Israel, because you have struggled with God and with men, and you have prevailed." (Genesis 32:28)

The name "Israel" comes from a word that means "to contend with," or "to fight or to struggle." The "el," as we saw earlier (lesson 7), references "God." The name "Israel," then, implies "one who struggles with God." And isn't that what we are all supposed to do? We are not to show indifference to God, but struggle with Him, "struggle" in the sense of learning about Him—who He is, what He is like, what He desires, and what His plans are.

Abraham's descendants through Jacob (Israel) will now be referred to as the "sons of Jacob" or the "children of Israel." These twelve sons become the "twelve tribes of Israel."

There are other terms for these descendants. When God provides His covenant promises to Abraham, He establishes circumcision as the sign of the covenant (Genesis 17:9–14). The sons of Israel and their male descendants are to be circumcised, reflecting their special relationship with the faithful God of promise. For this reason, these people are also referred to as the "circumcised."

In the New Testament, Paul will often use the word "circumcised" to represent the children of Israel (both male and female), and the word "uncircumcised" to refer to Gentiles. Sometimes Paul is talking about a physical characteristic and difference—and sometimes he is talking about a spiritual characteristic and difference.

There are additional terms used for these specific people. They are also called the "Hebrew" people, as well as the "Jews." Where do these terms come from?

We find the term "Hebrew" in Genesis 14:13 –

> Then an escapee came and reported this to Abram the <u>Hebrew</u>.

Scholars believe the term "Hebrew" came from the name "Eber," who is listed in Genesis 24 and is related to Noah's son, Shem (and is an ancestor of Abraham). Another possibility is that this comes from a Hebrew word meaning "from the other side" or "to cross over." This could imply the term "Hebrew" carries the connotation of "foreigner" or "immigrant."

In the above verse, we saw the term was used as a descriptor for Abram (Abraham). But it is also used to designate Abraham's descendants. When the people of God are in Egypt, note how the Israelite women are described:

> The midwives answered Pharaoh, '<u>The Hebrew women</u> are not like the Egyptian women, for they are vigorous and give birth before a midwife arrives.' (Exodus 1:19)

The Hebrew people are also referred to as "Jews." Where did this term come from?

There was a time in the history of these descendants when their land was divided (we'll get to this later in our study). The northern kingdom (the tribes or descendants living in the north) became known as "Israel." The south was referred to as "Judah," named after the major tribe of people occupying this section of the land. These were mainly descendants of Jacob's son named Judah. The word "Jew" comes from this word "Judah."

There is an additional term for these descendants. Because God chose and made His covenant with Abraham and his descendants through Isaac and Jacob, they are also referred to as "God's chosen people." By now it should be evident why this is the case. God selects these descendants of Abraham as His representatives. He provides His instructions to them. He raises up leaders and prophets among them. Most importantly, it will be through these chosen people—the Jews—that God will bless all of the nations on the earth in fulfillment of the Abrahamic Covenant. Jesus—the seed of woman of Genesis 3:15 and the one who will bring Satan and sin to defeat—will be a Jew.

Throughout history, much of the world has been anti-**Semitic**—hostile or prejudiced against the Jews—and Christians have been a significant part of this anti-Semitism. Some churches taught that it was the "**Jews that killed Jesus**." All of this is part of Satan's warfare against God and His plan of redemption. There is no place within the Christian family for anti-Semitism. This form of evil should be recognized as the direct activity of Satan and "**his seed**."

We should remind ourselves of what God's covenant with Abraham says:

> I will make you into a great nation,
>   and I will bless you;
> I will make your name great,
>   so that you will be a blessing.
> I will bless those who bless you
>   and curse those who curse you;
> and all the families of the earth
>   will be blessed through you.

Don't overlook the phrase, "and curse those who curse you." A reminder, the Hebrew can be translated: "I am going to utterly destroy anyone who disrespects you or makes light of you."

God takes His covenant seriously. Anyone who goes against Abraham's children of promise will face the curse of God—utter destruction.

And a reminder: God's covenant with Abraham is unconditional, as was stated previously. There were no conditions placed upon Abraham. God will fulfill the terms of the covenant no matter what.

And, the Abrahamic Covenant is everlasting. There is no end to this promise.

So, when we see God's warning that He will curse those that go against His chosen people, even by showing disrespect, this remains as true today as it was when God established His covenant with Abraham four thousand years ago.

From lesson 12: What do we learn about God?

- As God orchestrates His plan of redemption, the descendants of Abraham become central to the Biblical Story.
- These are the Jewish people—the chosen people of God and the children of promise.

Scholars: The first century Jewish historian Flavius Josephus writes, "Sala was the son of Arphaxad; and his son was Heber, from whom they originally called the Jews Hebrews" (Josephus, *Antiquities of the Jews* 1.6.4)

Semitic: Technically, the term "Semitic" refers to a family of languages that includes Hebrew, Arabic, and Aramaic. Normally, though, the term anti-Semitic equates to "anti-Jew."

Jews that killed Jesus: Who killed Jesus? Jesus tells us, and I think we should trust what he has to say when he talks about who took his life:

> "No one takes it from Me, but I lay it down of My own accord. I have authority to lay it down and authority to take it up again. This charge I have received from My Father." (John 10:18)

God's righteous judgment required sin to be punished. We said earlier that the seed of woman would face death. Salvation was made possible by the blood of Christ. All of this was God's plan to redeem fallen humanity. This is why Jesus can say,

> "I am the way, and the truth, and the life. No one comes to the Father except through Me." (John 14:6)

In that my sins required the death of Christ, Jesus died because of me. In that sense, I killed Jesus—and through his death I am able to live.

"his seed": In the Genesis 3:15 text, we see God announcing there will be hostility between Satan's offspring and woman's offspring. What is meant by "Satan's offspring"? We've discussed this previously, but it deserves being repeated. The "seed of Satan" are people in all walks of life and on every continent on earth that are part of Satan's kingdom. Whether purposefully, or inadvertently, they follow Satan and rebel against God.

The seed of Satan are all of those who have not placed their trust in Jesus. This sounds harsh—but that's what the Bible clearly teaches. There are only two groups of people (see John 10:10, for example).

If you do not belong to Christ, by definition, you belong to Satan. In volume 2, we are going to find out that following Satan is not a choice. Satan is our default master. Hell is our default destination. To assure ourselves of hell as our final destination, we don't have to change anything or make any decisions. We are on a journey to hell—unless God does something.

13

"The LORD was with him..."

The Biblical Story continues with a focus on Jacob's family. At this time in history, Jacob and his twelve sons are living in the land occupied by the Canaanites. Jacob's sons become envious of their younger brother, Joseph, the favorite of their father. They plot to kill Joseph, but he is spared and instead sold into slavery and taken to Egypt. This story is found in Genesis 37.

Note the last verse of this chapter (chapter 37):

> Meanwhile, the Midianites sold Joseph in Egypt to Potiphar, an officer of Pharaoh and captain of the guard. (Genesis 37:36)

For now, skip over chapter 38 and note the first verse of chapter 39:

> Meanwhile, Joseph had been taken down to Egypt, where an Egyptian named Potiphar, an officer of Pharaoh and captain of the guard, bought him from the Ishmaelites who had taken him there. (Genesis 39:1)

Between these two verses, Genesis 37:37 and Genesis 39:1, there is a complete chapter that has nothing to do with Joseph. It not only seems out of place; one wonders why the story is recorded in scripture to begin with.

It is an embarrassing, unflattering story. And yet, here it is—contained in the Holy Bible.

God must have had a reason for this being recorded. And as we have learned already, when we are given something in the Bible that seems odd, there is probably something special for us to learn.

We saw this earlier. When we looked at Genesis 5, we were surprised to see a listing of names associated with pre-flood individuals. Looking deeper, we found that the Hebrew names, when translated, point toward God's plan of redemption (see lesson 7). When we discussed the flood, we found it interesting that we are given the exact calendar day that the ark came to rest. Looking deeper into this, it seems God arranged His new beginning for the earth, with the flood waters having receded and the ark coming safely to rest, to coincide with the exact day several thousands of years later when Jesus leaves the tomb and provides a new beginning for those who seek refuge in him (see lesson 8).

We learned from those two examples that there is rich and valuable information in all of the Bible—but we may have to look for it. So here, sandwiched between Genesis 37 and 39 is a chapter on one of the brothers. Why? And when we read about him, having this part of his story for all who read the Bible to see—century after century—makes its presence even more startling.

The story in this seemingly "out-of-place" or "why bother" chapter focuses on Judah, one of Jacob's twelve sons and a brother of Joseph. Included in the story is Tamar, Judah's daughter-in-law. This is an "ugly" story—one which is a bit embarrassing. Judah is shown to be untrustworthy and a liar. He seeks out a prostitute and ends up mistakenly impregnating his daughter-in-law—a daughter-in-law playing the part of a prostitute! Do we really need to hear all of this?

But Judah is relevant. So is Tamar. Later in the Biblical Story, we learn that the seed of woman will be a descendant of this man—and this woman. He will come from the line (tribe) of Judah—and Tamar is included in the genealogy of Jesus. You might take time to read Genesis 38 and also note the genealogy of Jesus given by Matthew that includes Judah and Tamar (Matthew 1:2, 3).

I need to repeat this, and never tire of saying it, all of **the Bible is about Jesus**. This somewhat unusual story of Judah is included because Jesus will come from this family.

Continuing Joseph's story, which resumes in Genesis 39, we learn more about the God of the Bible:

> And the LORD was with Joseph, and he became a successful man, serving in the household of his Egyptian master. (Genesis 39:2)

> While Joseph was there in the prison, the LORD was with him and extended kindness to him. (Genesis 39:20, 21)

> The warden did not concern himself with anything under Joseph's authority, because the LORD was with him and gave him success in whatever he did. (Genesis 30:23)

What is the repeated message here?

Joseph has been cast away from his family. He is living in a strange land, with strange people, strange customs, and a strange language. To add to his troubles, he is imprisoned unjustly.

Joseph has been abandoned by his brothers—but he has not been abandoned by God. God continually watches over Joseph, and ultimately, through God's blessing, Joseph triumphs.

At the end of Joseph's story, he is reunited with his father, Jacob. And he is also reunited with the brothers who had cast him off from the family many years earlier.

As the book of Genesis comes to a close, Jacob, Joseph's father, is on his death bed and, as was the custom, he blesses each of his sons.

Two items should be noted.

While in Egypt, two sons are born to Joseph: Ephraim and Manasseh. Joseph's father, Jacob (Israel), blesses these sons as if they are his own. This means there are more than the commonly used term, "twelve tribes of Israel." Lists of the "tribes" in the Bible will only show twelve, but which tribes make up the twelve vary. For example, Revelation 7:5–8 lists twelve tribes by name, but omits the tribe of Dan. Often the tribe of Levi is omitted (for example, see Ezekiel 48 or Numbers 1:5–15).

Secondly, when Jacob blesses his son, Judah, he says:

> Judah, your brothers shall praise you.
> Your hand shall be on the necks of your enemies;
> your father's sons shall bow down to you. (Genesis 49:8)

There is something special about the descendants of Judah. The other tribes will bow down to this tribe. In other words, the descendants of Judah will be "over" the descendants from the other tribes. As we proceed with the Biblical Story, this prediction is fulfilled. When the descendants of Israel are in the Promised Land, a nation is formed and individuals from the tribe of Judah (the family of Judah) are designated as the nation's rulers. King David, Israel's greatest king, is a descendant of Judah. The last king, Zedekiah, is from the tribe of Judah. Jesus, the King of Kings and Lord of Lords, is from the tribe of Judah.

But there is an additional item of significance. Jacob predicts,

> The scepter will not depart from Judah,
> nor the staff from between his feet,
> until <u>Shiloh</u> comes
> and the allegiance of the nations is his. (Genesis 49:10)

What is meant by "scepter"? And who, or what, is Shiloh?

The "scepter" is an ornamental staff. It was carried by rulers on ceremonial occasions to represent one's authority to rule. The individual holding the scepter or in possession of the scepter is the ruler. This rule over God's chosen people was vested in the tribe of Judah. This rule, this scepter, would not depart from Judah until "Shiloh" comes. Let's investigate this term "Shiloh" and how it relates to the scepter.

We will see later in the Biblical Story that Moses delivers to the chosen people God's laws and instructions—referred to as the "Mosaic Law." In ruling over God's people, the tribe of Judah will continually possess the right to enforce the Mosaic Law, even to the extent of carrying out capital punishment if need be. This right won't be removed (the scepter won't be taken from Judah) until Shiloh comes.

Who, or what, is "Shiloh"?

This is a reference to the Messiah. Some translations of this verse and term use phrases such as "the one whom *it* belongs." In other words, the true, final, and everlasting authority to rule belongs to the Messiah. The scepter belongs to the Messiah.

There is more here, though, that deserves exploration and explanation. Note that the scepter *will not depart until the Messiah comes*. Once again, we are getting ahead of ourselves—but when the Biblical Story points to Jesus, we should pay attention and make the connection.

Assuming God's Word is true (a safe assumption), according to Genesis 49:10 and Jacob's blessing, Judah's rule, including the ability to exact capital punishment, would not be removed until such time as the Messiah (Shiloh) has come.

Was the scepter ever removed from Judah? Yes.

This should suggest the Messiah has come.

But more importantly, *when* was the scepter removed from Judah?

Throughout all of Jewish history, Israel had this right concerning discipline over its people. As we will learn later, there is a time when the nation is split into two, followed by defeat, captivity, and exile. But even when in exile in Babylon, the Jewish tribal system was maintained. This remained true after this period of captivity, when the people were able to return to Jerusalem and the land. It also remained true, for a time at least, when the people fell under Roman rule. This included the rule of King Herod (Herod the Great) who was appointed by Rome.

After King Herod's death, there was a brief period when one of Herod's sons, Archelaus, was placed on the throne. He owed his position to Caesar Augustus, the Roman emperor at the time, but his rule did not last long. He was removed around 7 **AD** and replaced by a Roman procurator named Caponius.

As part of this transition, greater controls and restrictions were placed upon the Jews—*and the right to perform capital punishment was removed from the Jewish ruling body*, the Sanhedrin. This was normal policy in lands under Roman control, but for the Jewish people, this meant *the scepter had been removed from Judah*. The adjudication of capital cases was lost, which is why the Jews had to hand Jesus over to Rome for their desire for capital punishment.

This transfer of power is mentioned by Josephus, a Jewish historian of the first century (and it is also mentioned in the Talmud—the body of Jewish civil and ceremonial law):

> After the death of the procurator Festus, when Albinus was about to succeed him, the high priest Ananius considered it a favorable opportunity to assemble the Sanhedrin. He therefore caused James, **the brother of Jesus**, who was called Christ, and several others, to appear before this hastily assembled council, and <u>pronounced upon them the sentence of death</u> by stoning. All the wise men and strict observers of the law who were at Jerusalem expressed their disapprobation of this act... Some even went to Albinus himself, who had departed to Alexandria, to bring <u>this breach of the law under his observation,</u> and to inform him that Aranius had acted illegally in assembling the Sanhedrin without the Roman authority (from Josephus, *Antiquities*, 20:9).

Here the Jewish historian Josephus mentions the Sanhedrin pronouncing the death sentence upon James (at the time, the leader of the Christian movement in Jerusalem). But Josephus recognizes *this was not legal. The scepter had departed from Judah!*

Jacob's death-bed pronouncement said this would not happen until the Messiah had come. But the **scepter had departed** from Judah. Was Jacob wrong?

No.

The Messiah *had* come! He had been born in Bethlehem about a dozen years before this occurred!

As we've said, the Biblical Story is all about Jesus.

As the book of Genesis comes to a close, Jacob (Israel) dies. This leaves Jacob's sons vulnerable to Joseph's vengeance, since they were the ones having separated Joseph from the family and having sold Joseph into slavery.

What does Joseph do?

Instead of revenge, he tells his brothers:

> "What you intended against me for evil, God intended for good, in order to accomplish a day like this—to preserve the lives of many people." (Genesis 50:20)

God took what was meant as evil and turned it into good. This is not a one-time event. The Apostle Paul writes:

> And we know that God works all things together for the good of those who love Him, who are called according to His purpose. (Romans 8:28)

Read this carefully. Paul is not saying that only good things happen to those who love God. Nowhere in the Bible are we promised that—and as we read about Joseph's life, including being cast off by his brothers and improperly imprisoned in Egypt, we know none of this was good. But Paul is saying, no matter what happens, good or bad, God will work these things for the ultimate good.

He does not work a few things for the ultimate good, or some things for the ultimate good. He works *all things* together for the good. Of course, this is not a blanket promise to anyone and everyone. It only applies to Christians. Paul tells us God will do this for "those who love Him, who are called according to His purpose."

That's exactly what the story of Joseph shows us. And that's precisely what Joseph shares in the Genesis 50:20 text above. Joseph tells his brothers, "You meant to harm me . . . but no, God uses this for the good!"

And that's exactly what the cross shows us. The Romans and disbelieving Jews nail the Messiah to the cross. Satan momentarily triumphs. But this is followed by resurrection. God uses all of this ugliness, failure, and animosity on the part of man for the ultimate good of salvation and redemption.

We come to the end of Genesis. Joseph will live to the age of 110 (Genesis 50:22, 26). Certain that all of the promises of God will be fulfilled, he confidently tells his family:

> "I am about to die, but God will surely visit you and bring you up from this land to the land He promised on oath to Abraham, Isaac, and Jacob."
>
> And Joseph made the sons of Israel take an oath and said, "God will surely attend to you, and then you must carry my bones up from this place." (Genesis 50:24, 25)

It is Joseph's desire that he be buried in the land God promised to his forefathers—Abraham, Isaac, and Jacob. His burial in the land will occur centuries later (Joshua 24:32). His bones are placed in Shechem—which has a rich history regarding the Biblical Story (it will be at this location where the tribes of Israel will shout blessings and curses, and years later, this is where Jesus will converse with the Samaritan woman at the well—Jacob's well).

It has been recognized that Genesis starts out on a high note: "In the beginning God." And it ends with the somber words, "...in a coffin in Egypt."

What a contrast.

Much has happened. But in some ways. God's story is just beginning to take off.

From lesson 13: What do we learn about God?

- God reveals that the Messiah will come from the tribe of Judah, one of Jacob's sons.
- As we read about Joseph, we learn that God remains with His people, regardless of the circumstances.
- We also learn that "God works all things together for the good of those who love Him, who are called according to His purpose."

the Bible is about Jesus: We tend to gloss over some of this. Moses gives us a full chapter on Judah—and an unflattering story centered on Judah (recognizing, of course, that the original Hebrew text was not segmented into chapters). I would think Moses might not have known why he was called by God to do this. On this side of the cross, we know the answer—Judah and Tamar are in the lineage of Jesus.

AD: In today's politically correct world, "B.C.E." (or "BCE") is used to designate "Before Common Era" and "C.E." (or CE) is used to designate "Common Era."

What is the "common era"? It starts with the birth of Christ.

Prior to this convention, the terms "BC" and "AD" (or "B.C." and "A.D.") were used. "BC" meant "before Christ," and "AD" meant "after the birth of Christ" (the "AD" stands for *Anno Domini*, which is Latin for "in the year of our Lord").

I still use BC and AD simply because to do otherwise is foolishness. The central point of world history is the incarnation of Jesus. The use of BC and AD reflect this. Going to BCE and CE did not change the importance of the Christ event, and the world's calendars are still based upon the arrival of Jesus. Just the terminology has been changed to reflect a secular world steeped in political correctness. Bah humbug.

the brother of Jesus: We will look at writings from Josephus in more detail in volume 2 of *A Forty-Day Study of the Biblical Story*. But for now, note what Josephus is saying. Josephus was a Jewish historian—and not a believer. Yet he confirms the historical Jesus, and that Jesus was referred to as the Christ (Messiah). He also confirms that Jesus had a brother named James.

This is just one of several references to Jesus that come from sources outside the biblical record—and non-Christian sources at that.

Another fact you'll see in volume 2, we have more references to a man called Jesus written within one hundred and fifty years of his life, than we do of Tiberius Caesar written within one hundred and fifty years of his life. To the Christian, that might not sound remarkable. But keep in mind, Jesus was a simple Jewish rabbi who lived in a tiny corner of the Middle East. Tiberius Caesar was the ruler of the largest empire of the world!

scepter had departed: For a more in depth treatment of this topic, see "The Scepter of Judah," available at https://www.khouse.org/articles/1999/187/ (accessed October 12, 2019).

14

"I AM"

The book of Genesis closes with the bones of Joseph being placed into a coffin in Egypt. The second book of the Bible, Exodus, begins with God's chosen people still in Egypt—and **four hundred years** have now passed. Their situation has turned from one of privilege to one of poverty and persecution. God's chosen people are now slaves in bondage to Pharaoh, the ruler of Egypt.

The offspring of Jacob (Israel) have greatly multiplied—troubling the Egyptian Pharaoh. He decrees any male born of Hebrew parents is to be put to death.

A Hebrew child is saved from this edict when his mother secures the baby in a basket and places it upon the Nile River. The daughter of Pharaoh retrieves the basket and recovers the infant boy, whom she names Moses (in Hebrew, the name we translate as "Moses" means "to draw out," as in "to draw out of the water").

Moses grows up in Pharaoh's Egyptian household. He is able to learn the language and customs of the Egyptians, but he also witnesses the harsh treatment of his own people—the Hebrews—at the hands of the Egyptians. In one incident, he sees an Egyptian beating a Hebrew slave. Angered by what he has witnessed, Moses kills the Egyptian, forcing Moses to flee Egypt.

God has not forgotten His covenant promise to Abraham. He will bring salvation to Abraham's descendants, God's chosen people (a reminder from lesson 8, "salvation" can mean saving one from enemies or from oppression and bondage).

God selects Moses to deliver His people. Why Moses? What did Moses do to deserve this calling? Like God's selection of Abraham generations before, He chose Moses because He wanted to. It is God's choice. Everything reflecting God's choice of the **patriarchs** (Abraham, Isaac, and Jacob) and Moses is simply due to God's sovereign decision and God's faithfulness to His covenant. Many years later, Moses tells the people:

> The LORD did not set His affection on you and choose you because you were more numerous than the other peoples, for you were the fewest of all peoples. But because the LORD loved you and kept the oath He swore to your fathers, He brought you out with a mighty hand and redeemed you from the house of slavery, from the hand of Pharaoh king of Egypt. (Deuteronomy 7:7, 8)

Note why God selects those whom He chooses. It is not because of their merits or anything they deserve; it is because of God's love and God's faithfulness. This is God's grace at work. We saw this trait of God with Abraham, and now we see it with Moses. We witness it throughout God's provisions and protection of the Israelites as they are brought to the land promised to them under the Abrahamic Covenant. And ultimately, we see God's love and faithfulness through the cross of Jesus.

The deliverance of Abraham's descendants from Egypt begins as God appears to Moses as a burning bush. God tells Moses:

> "Go! I am sending you to Pharaoh to bring My people, the Israelites, out of Egypt." (Exodus 3:10)

But Moses is reluctant:

> "Who am I, that I should go to Pharaoh and bring the Israelites out of Egypt?" (Exodus 3:11)

He then asks God,

> "Suppose I go to the Israelites and say to them, 'The God of your fathers has sent me to you,' and they ask me, 'What is His name?' What should I tell them?" (Exodus 3:13)

God responds,

> "I AM WHO I AM. This is what you are to say to the Israelites: 'I AM has sent me to you'." (Exodus 3:14)

You'll recall that we have said, perhaps a half-dozen or more times by now, all of scripture is about Jesus. In **John's Gospel**, Jesus echoes the "I AM" of the burning bush. His uses of this "I AM" term reflect one of the many ways Jesus authenticates he and God are One.

- Jesus feeds a multitude using a few pieces of bread and a couple of small fish. He proclaims, "I AM the bread of life" (John 6:35).
- Jesus announces to a humanity engulfed in spiritual darkness, "I AM the light of the world" (John 8:12).
- Jesus proclaims, "I AM the door of the sheep" (John 10:7). In the Old Testament, God is referenced as being the Shepherd

and His people are His sheep. Here the claim is being made that the only way to God is through Jesus.

- Jesus, God in human form, tells those around him, "I AM the good shepherd" (John 10:11). Not only is Jesus the way to God, Jesus is God. And, as a shepherd does so with the sheep, Jesus, as the Good Shepherd, will guide, protect, and nourish those who are his.

- Jesus, as the seed of woman, conquers Satan and death. It is fitting he tells those at the tomb of Lazarus, "I AM the resurrection and the life" (John 11:25).

- Jesus tells his disciples, "I AM the way, the truth, the life, no one comes to the Father but through me" (John 14:6). These are some of the last words Jesus shares before going to the cross. He tells those closest to him, he is the way to the Father—the only way.

Perhaps the most widely recognized verse in the Bible is John 3:16 –

> For God so loved the world that He gave His one and only Son, that everyone who believes in Him shall not perish but have eternal life.

God's promise is exclusive. It applies *only* to those who believe in Jesus. But it is also very inclusive. *Everyone* who believes in him will not experience God's wrath but will experience eternal life. We'll devote several lessons to this in volume 2.

- Jesus also tells the disciples, "I AM the vine, you are the branches" (John 15:5). Jesus will leave the disciples, but he will not abandon them. In his place, the Holy Spirit will come and indwell the people of God. Through God's Spirit, those who belong to Christ will remain connected to him and will receive life-giving, life-promoting sustenance from him.

Those who follow Jesus will face many obstacles. They will need to be fed by the Bread of Life and be kept from darkness by the Light of the World. They will require continual guidance and protection by the Good Shepherd. They will need to follow the Way, the Truth, the Life. Jesus is the vine and his followers are the branches connected to this vine. Jesus is the life-giving power of the believer. We can only thrive if we stay connected to Jesus.

These are known as the "seven I AM statements" as found in John's Gospel. Through the words of Jesus, we clearly hear the echo of the voice in the burning bush.

John records other references to "I AM." One, in particular, should not go unnoticed.

Jesus confronts the people of Israel who are refusing to accept him as their long-awaited Messiah. He tells them:

> "Your father Abraham was overjoyed to see My day.
> He saw it and was glad." (John 8:56—this verse was
> discussed in lesson 9)

The people do not understand who Jesus is or what Jesus is telling them. "How could you have known Abraham?" they ask. Jesus responds,

> "Truly, truly, I tell you...before Abraham was born, I
> AM!" (John 8:58)

The "I AM" is Jesus claiming equality with the great "I AM who I am" of the burning bush.

Aren't we assuming too much when we suggest Jesus' use of the phrase "I AM" is a declaration of equality with God? Is this reading too much into the text?

No.

The people's reaction confirms what Jesus is claiming.

John tells us,

> At this, they picked up stones to throw at Him. But Jesus was hidden and went out of the temple area. (John 8:59)

The people knew what the words "before Abraham was born, I AM" meant. Jesus was claiming equivalence with God. To the people remaining in spiritual darkness, this was blasphemy—and, according to the Mosaic Law, the blasphemer was to be put to death (we'll learn about the Law of Moses shortly). When John tells us, "At this, they picked up stones to throw at Him," we can be assured the people clearly understood what was meant when Jesus used "I AM."

All of scripture is about Jesus.

From lesson 14: What do we learn about God?

- As we saw in previous lessons, God orchestrates historical events to accomplish His purposes and to fulfill His promises.
- Here we see His commitment to His chosen people, and His selection of a deliverer, Moses, to bring salvation.
- God provides Moses with His name: I AM. Jesus will use this term to authenticate his Messiahship and Deity.

Four hundred years: According to Exodus 12:40 the duration of the Israelites in Egypt lasted 430 years. However, this is based on the Masoretic Text of the Hebrew Scriptures, and there is evidence that the 430-year period includes time not just in Egypt but also in

Canaan itself. For one interesting viewpoint, which is questioned by some scholars, see https://www.youtube.com/watch?v=VI1yRTC6kGE&feature=youtu. be (accessed November 8, 2019). It should be noted that there is healthy scholarly debate concerning such things as the timing of Egyptian events, the period when the Israelites were in bondage, and the timing of the Exodus. That the Israelites spent time in Egypt is affirmed through archeology.

patriarchs: From a biblical perspective, the patriarchs are the forefathers of the twelve sons of Jacob (Israel) and the Jews: Abraham, Isaac, and Jacob.

John's Gospel: Volume 2 devotes an entire lesson to the seven "I AM" statements as found in John's Gospel. See lesson 23 in *A Forty-Day Study of the Biblical Story: The Story of Christ, Volume Two: The Arrival of the Christ.*

15

Salvation of God's Chosen People

Let's return to the story of Moses. He is instructed by the great "I AM" to go to Egypt, free God's chosen people, and lead them to the land God promised as part of His covenant with Abraham.

This is no simple task. Moses is to confront the most powerful man on earth, Egypt's Pharaoh.

It is here in the Biblical Story (the book of Exodus) that we read of the encounter between Moses and Pharaoh—and the one true God of the Bible and the false gods of the Egyptians. The Egyptians were a "polytheistic" culture ("poly" meaning "many," "theistic" relating to "God" or "gods"). The Egyptians worshipped numerous gods. God orchestrates a series of ten plagues, each one to show the **futility of these Egyptian gods**.

I have found that God tends to show up and communicate in the language that people can understand. God's choice of plagues could be readily understood by the Egyptians. God attacks the objects of Egyptian worship—showing He is more powerful than these "gods" invented and worshipped by man.

God communicates this same way today. As an example, the tribal people in **Vietnam** still have the equivalent of what we label as "witch doctors." Some tribes rely upon this individual and the performance of various rituals to bring health to someone who is sick or has suffered injury. The "witch doctors" are ineffective—but the tribespeople have no other option than to rely upon their pagan practices.

This changes when a member of the tribe becomes a Christian, or when a Christian missionary visits the tribe. What often happens is that the Christian is able to pray over the afflicted and a supernatural healing occurs. Vietnamese communities also experience demon possession—and we see this same supernatural power and effectiveness when Christians are able to cast out (exorcise) demons. Numerous people have also experienced visions that have led them to Christ.

God is at work in Vietnam, and conversions to Christianity are occurring throughout the tribal areas of Vietnam—and all of Vietnam—because God is communicating with these people in ways they can understand.

Thousands of years ago, we see this same approach as God sends ten plagues upon Egypt to show the futility of their worship of false gods. We won't go through all ten plagues, but we will look at several as being representative of the acts of God.

For the Egyptian, the Nile River could bring life or death. An abundant flow of the Nile provided food and promoted prosperity. A lethargic Nile meant famine. The Egyptians worshipped Hapi, the god associated with the Nile.

What does God do?

He turns the Nile to blood.

The Egyptians worshipped the sun-god, Ra. This god brought sustenance to the people and their crops—or so the people thought.

What does God do?

He turns the sun into darkness.

And, the Egyptians worshipped Pharaoh. The last plague was the killing of the firstborn throughout all of Egypt. This targeted both the people, and their most visible god—Pharaoh himself. The death of Pharaoh's oldest son took away the successor to Pharaoh's throne.

This was the final and most destructive plague. It is after this that Pharaoh lets the people of God leave the land.

This last plague is memorialized forever in Jewish life—and in Christianity. For Judaism, it established the religious calendar (see Exodus 12:1, as discussed in lesson 8) and their religious festivals center on this event (see Leviticus 23). It has been honored each year for over three thousand years, and today it is honored each year throughout the Christian community.

Let's look at the events surrounding the last plague.

> Then the LORD said to Moses, "I will bring upon Pharaoh and Egypt one more plague. After that, he will allow you to leave this place. And when he lets you go he will drive you out completely." (Exodus 11:1)

God's chosen people are warned of the plague that is about to happen:

> This is what the LORD says: 'About midnight I will go throughout Egypt, and every firstborn son in the land of Egypt will die, from the firstborn of Pharaoh who sits on his throne, to the firstborn of the servant girl behind the hand mill, as well as the firstborn of all the cattle. Then a great cry will go out over all the land of Egypt, the likes of which have never been heard before and will never be heard again.' (Exodus 11:4–6)

The only way, the *only* way the Hebrews will be saved from God's wrath, is if they follow God's instructions:

- On the tenth day of the month, each family is to take a lamb without blemish.
- This sacrificial lamb is kept until the fourteenth of the month, at which time the community is to slaughter each of the lambs.
- The blood of lambs is put upon the side posts and tops of the doorframes of each dwelling.

God tells the Israelites:

> On that night I will pass through the land of Egypt and strike down every firstborn male, both man and beast, and I will execute judgment against all the gods of Egypt. I am the LORD. (Exodus 12:12)

And adds:

> When I see the blood, I will pass over you. No plague will fall on you to destroy you when I strike the land of Egypt. (Exodus 12:13)

If they follow God's instructions, if they place their trust in the blood of the lamb, God's wrath will pass over them. This is where the term "Passover" comes from.

God's instructions include each family partaking of the lamb—the Passover Meal.

As we saw in the naming of Adam's descendants up to Noah, as well as when God tells us the exact date the ark came to rest, God provides details which ultimately point to Christ. On this side of the cross, we have the completed picture—and all of this makes sense. But for centuries, the Jewish people celebrated Passover without recognizing its true relationship to the Messiah. The only way, the *only* way to be saved from God's wrath is to rely upon the blood of Jesus, the Lamb of God that takes away the sins of the world.

Jesus' last meal with his disciples is the celebration of the Jewish Passover. It is here that he refers to the cup of wine as being representative of his blood. And he tells the disciples:

> "This cup is the new covenant in My blood, which is poured out for you." (Luke 22:20)

We have already discussed God's covenant with Abraham, and soon we'll be discussing God's covenant with Moses. Here, though, Jesus refers to a different covenant—a new covenant. We will get to this later in the Biblical Story. It is the covenant you and I live under—inaugurated by the cross and validated by the resurrection.

The Jewish Passover is about Jesus. The entire Bible is about Jesus.

From lesson 15: What do we learn about God?

- There is only one God, yet throughout the history of mankind, people have worshipped other gods. This is true of the Egyptians at the time of Moses, and God uses a series of plagues to readily show the futility of worshipping anything or anyone other than the God of creation who has been revealed to the Hebrew people.
- The last plague involves death. Salvation is offered to the Israelites. They can escape death by obeying God's instruction. This involves placing the blood of a lamb upon their doorposts. All of this prefigures the Lamb of God whose spilled blood offers salvation to those who place their trust in him.

futility of the Egyptian gods: Jewish rabbinical writings (writings outside the Hebrew Scriptures, or Old Testament), suggest the plagues of Exodus were not punishment for the mistreatment of the Hebrews, but instead were retribution for Pharaoh's rejection of God and Egypt's worship of other gods (idols). This Bible supports this. In Exodus 12:12, God says,

> On that night I will pass through the land of Egypt and strike down every firstborn male, both man and beast, and I will execute judgment against all the gods of Egypt. I am the LORD.

In recording their exodus from Egypt, Moses writes,

> On the fifteenth day of the first month, on the day after the Passover, the Israelites set out from Rameses. They marched out triumphantly in full view of all the Egyptians, who were burying all their firstborn, whom the LORD had struck down among them; for the LORD had executed judgment against their gods. The Israelites set out from Rameses and camped at Succoth. (Numbers 33:3–5)

Vietnam: In my early days of teaching various Vietnamese pastors and church leaders, I was curious to hear their stories as to how they became believers in Christ—especially those coming from places where there are no Bibles, no churches, and no pastors.

Many came to Christ due to the witnessing of healings or exorcisms. Some experienced visions. I decided on one of my visits to quantify their experiences. I surveyed twenty-two people, representing five different churches. Seventeen were pastors or church leaders. The results are as follows:

	Yes	Not Sure	No
Had some type of religious vision:	14	7	1
Personally healed (supernaturally):	16		6
Knew someone physically healed:	20	1	1
Witnessed an exorcism:	11	1	10

The majority of those interviewed had experienced some form of religious vision, or had either personally been healed, or had witnessed a supernatural healing. Half had personally witnessed an exorcism.

While these types of events seem strange to those of us in the West, they are very common within the Christian community of Vietnam. My discussions with pastors and church leaders from other parts of the world, particularly South American tribal areas and Africa, support similar findings for those geographic regions as well.

God speaks in the language the people being spoken to can understand.

16

The Wilderness Journey

One of the great migrations in human history is the exodus of God's chosen people from Egypt and their forty-years of journey to the Promised Land. God's mighty acts lead Pharaoh to release the Hebrew people. Throughout their wilderness journey, God instructs and continually sustains them.

The biblical books Exodus, Leviticus, Numbers, and Deuteronomy all cover this period in Israel's history. Adding Genesis to this creates the "**Pentateuch**"—the first five books of the Bible. These are the sacred writings of Moses. The Pentateuch ends with the death of Moses and the children of Israel on the doorstep of Canaan—the Promised Land.

This history is important because this ties to Genesis 3:15 and centers on the Abrahamic Covenant. God tells Abraham:

> "Leave your country, your kindred, and your father's household, and go to the land I will show you.
>
> I will make you into a great nation and I will bless you...
>
> > ...and all the families of the earth
> > will be blessed through you" (Genesis 12:1–3)

As we saw in our review of Genesis, the seed of woman will come through Abraham, Isaac, and Jacob—the patriarchs and ancestors of the Israelites. And a great nation will be established in a land promised to these people. These are God's actions in history as His plan of redemption continues to unfold.

At Mount Sinai, God gives Moses the Ten Commandments and provides instructions and requirements for the Israelites. We refer to this relationship between God and His people as the "Mosaic Covenant," and His commands and instructions as the "Mosaic Law." This will become the focal point for Jewish life for the next three thousand years. Today's orthodox Jews devote their existence to following the Mosaic Law. Believers in Jesus do not do this in that the Mosaic Covenant has been replaced by the New Covenant.

Reading the Pentateuch is fascinating. We continually see God providing for His covenant people—and yet their responses are those of stubbornness, ungratefulness, and obstinance. It's been said that the opposite of love is not hate—it is indifference. The Israelites did not hate God—far from it. But over and over again, we see their indifference to God.

Unlike God's covenant with Abraham, which was unconditional and everlasting, God's covenant with Moses is both conditional and finite. As to its temporary nature, Moses foresees the people's inability to live up to the covenant. He talks about punishment for disobedience and tells the people:

> The generation to come—your sons who follow you and the foreigner who comes from a distant land—will see the plagues of the land and the sicknesses the LORD has inflicted on it. All its soil will be a burning waste of sulfur and salt, unsown and unproductive, with no plant growing on it, just like the destruction

of Sodom and Gomorrah, Admah and Zeboiim, which the LORD overthrew in His fierce anger.

All the nations will ask, 'Why has the LORD done such a thing to this land? Why this great outburst of anger?'

And the people will answer, 'It is because they abandoned the covenant of the LORD, the God of their fathers, which He made with them when He brought them out of the land of Egypt. They went and served other gods, and they worshiped gods they had not known—gods that the LORD had not given to them. Therefore the LORD's anger burned against this land, and He brought upon it every curse written in this book. The LORD uprooted them from their land in His anger, rage, and great wrath, and He cast them into another land, where they are today.' (Deuteronomy 29:22–28)

As to the conditional nature of the Mosaic Covenant, the term "conditional" means God places conditions on His promises. Here, God's covenant blessings are directly related to Israel's obedience. If Israel is obedient to the Law and faithful to God, God will bless them. But if they disobey, God will punish them. The blessings and curses associated with this conditional covenant are found in detail in the 28th chapter of Deuteronomy—some of the last words written by Moses.

God tells the people to expect punishment when He is disobeyed. An example of this occurs at the wilderness oasis of Kadesh Barnea—the doorstep of the land God has promised to them. By the time we get to the thirteenth chapter of Numbers, the third book of the Bible, the Israelites have been in the wilderness for a year. They have received a great portion of the Mosaic Law. A special portable structure, the tabernacle, has been built for their worship of God. And, their journey to the Promised Land is about to end.

Except . . .

Except they refuse to enter the land.

Moses sends twelve "spies" to scout out the land—leaders from each of the twelve tribes of Israel. They return with a large cluster of grapes—so heavy that it takes two men to lift them on poles that they **carry between their shoulders**. They also bring back pomegranates and figs. This was truly a land of abundance, a land "**flowing with milk and honey**" (described this way twenty-four times in the Bible). The twelve spies announce the wonders and bountiful provisions that await the people of God.

The land is one more affirmation of God's faithfulness. This is the land God promises to Abraham (Genesis 15:18–21). It is the land that God promises to Abraham's son Isaac (Genesis 26:3). And this is the land that God promises to Abraham's grandson, Jacob, or Israel (Genesis 28:13).

And Jacob was so sure of God's fulfillment of His promise, he asks that his remains be taken there for burial (Genesis 47:30, see also Joshua 24:32). Over and over, God promises this land to His people.

But when the spies return, the people's focus is not on the promises of God. Nor is it on the bountiful provisions of the land that God is giving to them. Instead, those sent to survey the land, or at least all but two of those sent, are fearful. In their anguish and apprehension, they moan about the numerical strength and military superiority of the people living in the land—the Canaanites. They even claim to have seen Nephilim in the land—offspring from the Genesis 6 fallen angels as was discussed in lesson 8.

The two that encourage the people to trust in God and enter the land are Caleb and Joshua.

But the people do not listen to these two. They listen to the ten. Strong in fear and weak in faith, they revolt against Moses and **Aaron**:

> All the Israelites grumbled against Moses and Aaron, and the whole congregation said to them, "If only we had died in the land of Egypt, or if only we had died in this wilderness! Why is the LORD bringing us into this land to fall by the sword? Our wives and children will become plunder. Would it not be better for us to go back to Egypt?"
>
> So they said to one another, "Let us appoint a leader and return to Egypt." (Numbers 14:2–4)

This is not the first time the people have complained. Up to this point, they have repeatedly disobeyed God. And now they refuse to place their trust in God's promises—having a stronger desire to return to Egypt and live under Egyptian bondage than to rely upon God and His faithfulness.

Moses petitions God to forgive the sins of these obstinate, stiff-necked people.

How does God respond?

> "I have pardoned them as you requested," the LORD replied. "Yet as surely as I live and as surely as the whole earth is filled with the glory of the LORD, not one of the men who have seen My glory and the signs I performed in Egypt and in the wilderness—yet have tested Me and disobeyed Me these ten times—not one will ever see the land that I swore to give their fathers.

None of those who have treated Me with contempt will see it." (Numbers 14:20–23)

The people had disobeyed God ten times, but this passage begins: "I have pardoned them as you requested." The people's sin and indifference to God is met with God's forgiveness and grace.

God pardons the people—but that does not mean He allows sin to go unpunished. Sin must be punished (if this were not the case, there would be no need for the cross). Even though God forgives the people, none of the adult males will live to step foot into the Promised Land, other than Joshua and Caleb—the two who wanted their fellow Israelites to trust in God's promises and enter the land. Even Moses, who sins against God, will not be allowed to enter the land.

There are several more events in the book of Numbers that deserve attention. Further into their wilderness journey, we once again witness a rebellious people:

The people grew impatient on the journey and spoke against God and against Moses: "Why have you led us up out of Egypt to die in the wilderness? There is no bread or water, and we detest this wretched food!" (Numbers 21:4, 5)

Again, we see punishment:

The LORD sent venomous snakes among the people, and many of the Israelites were bitten and died. (Numbers 21:6)

But God, once more, shows His mercy:

Then the LORD said to Moses, "Make a fiery serpent and mount it on a pole. When anyone who is bitten looks at it, he will live." So Moses made a bronze snake and mounted it on a pole. If anyone who was bitten looked at the bronze snake, he would live. (Numbers 21:8, 9)

In lesson 9, we talked about some of the ways of God that seem so strange to us—yet help us understand faith and build faith. Examples cited included Noah building a boat when it had never rained before, and Joshua walking around fortifications and blasting horns to take down the walls of Jericho. Here, in the book of Numbers, is another example. Moses is told to fashion a bronze snake and put it on a pole. Those struck by a snake—in other words, those afflicted by God's judgment, condemnation, and wrath—could lift their eyes to that which was raised before them and be saved.

It would be fifteen hundred years after this event until we are told what this meant. And it is Jesus who tells explains it. A man named Nicodemus approaches Jesus at night and is told by Jesus that no one can see God without being born of the Spirit. And then Jesus adds,

> Just as Moses lifted up the snake in the wilderness, so the Son of Man must be lifted up, that everyone who believes in Him may have eternal life. For God so loved the world that He gave His one and only Son, that everyone who believes in Him shall not perish but have eternal life. (John 3:14–16)

The Biblical Story centers on Jesus. In their wilderness journey, God offers His chosen people salvation—a way to escape punishment. But the people, in order to live, must place their faith and trust in God and His provision for their salvation.

Years later, through the lifted cross of Jesus, God will offer to the world salvation from punishment. But, in order to escape God's punishment, people must place their faith and trust in God and His provision for their salvation—the blood of Christ.

Moses is perhaps the most revered individual in Judaism, and the Mosaic Law has been the focal point of Jewish life for thousands of years. We clearly see God's providence in the life of Moses:

- At his birth, Moses is protected by God.
- In his later years, Moses is chosen to become God's servant.
- Through the power and presence of God, Moses delivers the people of God from Egyptian bondage and leads them toward the Promised Land.
- And at the end of his life, Moses is buried by God himself (Deuteronomy 34:6).

Deuteronomy, the last book of the Pentateuch, closes with the words:

> Since that time, no prophet has arisen in Israel like Moses, whom the LORD knew face to face, who did all the signs and wonders that the LORD sent him to do against the land of Egypt—to Pharaoh and all his officials and all his land— by all the mighty acts of power and awesome deeds that Moses performed in the sight of all Israel. (Deuteronomy 34:10–12)

Moses was truly a great prophet. But before we leave the writings of Moses, we need to look at another key revelation concerning the seed of woman—the Redeemer. Before his death, Moses tells the people:

> The LORD your God will raise up for <u>you a prophet</u> like me <u>from among your own brothers</u>. <u>You must listen to him.</u> (Deuteronomy 18:15)

God is going to raise up a future prophet. He is the one the people *must* listen to. On this side of the cross. we know this "Greater Prophet" is Jesus. Much can be said here.

- Moses parts the waters. Jesus walks upon the water.

- Moses delivers the people of God from Egyptian bondage. Jesus provides the people of God deliverance from bondage to sin and Satan.
- Moses brought us the commandments from God. Jesus fulfills the commandments of God.
- Through Moses, the people are fed manna from heaven. Jesus is the Bread of Life.
- Moses brings the people to the doorstep of the Promised Land. Jesus brings God's people to the dwelling place of God Himself.
- Moses was a servant of God. Jesus is the Son of God.

Note that Moses predicts the prophet will come from Israel ("... among your own brothers...") and says, "You must listen to him." Centuries later, Jesus will travel to Caesarea Philippi, where his disciples acknowledge him as the Messiah. He then proceeds to take three of his disciples, Peter, James, and John, to a mountain where his transfiguration occurs. Moses and Elijah appear, and a bright cloud surrounds them. The voice of God says,

> "This is My beloved Son, in whom I am well pleased. <u>Listen to Him</u>!" (Matthew 17:5)

On another occasion, Jesus walks among the people in Galilee. A large gathering of people follows him and are listening to his teachings. It is here that Jesus feeds the people. Unlike Moses, he does not call down manna from heaven. Instead, he takes the loaves and fish, blesses them, and then multiples them so that all can be fed. How do the people respond?

> When the people saw the sign that Jesus had performed, they began to say, "Truly this is <u>the Prophet</u> who is to come into the world." (John 6:14)

After the resurrection of Jesus, Peter preaches to the people and reminds them of this Greater Prophet:

> "And now, brothers, I know that you acted in ignorance, as did your leaders. But in this way God has fulfilled what He foretold through all the prophets, saying that His Christ would suffer. Repent, then, and turn back, so that your sins may be wiped away, that times of refreshing may come from the presence of the Lord, and that He may send Jesus, the Christ, who has been appointed for you.
>
> Heaven must take Him in until the time comes for the restoration of all things, which God announced long ago through His holy prophets. For Moses said, 'The Lord your God will raise up for you a prophet like me from among your brothers. You must listen to Him in everything He tells you. Everyone who does not listen to Him will be completely cut off from among his people." (Acts 3:17–22)

Moses was truly a great prophet. But Jesus is the Greater Prophet.

We must listen to him!

Before we leave this section, there is one additional item we should touch upon. Moses predicted a day when,

> The LORD your God will circumcise your hearts and the hearts of your descendants, and you will love Him with all your heart and with all your soul, so that you may live. (Deuteronomy 30:6)

Moses foresees a new covenant between God and his people. The Israelite prophets, Jeremiah and Ezekiel, also anticipate a replacement to the Mosaic Covenant. Jeremiah tells the Israelites:

Behold, the days are coming, declares the LORD,
    when I will make a new covenant
with the house of Israel
    and with the house of Judah. (Jeremiah 31:31)

This new covenant will involve "circumcised hearts":

"But this is the covenant I will make with the house
of Israel
    after those days, declares the LORD.
I will put My law in their minds
    and inscribe it on their hearts.
And I will be their God,
    and they will be My people." (Jeremiah 31:33)

Through Ezekiel, God says to His people,

I will give you a new heart and put a new spirit within
you; I will remove your heart of stone and give you
a heart of flesh. And I will put My Spirit within you
and cause you to walk in My statutes and to carefully
observe My ordinances. (Ezekiel 36:36, 37)

The Mosaic Covenant is replaced by the New Covenant—which
Jesus inaugurates through his blood, the "blood of the new covenant"
(Luke 22:20). All of this will be discussed in detail in volume 2. But
we are a long way from there. There is much in Israel's history to
discuss—and it all points to Jesus. And it points to why we need
Jesus.

From lesson 16: What do we learn about God?

- God remains faithful to His people and His promises.
- He establishes a covenant with His chosen people and includes instructions as to how He wants them to live.
- This covenant is the Mosaic Covenant and includes the Ten Commandments and the rest of the Mosaic Law.
- The Mosaic Covenant is conditional and temporary. If the people obey, they will be blessed; if they disobey, they will be subject to a loss of blessings and punishment. It is replaced by the New Covenant—inaugurated by the blood of Christ and his resurrection.

Pentateuch: These are the first five books of the Bible (and the Hebrew Scriptures). This word derives from the Greek *"pentateuchos,"* or "five books" (or "five scrolls"). These are also referred to in Judaism as the Torah, coming from a Hebrew word that implies "instruction" or "teaching."

carry between their shoulders: The symbol for tourism in modern-day Israel is an artist's rendering of two men carrying a large cluster of grapes hung in the middle of a pole. The grapes are heavy enough to require the two men to carry them. This depiction comes from Numbers 13:23 and the spies returning from the land of promise.

flowing with milk and honey: We see this term in four of the five books of the Pentateuch (as examples, Exodus 3:8; Leviticus 20:24; Numbers 14:8; and Deuteronomy 6:3). We also see this in the Song of Solomon, as well as in Isaiah, Jeremiah, and Ezekiel.

If you have been to Israel, you might wonder where all of the cows and bees are. In context, milk refers to goat's milk. In biblical times, an abundance of goats was a reflection of wealth. And honey refers to the honey obtained from dates. Both reflect a land of extraordinary richness and fertility.

Aaron: Aaron is the brother of Moses. As part of God's instructions in the Mosaic Law, Aaron and his descendants were to represent the people before God. These individuals would be Israel's priests. In that Aaron and his descendants are Levites (descendants of Jacob's son, Levi), this is referred to as the "Levitical priesthood."

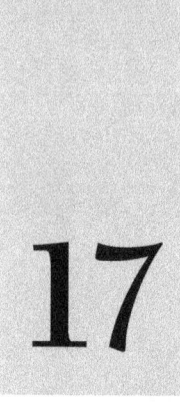

17

Conquest of the Land

The Pentateuch, the first five books of the Bible, ends with the death of Moses. This is followed by the book "Joshua," named after its central character.

You will recall from our last lesson, Joshua was one of the twelve spies sent into the land. He and Caleb were the only two that offer encouragement to the people upon returning from this mission. They want their fellow Israelites to trust in the faithfulness of God and His promises and enter the land. But the people listen to the ten who describe fortified cities and fear the strength of the Canaanites. They refuse to place their faith in God, resulting in their punishment from God. Of the adult males living at the time the spies returned, only Joshua and Caleb will enter the land—and this will not occur until forty years have passed.

The book of Joshua is about Joshua's leadership, the conquering of the land, and the parceling of the land to each of the tribes. The first Canaanite city they must conquer is that of Jericho, protected by its massive walls. Archeologists suggest these walls were from five to seven feet thick, and at least thirteen feet in height. There were watchtowers along the walls that could have been twenty-eight feet in height.

Before the Israelites cross the Jordan River, two spies are sent to inspect Jericho and the land. At Jericho, they are offered protection by a prostitute named **Rahab**. Though she is a Canaanite Gentile, note what she says, both about her people's fear and also about the God of the Israelites:

> "I know that the LORD has given you this land and that the fear of you has fallen on us, so that all who dwell in the land are melting in fear of you. For we have heard how the LORD dried up the waters of the Red Sea before you when you came out of Egypt, and what you did to Sihon and Og, the two kings of the Amorites across the Jordan, whom you devoted to destruction. When we heard this, our hearts melted and everyone's courage failed because of you, for the LORD your God is God in the heavens above and on the earth below." (Joshua 2:9–11)

God provides directions to Joshua as to how he is to go about conquering Jericho. These instructions are detailed and clear.

But they make no sense whatsoever.

That is, the instructions make no sense unless God is teaching His chosen people a lesson on faith, and a lesson on the necessity of trusting and depending upon God. God tells Joshua,

> "March around the city with all the men of war, circling the city one time. Do this for six days. Have seven priests carry seven rams' horns in front of the ark. Then on the seventh day, march around the city seven times, while the priests blow the horns. And

when there is a long blast of the ram's horn and you hear its sound, have all the people give a mighty shout. Then the wall of the city will collapse, and the people will go up, each man straight ahead." (Joshua 6:3)

We've seen this trait of God before. It made no sense for Noah to build a boat—it had never rained. It made no sense for Abraham, at age 100, to count on God who promised him many descendants. It made no sense for Moses to confront Egypt's Pharaoh—the most powerful man in the world. And it makes no sense to walk around these five- to seven-foot-thick walls and blow shofars—ram's horns—and expect the walls to crumble.

But Joshua is a man of faith. We saw this when he and the eleven other spies returned to Kadesh Barnea after scouting out the land. And we see this same faith in the conquest of Jericho:

On the seventh day, they got up at dawn and marched around the city seven times in the same manner. That was the only day they circled the city seven times. After the seventh time around, the priests blew the horns, and Joshua commanded the people, "Shout! For the LORD has given you the city!"

So when the rams' horns sounded, the people shouted. When they heard the blast of the horn, the people gave a great shout, and the wall collapsed. The people charged into the city, each man straight ahead, and captured the city. At the edge of the sword they devoted to destruction everything in the city—man and woman, young and old, oxen, sheep, and donkeys. (Joshua 7:15, 16, 20, 21)

The **walls come down**. There is total destruction. Only Rahab and her family are saved.

Unlike most victories in ancient times, where soldiers are given the spoils of war, the Israelites are commanded by God to take nothing from Jericho. For this specific conquest, the first victory within the Promised Land, articles of silver, gold, bronze, and iron are to be used in the honoring of God. Everything else is to be set aside for destruction. Joshua tells the people:

> "Now the city and everything in it must be devoted to the LORD for destruction. Only Rahab the prostitute and all those with her in her house will live, because she hid the spies we sent. But keep away from the things devoted to destruction, lest you yourself be set apart for destruction. If you take any of these, you will set apart the camp of Israel for destruction and bring disaster upon it. For all the silver and gold and all the articles of bronze and iron are holy to the LORD; they must go into His treasury." (Joshua 6:15–19)

In some ways, entry into the Promised Land represents a new beginning. Joshua represents new leadership—a new servant of God. God tells Joshua,

> No one shall stand against you all the days of your life. As I was with Moses, so will I be with you; I will never leave you nor forsake you. (Joshua 1:5)

He adds:

> Above all, be strong and very courageous. Be careful to observe all the law that My servant Moses commanded you. Do not turn from it to the right or to the left, so that you may prosper wherever you go. This Book of the Law must not depart from your mouth; you are to recite it day and night so that you may be careful to

do everything written in it. For then you will prosper and succeed in all you do. (Joshua 1:7, 8)

How do the people handle this new beginning?

> The Israelites, however, acted unfaithfully regarding the things devoted to destruction. Achan son of Carmi ... of the tribe of Judah, took some of what was set apart. So the LORD's anger burned against the Israelites. (Joshua 7:1)

Once again, we see the people's indifference toward God. In this case, it is only one Israelite that disobeys God's command, a man named Achan. But because of this one man's sin, all of the Israelite community suffers.

There is minimal delay in God's punishment. The suffering begins immediately after the successful conquest of Jericho. The Israelites set out to defeat the second Canaanite city in their path, the small settlement of Ai. But they fail at this as God is not with them. They must retreat, and for the first time the Israelites lose men in battle.

The initial conquest of Ai was a relatively small skirmish—but we cannot overlook what this defeat of the Israelites meant. God had promised the Israelites the land. God would go before them in battle. The victory at Jericho was God's victory. But at Ai, the Israelites had to turn and run.

You will recall, Rahab had talked about the fear of the Canaanite people in hearing of the successful exploits of the Israelites. Hearts had melted and courage had failed—and those in Jericho were recipients of the power of Israel's God. There was truth in the words of the two spies returning to Joshua prior to Jericho's destruction: "Indeed, all who dwell in the land are melting in fear of us" (Joshua 2:24).

But now, the Israelites are shown to be vulnerable. They were the ones that lost men and had to retreat.

Joshua's reaction to this loss at Ai shows his distress:

> Joshua tore his clothes and fell facedown before the ark of the LORD until evening, as did the elders of Israel; and they all sprinkled dust on their heads.
>
> "O, Lord GOD," Joshua said, "why did You ever bring this people across the Jordan to deliver us into the hands of the Amorites to be destroyed? If only we had been content to stay on the other side of the Jordan! O Lord, what can I say, now that Israel has turned its back and run from its enemies? When the Canaanites and all who live in the land hear about this, they will surround us and wipe out our name from the earth. Then what will You do for Your great name?" (Joshua 7:6–9)

The Israelites are the covenant people of God, and the Mosaic Covenant is alive and well. If the people follow God and obey His instructions, they will be blessed. If not, they will forfeit His blessings. God had told the people to keep away from the things devoted for destruction: "If you take any of these, you will set apart the camp of Israel for destruction and bring disaster upon it" (Joshua 6:18). Achan disobeys and disaster follows.

God tells the people:

> Israel has sinned; they have transgressed My covenant that I commanded them, and they have taken some of what was devoted to destruction. Indeed, they have stolen and lied about it, and they have put these things with their own possessions. (Joshua 7:11)

Get up and consecrate the people, saying, 'Consecrate yourselves for tomorrow, for this is what the LORD, the God of Israel, says: Among you, O Israel, there are things devoted to destruction. <u>You cannot stand against your enemies until you remove them.</u> (Joshua 7:13)

When it is determined that Achan had taken these things, he is removed from the camp. He is put to death. His sons are put to death. His daughters are put to death. All of Achan's possessions are destroyed.

The punishment upon Achan and his family seems harsh—and it was.

About a hundred years after Christ walked the earth, there was a wealthy man living within the Roman empire. His name was Marcion. Marcion started a movement to "reform" Christianity. He studied the writings circulating throughout the early church—including the Hebrew Scriptures. According to Marcion, the God of Judaism could not be the God of what later became known as the New Testament.

No, the God of the Hebrews is belligerent and mean. He is characterized by pettiness and wrath. He has no place in Christianity. He is not the God of love we can approach as "Abba, Father."

Marcion wanted to banish from the Christian Bible the Hebrew Scriptures, our Old Testament.

His views were inaccurate, at best. Throughout the Old Testament, we continually see God's patience and His grace and mercy. But **even today** there is sometimes uneasiness with God as He is depicted in the Old Testament compared with God as found in the New Testament. Of course, they are one and the same. But if a person only gives the God of the Old Testament a cursory glance, without placing His actions into the context of man's rebellion and such things as the Mosaic Covenant, their view of God may get distorted. Similarly, if one focuses on the New Testament text without hearing the clear warnings on the reality of eternal damnation for those who do not accept Christ, the view of God may also get distorted.

God is God. And God says what He means and means what He says.

The punishment upon Achan and his family was harsh, as was the initial defeat of the Israelites at Ai. But let's put this into perspective:

- Achan placed his desire to possess items taken from war over his desire to obey God (Joshua 7:21).
- God had clearly warned His people of what would occur should they disobey (Joshua 6:18).
- God gave Achan a night to consider what he had done; time where Achan could have confessed his sin both to God and to the community (Joshua 7:13).
- Achan's sin affected the entire nation of Israel. Only Achan had violated God's command, but note the text:

> The Israelites, however, acted unfaithfully...the LORD's anger burned against the Israelites. (Joshua 7:1)

  The nation as a whole was in a covenant relationship with God. When one member transgresses the covenant, the entire nation's relationship with God is damaged.
- And this covenant, the Mosaic Covenant, was operative. God promises to bless the people when they obey—but remove the blessings when they disobey. God withheld his blessings when the Israelites went against Ai—and thirty-six of their men died (Joshua 7:4, 5). God made it clear why this happened:

This is why the Israelites cannot stand against their enemies. They will turn their backs and run from their enemies, because they themselves have been set apart for destruction. I will no longer be with you unless you remove from among you whatever is devoted to destruction. (Joshua 7:12)

Achan stole from that which was "devoted to destruction." His failure to follow the commands of God brought destruction to others.

- And ultimately, Achan stole from God. Articles of gold, silver, bronze, and iron from this first conquest were to be dedicated to God. Part of what Achan had taken was both gold and silver.

Achan's sin affected those around him and did not go unpunished. Sin always affects others—and always requires punishment.

There are no exceptions.

The book of Joshua continues, as the Israelites resume their conquest of the land and captured territories are given to each of the various tribes. The book comes to a close with words that are instructive:

The LORD has driven out great and powerful nations before you, and to this day no one can stand against you. One of you can put a thousand to flight, because the LORD your God fights for you, just as He promised. Therefore, watch yourselves carefully, that you love the LORD your God. (Joshua 23:9–11)

Now behold, today I am going the way of all the earth, and you know with all your heart and soul that not one of the good promises the LORD your God made to you has failed. Everything was fulfilled for you; not one promise has failed. (Joshua 23:14)

God has been faithful. The land has been delivered to the people. But the Israelites must be reminded once again of the conditional nature of the Mosaic Covenant:

> But just as every good thing the LORD your God promised you has come to pass, likewise the LORD will bring upon you the calamity He has threatened, until He has destroyed you from this good land He has given you. If you transgress the covenant of the LORD your God, which He commanded you, and go and serve other gods and bow down to them, the LORD's anger will burn against you, and you will quickly perish from this good land He has given you. (Joshua 23:15, 16)

God's gifts to Jacob's children included a land on which they did not toil and cities that they did not build. They now eat from vineyards and olive groves that they did not plant (Joshua 24:13). God has been faithful in His covenant promises to Abraham and his descendants, the Israelites—the chosen people of God. They have been blessed.

Joshua tells the people,

> "Now, therefore, fear the LORD and serve Him in sincerity and truth; cast aside the gods your fathers served beyond the Euphrates and in Egypt, and serve the LORD. But if it is unpleasing in your sight to serve the LORD, choose for yourselves this day whom you will serve, whether the gods your fathers served beyond the Euphrates, or the gods of the Amorites in whose land you are living. As for me and my house, we will serve the LORD!" (Joshua 24:14, 15)

What is the response of the Israelites?

> "Far be it from us to forsake the LORD to serve other gods! For the LORD our God brought us and our fathers out of the land of Egypt, out of the house of slavery, and performed these great signs before our eyes. He also protected us throughout our journey and among all the nations through which we traveled. And the LORD drove out before us all the nations, including the Amorites who lived in the land. We too will serve the LORD, because He is our God!" (Joshua 24:16–18)

Joshua knows the people all too well. He has been with them throughout the wilderness journey. He has seen their repeated failure to place trust in God and witnessed the numerous times when they had gone against God's commands. He tells the Israelites,

> "You are not able to serve the LORD, for He is a holy God; He is a jealous God; He will not forgive your rebellion or your sins. If you forsake the LORD and serve foreign gods, He will turn and bring disaster on you and consume you, even after He has been good to you." (Joshua 24:19, 20)

There is an emphatic response from the Israelites,

> "No!" replied the people. "We will serve the LORD!"

The text continues,

> Then Joshua told them, "You are witnesses against yourselves that you have chosen to serve the LORD."

> "We are witnesses!" they said.

"Now, therefore," he said, "get rid of the foreign gods among you and incline your hearts to the LORD, the God of Israel."

So the people said to Joshua, "We will serve the LORD our God and obey His voice."

On that day Joshua made a covenant for the people, and there at Shechem he established for them a statute and ordinance. Joshua recorded these things in the Book of the Law of God. Then he took a large stone and set it up there under the oak that was near the sanctuary of the LORD. And Joshua said to all the people, "You see this stone. It will be a witness against us, for it has heard all the words the LORD has spoken to us, and it will be a witness against you if you ever deny your God."

Then Joshua sent the people away, each to his own inheritance. (Joshua 24:22–28)

As the book of Joshua comes to a close, the bones of Joseph that had been brought from Egypt are buried in Shechem, the site of Jacob's well. And we also learn of Joshua's death at the age of 110.

God has delivered His people to the Promised Land.

But all is not well. God told Joshua,

> I have given you every place where the sole of your foot will tread, just as I promised to Moses. (Joshua 1:3)

But Joshua's conquest of the land was incomplete. There were areas still occupied and controlled by the Canaanites. Conflict would continue. And, despite the people's declaration that they would serve God and obey His voice, this will soon change. As the story continues, we see the repeated failure of the people. They turn from God. They do evil in God's sight. All of this shows us why God must eventually send a Savior.

This story of the conquest of the land is instructive.

- God delivered the land to the people—but the people had to enter the land and take possession of it. Yes, the land is promised to Abraham, Isaac, and Jacob—and Moses. But the people must take possession. Over and over again in the **biblical text**, there are the twin themes of God providing, but the people having to take possession of that which God is providing.
- God does not use His sovereign power to force His people to cooperate with His plans. Joshua proclaims to his fellow Israelites:

  > As for me and my house, we will serve the LORD! (Joshua 24:15)

  But this is Joshua's choice. It is his decision whether to follow God.
- Our journey with Christ is no different. God forces no one to accept His plan of salvation. And while God has provided redemption through the blood of Christ, we must take possession of this unmerited gift from God.

If we want to be saved from God's wrath—and if we want to receive God's blessings as participants in His kingdom, we must approach the cross with the empty, unworthy hands of faith and accept God's provision for salvation.

And God's provision is Jesus Christ.

From lesson 17: What do we learn about God?

- God remains faithful to His people and His promises.
- The victory in conquering the land comes from God—His sovereign will and His power—and not due to the people and their abilities (see Exodus 23:30, for example).
- God blesses the people when they uphold the covenant and obey His instructions—an example being their victory over Jericho. But His blessings are removed when they are disobedient, as seen in the initial defeat at Ai and the punishment given to Achan and his family.
- God expects obedience—but we can choose not to obey.
- God provides, but we must take possession of that which He is providing.

Rahab: Why devote an entire chapter to a prostitute living in Jericho? We've said a few times now, the Biblical Story is about Jesus. Rahab will have a son named Boaz. Boaz is the great grandfather of King David. Rahab, Boaz, and David are all in the family tree of Jesus.

walls to crumble: In ancient times, when an army attacked the fortified walls of a city, the walls would crumble inward, as one would expect. Archeologists have discovered the original walls of Jericho at the time of Joshua. Strangely, the walls fell outward, causing some skeptical of the biblical account to suggest the walls were destroyed by earthquake.

even today: People still struggle reconciling the "God of the Old Testament" with the "God of the New Testament"—even though they are one and the same. Throughout all of scripture, we see a God of grace and mercy, as well as a God of wrath and righteous judgment. As one example of the ongoing interest in this topic and dialogue, in 2019 Denver Seminary held a panel discussion titled: "The False Dichotomy of the Old Testament God and the New Testament God" (September 10, 2019).

biblical text: Specific to the land, over and over again we hear of God's promise. He will drive out the occupants of the land, but the people must take possession of the land. To cite just a few examples, see Exodus 23:30; Numbers 33:53; Deuteronomy 1:29; and Joshua 1:11.

The Period of the Judges

The book of Judges follows the book of Joshua, and God continues to bless His people.

> The LORD delivered the Canaanites and Perizzites into their hands. (Judges 1:4)

> The LORD was with Judah, and they took possession of the hill country. (Judges 1:19)

> And the LORD was with them. (Judges 1:22)

We are reminded of the conditional nature of the Mosaic Covenant and the reasons for God's blessings:

> The people served the LORD throughout the days of Joshua and of the elders who outlived him and who had seen all the great works that the LORD had done for Israel. (Judges 2:7)

But things change. Actually, that is not correct. The people change.

After that whole generation had also been gathered to their fathers, another generation rose up who did not know the LORD or the works that He had done for Israel. And <u>the Israelites did evil in the sight of the LORD</u> and served the Baals.

Thus, they forsook the LORD, the God of their fathers, who had brought them out of the land of Egypt, and they followed after various gods of the peoples around them. They bowed down to them and provoked the LORD to anger, for they forsook Him and served Baal and the Ashtoreths. (Judges 2:10–13, 15)

"The Israelites did evil in the sight of the LORD..." This is a repeated theme in the book of Judges. We will see this phrase **seven times** (Judges 2:10; 3:7; 3:12; 4:1; 6:1; 10:6; and 13:1).

A major source of evil is their worship of Baal. For those new to the Bible, Baal was the major god of the Canaanites. He is the "storm god" (and also the "sun god") who was thought to be responsible for bringing rain and replenishing the land. If angered, Baal could withhold the rain and cause famine. Ashtoreth (Judges 2:15, above) was a goddess and considered to be the consort of Baal. She represented nature or nature's fertility. The Israelites, in their idolatry, begin to worship both. There are numerous biblical references to the "high places" and the "Asherah poles" that signify worship sites.

Theologically, when a society blends together two or more religious belief systems, it is called "syncretism." When God gave Moses the Ten Commandments, the very first commandment addresses syncretism:

"You shall have no other gods before Me." (Deuteronomy 5:7, see also Exodus 20:3)

This comprises just **seven words** in the Hebrew. There is only one God, and nothing is to replace God. Period.

To this, God adds His second commandment—also targeting syncretism and idolatry:

> You shall not make for yourself an idol in the form of anything in the heavens above, on the earth beneath, or in the waters below. You shall not bow down to them or worship them; for I, the LORD your God, am a jealous God, visiting the iniquity of the fathers on their children to the third and fourth generations of those who hate Me, but showing loving devotion to a thousand generations of those who love Me and keep My commandments. (Deuteronomy 5:8–10)

We are reminded of some of Joshua's last recorded words:

> "Now, therefore," he said, "get rid of the foreign gods among you and incline your hearts to the LORD, the God of Israel." (Joshua 24:23)

We are also reminded of how the people respond:

> "We will serve the LORD our God and obey His voice" (Joshua 24:24)

But that generation has passed, and the Israelites no longer serve the LORD or obey His voice. Now we see phrases like,

> ... provoked the LORD to anger (Judges 2:12),

and,

> ... the hand of the LORD was against them (Judges 2:15),

and,

> ... the anger of the LORD burned against Israel (which appears three times: Judges 2:14, 2:20, and 3:1).

What follows in the book of Judges are stories of the plight of the people because of their sin. Judges appear—military leaders called by God to serve the people in times of crises (12 named judges are found in the book of Judges). We see a recurring cycle:

- The people of Israel serve the LORD.
- They then fall into sin and idolatry.
- God removes His blessings and the people are subdued by their enemies.
- Israel cries out to God for help.
- God raises up a judge—a deliverer—to rescue the people.
- Israel is delivered and there is a time of peace.

At the end of the cycle, Israel returns to serving the LORD, only to again fall into sin and idolatry, and the cycle is repeated.

And repeated. And repeated. This pattern dominates three hundred years of Israel's history. Throughout this period, the Israelites face the Edomites, Moabites, Canaanites, Midianites, and Ammonites— virtually all of the "-ites" except for the Mosquitobites (as one of my pastor friends says). Their conquerors also include the Philistines, which brings us to the last judge mentioned in this book, Samson (and the story of Samson and Delilah, Judges 13–16).

The book of Judges ends with three tragedies. Each is introduced with the phrase:

> In those days there was no king in Israel; everyone did what was right in his own eyes. (Joshua 17:6, 18:1, 19:1)

The introduction of this theme is significant. The book of Judges closes with this verse as well (21:25). The problem with Israel, according to the **author of Judges** and what the book suggests, is not the people's betrayal of the covenant. It is not their indifference to God and the introduction of syncretism and their worship of other gods (idolatry).

No. The problem is that they have no king. A king will solve all of their problems, or so they thought.

The Biblical Story continues with Israel's establishment of a monarchy—their "solution" to the problem. But before we get to this, the Bible contains the small book called "Ruth"—the subject of our next lesson.

From lesson 18: What do we learn about God?

- Despite repeated cycles of disobedience—including the sin of idolatry and the worshipping of other gods, God delivers the people by raising up a series of judges.
- There is a consistent theme in the Biblical Story of God providing salvation to His chosen people—despite their on-going rebellion, unfaithfulness, and unworthiness.

seven times: We see "did evil in the eyes of the LORD" spread throughout the book of Judges. But this is the tip of the iceberg. If you are reading the Bible alongside this study, when you get to 1st and 2nd Kings, see if you can count how many times "evil in the eyes of the LORD" is mentioned. God's chosen people go from bad—to worse—to disaster.

seven words: The phrase "did evil in the eyes of the LORD" is mentioned seven times in the book of Judges. The number seven is an important number in scripture. We mentioned how the opening words of the Bible, "In the beginning God created the heavens and the earth" are seven words in the Hebrew. Here we see that the very first commandment is seven words in the Hebrew.

We have also mentioned the "seven I AM's" in John's Gospel. He also provides the reader with seven signs performed by Jesus.

By the time we get to the last book of the Bible, Revelation, the sevens are too numerous to count. And sometimes one has to look closely to see some of the sevens that are hidden in the text. For example, look at Revelation 5:12,

> Worthy is the Lamb who was slain,
> > to receive power and riches
> and wisdom and strength
> > and honor and glory and blessing!

Jesus is worthy of power (1), riches (2), wisdom (3), strength (4), honor (5), glory (6) and blessing (7).

What's even more amazing is when examples of "seven" cross over between several authors. The Gospels record Jesus as saying seven statements from the cross (we will cover these in volume 2). But no single Gospel contains all seven. You can only get to the number "seven" if you look at each of the discrete sayings from each Gospel writer and add them together. It's hard to imagine the writers planning and colluding such that the statements add up to seven. They add up to seven because God planned it this way.

author of Judges: The author of Judges is believed to have been Samuel, whom we'll learn about shortly.

19

Ruth

We now come to a small book in the Bible sandwiched between Judges and 1ˢᵗ and 2ⁿᵈ Samuel. It is located here in that the events being described occur at the time of the Judges. It's the story about a woman named Ruth.

If we look ahead to the first book of the New Testament, Matthew's Gospel, we see it begins with a genealogy from Abraham to Jesus. Excluding Mary, the mother of Jesus, the list includes four women—highly unusual for genealogies of that era and for genealogies contained in the Bible.

The first woman cited is Tamar—the daughter-in-law of Judah mentioned in Genesis 38 (lesson 13). The second is the prostitute Rahab, introduced in Joshua 2 (lesson 14). Both Tamar and Rahab are not descendants of Abraham, Isaac, and Jacob—they are Canaanites.

The third woman listed in Matthew's genealogy is Ruth. She is also a non-Israelite. Yet she, too, is in the family tree of Jesus.

What do we learn about Ruth? Why does the Bible contain a book devoted to her story? How does all of this connect to Jesus?

Let's find the answers.

As the book of Ruth begins, we learn of a famine in the land of the Israelites and are introduced to an Israelite family: Naomi and her husband and two sons. They are living in Bethlehem but must seek refuge in distant Moab to escape the famine.

In Moab, the two sons marry Moabite women—one marrying a Moabitess name Ruth. By the time ten years have passed, Naomi's husband and the two sons have died. This leaves Naomi and the two daughters-in-law destitute.

Naomi decides to return to her home in Bethlehem. She encourages the two daughters-in-law to make new lives for themselves and remain in Moab with their own people.

Ruth, though, insists on staying with Naomi. She tells Naomi:

> "Do not urge me to leave you
>   or to turn from following you.
> For wherever you go, I will go,
>   and wherever you live, I will live;
> your people will be my people,
>   and your God will be my God.
> Where you die, I will die,
>   and there I will be buried.
> May the LORD punish me,
>   and ever so severely,
> if anything but death
>   separates you and me." (Ruth 1:16, 17)

Could there be a more poignant passage in scripture that displays a person's total devotion and commitment? Ruth joins Naomi in the journey to the land of Naomi's people—the land of the Israelites.

When they reach Bethlehem, Naomi tells the townspeople she is no longer to be called Naomi, a Hebrew word meaning "pleasant."

> "Call me Mara, because the Almighty has dealt quite bitterly with me. I went away full, but the LORD has brought me back empty. Why call me Naomi? After all, the LORD has testified against me, and the Almighty has afflicted me." (Ruth 1:20, 21)

"Mara" means "bitter." Naomi has lost her husband. She has lost her two sons. She and Ruth are destitute. And Naomi is bitter. From her perspective, God is the source of her afflictions.

We need to think about Naomi's plight and her bitterness. The two most vulnerable people groups in ancient times were the widows and the fatherless (orphans). There was no social security—no safety net—to care for these people. Unless support came from the kindness of friends and relatives, or the generosity of the community, the widows and orphans did not survive. And of course, we are called today to make sure widows and orphans and the most vulnerable in our society are cared for. In the New Testament, James tells us:

> Pure and undefiled religion before our God and Father is this: to care for orphans and widows in their distress. (James 1:27)

The prophet Isaiah tells the Israelites:

> Learn to do right, seek justice,
>   correct the oppressor,
> defend the fatherless,
>   plead for the widow. (Isaiah 1:17)

Caring for the fatherless and widows were not just suggestions. This was part of God's law given to the people:

You must not mistreat any widow or orphan. If you
do mistreat them, and they cry out to Me in distress,
I will surely hear their cry. My anger will be kindled,
and I will kill you with the sword; then your wives will
become widows and your children will be fatherless.
(Exodus 22:22–24)

Naomi and Ruth were widows. And struggling to survive in the land
without a husband left the two of them impoverished and vulnerable.

Secondly, note what Naomi says,

... the Almighty has dealt quite bitterly with me.
... the LORD has brought me back empty.
... the LORD has testified against me,
... the Almighty has afflicted me. (from Ruth 1:20, 21)

Part of Naomi's bitterness centered on a misconception concerning
God—one that many people today seem to have. Specific to the
Israelites, the Mosaic Covenant promised blessings to God's covenant
people for their faithfulness, and curses should they disobey. But this
did not imply that every single Israelite would be blessed, or every
single Israelite would be cursed. The covenant was with the covenant
community—the people at large. But the mindset became one where
any affliction was blamed on God. If bad things were happening, the
person must have done something to anger God.

This mindset carries into the New Testament. As one example, John
shares the story of a man blind since birth who is given sight by
Jesus (Jesus uses this to teach the Pharisees about their spiritual
blindness). But note how the story begins:

Now as Jesus was passing by, He saw a man blind
from birth, and His disciples asked Him, "Rabbi, who

sinned, this man or his parents, that he was born blind?" (John 9:1, 2)

Here is a man who is blind, but he was born that way. Is his affliction from God due to the sins of his parents? Or is this due to his own sin—even though he is born with this affliction and it is hard to see how he could have sinned prior to the blindness?

It is actually a profound question, but it is asked in a profoundly wrong way. Note that the question assumes affliction is from God. And this is the assumption Naomi makes.

This brings up an issue near to the heart of every human who experiences suffering: Why do bad things happen to good people? The biblical book of Job centers on answering this—and we'll address this issue when we get to portions of the New Testament in volume 2 as well as two separate publications to follow: *A Forty-Day Study on the Book of John: Who is Christ?* and *A Forty-Day Study of the Book of Romans: What is a Christian.* We'll provide at least ten biblically based reasons why God causes suffering or permits suffering.

But for now, let's continue our review of the book of Ruth. There are two important concepts to introduce. In the Pentateuch, where God provides instructions to the Israelites, He makes provisions so that people like Naomi and Ruth can survive. One provision is referred to as the Law of Gleaning, found in Leviticus 19:9–10 and Deuteronomy 24:19–22,

> If you are harvesting in your field and forget a sheaf
> there, do not go back to get it. It is to be left for the
> foreigner, the fatherless, and the widow, so that the
> LORD your God may bless you in all the work of
> your hands.

When you beat the olives from your trees, you must not go over the branches again. What remains will be for the foreigner, the fatherless, and the widow.

When you gather the grapes of your vineyard, you must not go over the vines again. What remains will be for the foreigner, the fatherless, and the widow. Remember that you were slaves in the land of Egypt. Therefore, I am commanding you to do this. (Deuteronomy 24:19–22)

At harvesttime, Israelites can only pass through their crops once. What is missed and remains among the fields and vineyards can be gleaned by those in need. Naomi and Ruth return to Bethlehem at the beginning of the harvest (Ruth 1:22) and Ruth is sent into the fields to glean heads of grain (Ruth 2:3).

It is here in the story that we are introduced to Boaz, a blood relative of Naomi's deceased husband. Boaz owns a portion of the land being harvested. He meets Ruth and shows kindness to her. Ruth asks why she receives such favored treatment, and Boaz tells her:

> "I have been made fully aware of all you have done for your mother-in-law since the death of your husband, how you left your father and mother and the land of your birth, and how you came to a people you did not know before. May the LORD repay your work, and may you receive a rich reward from the LORD, the God of Israel, under whose wings you have taken refuge." (Ruth 2:11, 12)

We now need to introduce the second important concept. It is known as the Law of Redemption and is also a part of God's instructions to His people:

> If a foreigner residing among you prospers, but your countryman dwelling near him becomes destitute and sells himself to the foreigner or to a member of his clan, he retains the right of redemption after he has sold himself. One of his brothers may redeem him: either his uncle or cousin or any close relative from his clan may redeem him. Or if he prospers, he may redeem himself. (Leviticus 25:47–49)

This is the concept of a *"goel"*—derived from a Hebrew term which comes from the word we translate "to redeem" or "to deliver." The goel is also referred to as "kinsman-redeemer," as seen throughout the book of Ruth in the Berean Study Bible translation (for example, Ruth 2:20 and 3:9). Other translations call this a guardian-redeemer (NIV) or simply refer to "close relative" or "kin"—but omit a key part of this designation, that of "redeemer."

In the context of Judaism and the Hebrew Scriptures, the kinsman-redeemer is a male relative having the privilege, or charged with the responsibility, of restoring the rights of a relative or avenging his or her wrongs. The kinsman-redeemer could voluntarily come to the aid of a relative in trouble or danger, or in need of vindication.

Boaz assumes the role of Naomi's kinsman-redeemer. He absolves Naomi's debt, restoring her husband's land to her. Separate from this, Boaz takes Ruth as his wife.

So why do we have the book of Ruth in the Bible?

The inclusion of this story in the Hebrew Scriptures makes sense in that it ends with an important genealogy:

> Boaz was the father of Obed,
> Obed was the father of Jesse,
> and Jesse was the father of David. (Ruth 4:21, 22)

Boaz is the great grandfather of King David, and Ruth is David's great grandmother. Both are in the lineage of Jesus—hence their inclusion in Matthew's genealogy (Matthew 1:5, 6).

Another item of significance is Naomi's connection with Bethlehem and the land of her deceased husband. This links David to Bethlehem and ultimately Bethlehem becomes the birthplace of Jesus.

But perhaps the most significant connection to the Biblical Story, and to Jesus, is this concept of kinsman-redeemer. As we've said, a goel—a kinsman-redeemer—is a deliverer, and here we see parallels.

Let's look at the requirements for the person accepting the obligation of being a kinsman-redeemer:

- They have to be a relative (a kinsman). A stranger could not perform this role.
- They have to be able to meet the obligation incurred by the relative. For example, in the case of Naomi, Boaz had to have the means to acquire her deceased husband's property.
- Lastly, the kinsman-redeemer has to be willing to meet the obligation. His actions are voluntary, and he is under no obligation to assume the role of a kinsman-redeemer.

With this as background, we can now connect the book of Ruth as a foreshadowing of Jesus—and there is a lot here.

Jesus is our kinsman-redeemer. He provides redemption and restoration. He removes from us the debts of our sin.

But one requirement of a kinsmen-redeemer is that he has to be a blood relative. Does Jesus meet this condition? Jesus is both fully God and became fully man. In describing the humanity of Jesus, the author of Hebrews writes:

For this reason, He had to be made like His brothers in every way, so that He might become a merciful and faithful high priest in service to God, in order to make atonement for the sins of the people. (Hebrews 2:17)

By becoming fully human ("made like His brothers in every way"), Jesus creates a blood relationship between himself and all of humanity.

The kinsman-redeemer has to be able to meet the obligations incurred by the one in need. Was Jesus able to pay off the debt associated with our sin? According to the Levitical priestly functions and practices called out in the Old Testament, this required the shedding of blood:

For the life of the flesh is in the blood, and I have given it to you to make atonement for your souls upon the altar; for it is the blood that makes atonement for the soul. (Leviticus 17:11)

The author of Hebrews tells us,

Without the shedding of blood there is no forgiveness. (Hebrews 9:22)

Jesus, and Jesus alone, lived without sin and kept God's law perfectly. He was the only one ever qualified to offer redemption through the shedding of innocent human blood. He is the unblemished Lamb of God, able to take away the sins of the world.

Lastly, the kinsman-redeemer was not forced to take on this role. Was Jesus' sacrifice on the cross done voluntarily? Referring to his life, Jesus says,

"No one takes it from Me, but I lay it down of My own accord. I have authority to lay it down and authority to take it up again." (John 10:18)

Jesus accepted crucifixion and became our Redeemer voluntarily. He was not forced to do this. He was motivated by love. And there is no greater love than that of giving one's life for friends (John 15:13).

There are more ways we can connect the story of Ruth with Jesus. In the book of Ruth, Boaz, the kinsman-redeemer, is a type of Christ. The name "Boaz" means "ability." Boaz has the ability to be Naomi's kinsman-redeemer. He can meet the demands of her debt. Jesus, as our kinsman-redeemer, has the ability to redeem fallen humanity.

Naomi can be viewed as representing Israel—destitute and without hope. She becomes "Mara"—bitter. But she is ultimately redeemed and restored, just as Israel is destined for redemption, restoration, and eventual glorification through the return and millennial rule of Christ.

Ruth can be viewed as representing the Church. She is a Gentile but shows faithfulness to Israel's God and does not abandon Naomi (Israel). She, too, is rescued and delivered from need. In the story of Ruth, the kinsman-redeemer takes this Gentile as his bride. For our kinsman-redeemer, the Church is the **Bride of Christ**. And, though the Church is separate from Israel, the Church will remain faithful to Israel.

Before we leave the book of Ruth, there is perhaps one other connection to Jesus that we should notice. It is customary for the Jewish people to read this portion of their scripture during "Shavuot"—the feast of Weeks. This is one of seven Jewish festivals—this one associated with the grain harvest. It also commemorates when the Law was given to the Israelites. Why read Ruth during Shavuot?

Rabbi Rifat Sonsino **writes,**

> Ruth's acceptance of Judaism corresponds nicely
> with the Giving of the Torah in the desert to all of

humanity; and Ruth's loyalty symbolizes the fidelity to the Torah that is expected of all Jews.

That's the perspective from a non-Messianic Jew, that is, one who does not accept Jesus as the Messiah.

The Christian/Messianic Jewish perspective is different.

Shavuot is Pentecost. This is when the Church began. Our kinsman-redeemer voluntarily paid the price to purchase our redemption—this was the cross. And it was at Pentecost that the Holy Spirit began indwelling God's chosen people—the bride of Christ. The Holy Spirit continues to do his work, continuing God's great harvest to bring souls into His kingdom.

From lesson 19: What do we learn about God?

- A review of two of God's provisions, the Law of Gleaning and the Law of Redemption, shows God's desire to provide for those in need.
- Jesus is our kinsman-redeemer, redeeming us and delivering us from the penalty of sin.

Bride of Christ: Relevant passages include Ephesians 5:24–27; 2nd Corinthians 11:2; Revelation 19:7–9; and Revelation 21:1, 2.

writes: See "Why Ruth on Shavuot?" available at myjewishlearning.com.

20

The Kingdom

The last *verse* in the book of Judges reads:

> In those days there was no king in Israel; everyone
> did what was right in his own eyes. (Judges 21:25)

Judges is followed by the book of Ruth. The last *word* in the book of Ruth reads:

> ... David. (Ruth 4:22)

The book of Judges ends with a plea for a king. Ruth ends with a genealogy leading to David, Israel's greatest king. We are now ready to learn of the establishment of kings in the Promised Land.

It is not a pretty story.

Moses anticipated an eventual monarchy. He warns the Israelites:

> When you enter the land that the LORD your God is
> giving you and have taken possession of it and settled
> in it, and you say, "Let us set a king over us like all the
> nations around us," you are to appoint over yourselves

the king whom the LORD your God shall choose. Appoint a king from among your brothers; you are not to set over yourselves a foreigner who is not one of your brothers.

But the king must not acquire many horses for himself or send the people back to Egypt to acquire more horses, for the LORD has said, 'You are never to go back that way again.' He must not take many wives for himself, lest his heart go astray. He must not accumulate for himself great amounts of silver and gold.

When he is seated on his royal throne, he must write for himself a copy of this instruction on a scroll in the presence of the Levitical priests. It is to remain with him, and he is to read from it all the days of his life, so that he may learn to fear the LORD his God by carefully observing all the words of this instruction and these statutes. Then his heart will not be exalted above his countrymen, and he will not turn aside from the commandment, to the right or to the left, in order that he and his sons may reign many years over his kingdom in Israel. (Deuteronomy 17:14–20)

We learn about Israel's kings in 1st and 2nd Samuel and 1st and 2nd Kings, which follow Judges and the book of Ruth. In the Hebrew Scriptures, Samuel and Kings are each one long "book"—separated due to the length of ancient scrolls. Collectively, they describe all of the kings that ruled over the land (1st and 2nd Chronicles is a separate writing, written much later in Israel's history, but containing much of the same material).

1st Samuel begins with a transition between the period of the judges and the selection of a man named Saul as Israel's first king. The leader during this transition is **Samuel**, Israel's last great judge. As we saw in lesson 18, Israel continually experiences repeated cycles of falling away from God, most often by committing the sin of idolatry, followed by God raising up judges (military leaders) who deliver and restore His people. Each failure on the people's part is met with a display of God's grace and mercy.

At the time of Samuel, the Philistines are Israel's main adversary, and Samuel is raised up to confront them. He tells the Israelites,

> "If you are returning to the LORD with all your hearts, then rid yourselves of the foreign gods and Ashtoreths among you, prepare your hearts for the LORD, and serve Him only. And He will deliver you from the hand of the Philistines." (1st Samuel 7:3)

The Israelites respond favorably to Samuel's admonition:

> So the Israelites put away the Baals and Ashtoreths and served only the LORD. (1st Samuel 7:3, 4)

God, in turn, delivers the Israelites:

> So the Philistines were subdued, and they stopped invading the territory of Israel. And the hand of the LORD was against the Philistines all the days of Samuel. The cities from Ekron to Gath, which the Philistines had taken, were restored to Israel, who also delivered the surrounding territory from the hand of the Philistines. And there was peace between the Israelites and the Amorites. (1st Samuel 7:13, 14)

But all is not well. Toward the end of Samuel's life, he appoints his two sons as judges. The Bible tells us the sons turn toward *"dishonest gain,"* and that they accepted bribes and perverted justice

(1st Samuel 8:3). The two corrupt sons are rejected by the Israelites, who approach Samuel and present their own solution:

> So all the elders of Israel gathered together and came to Samuel at Ramah. "Look," they said, "you are old, and your sons do not walk in your ways. <u>Now appoint a king to judge us like all the other nations.</u>" (1st Samuel 8:4, 5)

Samuel prays to God concerning the wishes of the people, and God responds. But note His response:

> "Listen to the voice of the people in all that they say to you. For it is not you they have rejected, but <u>they have rejected Me as their king.</u> Just as they have done from the day I brought them up out of Egypt until this day, forsaking Me and serving other gods, so they are doing to you. Now listen to them, but you must solemnly warn them and show them the manner of the king who will reign over them." (1st Samuel 8:7–9)

God gives the people what they want—not what God wants for the people. They will get their king. This may be where the adage, "Be careful what you wish for" came from.

We should pause and remind ourselves something about God. God is all-powerful. He can make things happen according to His will. When events occur because they are what God wants, this is a display of God's *sovereign will*.

But God can also *permit* things to happen. This is His *permissive will*. We experience or see God's permissive will quite often as He allows us to have things our way—sometimes to our detriment. From Oscar **Wilde's** perspective, "When the gods wish to punish us, they answer our prayers."

The people will get their king, and Samuel warns them:

> "This will be the manner of the king who will reign over you: <u>He will take</u> your sons and appoint them to his own chariots and horses, to run in front of his chariots.
>
> He will appoint some for himself as commanders of thousands and of fifties, and others to plow his ground, to reap his harvest, to make his weapons of war, and to equip his chariots.
>
> And <u>he will take</u> your daughters to be perfumers, cooks, and bakers.
>
> <u>He will take</u> the best of your fields and vineyards and olive groves and give them to his servants. <u>He will take</u> a tenth of your grain and grape harvest and give it to his officials and servants. And <u>he will take</u> your menservants and maidservants and your best cattle and donkeys and put them to his own use.
>
> <u>He will take</u> a tenth of your flocks, and you yourselves will become his slaves. When that day comes, <u>you will beg for relief from the king</u> you have chosen, but the LORD will not answer you on that day." (1st Samuel 8:11–18)

The phrase "he will take" applying to a king is repeated six times (strangely enough, not seven—but if you add "he will appoint for himself," that makes seven). Nothing has changed over these past three thousand years! Actually, that is not true. Rulers over us don't take a tenth of our flocks—they take much more than that. And we certainly get fleeced. Oh, if they only took just ten percent. But I digress.

Saul is chosen as Israel's first king, and while his reign begins in a positive light, it ends in disaster. Samuel tells Saul:

> "You have acted foolishly . . . you have not kept the command the LORD your God gave you; if you had, the LORD would have established your kingdom over Israel for all time. But now your kingdom will not endure; the LORD has sought a man after His own heart and appointed him ruler over His people, because you have not kept the command of the LORD." (1st Samuel 13:13, 14)

God installs David on the throne, a man from the house of Judah, and a man after **God's own heart**.

For those familiar with the story of King David, it might be a bit of a struggle to relate David to the heart of God. David commits adultery with Bathsheba. He orchestrates the death of Bathsheba's husband, Uriah—an elite Hittite soldier in David's army protecting David and his throne. He raises a dysfunctional family. A daughter gets raped by her half-brother. This son is killed by another of David's sons, who ultimately is bent on killing his father, David. David was a mess. His family was a mess.

But David did have godly traits. Ron Edmonson, writing for BibleStudyTools.com, reviews some of the Psalms attributed to David and finds these characteristics of David: humility, reference, respect, trusting, loving, devoted, recognition of God, faithfulness, obedient, and repentant.

And God brings David to the throne.

Why David?

As we saw with Abraham and Moses, God chooses David simply because He wants to—an example of God's sovereign will. God initiates a set of circumstances that brings David to the forefront of the attention of King Saul and Israel. And, like God did with Abraham and with Moses, God also establishes a covenant with David:

> The LORD declares to you that He Himself will establish a <u>house</u> for you. And when your days are fulfilled and you rest with your fathers, I will raise up your offspring after you, who will come from your own body, and I will establish his <u>kingdom</u>. He will build a house for My Name, and I will establish the <u>throne</u> of his kingdom <u>forever</u>. I will be his Father, and he will be My son. When he does wrong, I will discipline him with the rod of men and with the blows of the sons of men.
>
> But My loving devotion will never be removed from him as I removed it from Saul, whom I moved out of your way. Your house and kingdom will endure forever before Me, and your throne will be established forever. (2nd Samuel 7:11–16)

Like God's covenant with Abraham, the Davidic Covenant is unconditional. God does not place any conditions on David or his heirs for its fulfillment. The covenant rests solely on God's faithfulness.

What does this covenant include? It focuses on the Son of God. It points to the Messiah.

Note the words in the covenant that are underlined above: "house," "kingdom," "throne," and "forever."

The word "house" signifies the Messiah will come through Israel. He will be a descendant of David.

The word "kingdom" implies the Messiah comes to reign.

And the word "throne" implies the Messiah will have authority.

This kingdom and rule are to be established "forever"—emphasizing the eternal nature of God's plan and promise.

There's more we could say about David, but we're going to follow in the footsteps of the Apostle Paul. During Paul's first missionary journey, he provides his audience with a brief sermon and mentions David. Most, if not all of his audience were Jews and would be able to relate to Paul's words:

> After removing Saul, He raised up David as their king and testified about him: 'I have found David son of Jesse a man after My own heart; he will carry out My will in its entirety.' (Acts 13:22)

But for Paul, the importance of God's act in history is not David. This is all he says about David, Israel's greatest king. Paul focuses the rest of his sermon on Christ. He begins,

> From the descendants of this man, God has brought to Israel <u>the Savior Jesus, as He promised.</u> (Acts 13:23)

And this is our focus. The Biblical Story is all about Jesus. If we add the Davidic Covenant to our list of God's revelations concerning Jesus, here is what we have so far:

- God will send a Redeemer who will be born of woman and who will ultimately defeat Satan and sin. But the Redeemer will face suffering and death (Genesis 3:15).
- Psalm 2 introduces us to the titles of this Redeemer: Messiah (verse 2), Son of God (verse 7), and King (verse 6).
- The Messiah will be a descendant of Abraham (Genesis 12:2).

- He will be a descendant through Isaac and not Ishmael (Genesis 26:2–4).
- He will be a descendant through Jacob and not Esau (Genesis 28:14, 15).
- He will come from the tribe of Judah (Genesis 49:10).
- He will be a prophet greater than Moses—we are to listen to him (Deuteronomy 18:15).
- Like Boaz in the story of Ruth, he will be a kinsman-redeemer.
- He will ultimately reign on David's throne. He will be the Son of God and his rule will be eternal (2nd Samuel 7:11–16).

The Biblical Story is all about Jesus.

From lesson 20: What do we learn about God?

- God has a sovereign will and also a permissive will. He allows the people of Israel to reject Him and to go their own way in establishing their first king (God's permissive will).
- But God will also intervene and do what is ultimately best for the people (God's sovereign will).
- God establishes a covenant with King David.
  - It will be from the line of David that the Messiah will come.
  - The Messiah will reign with authority—and his rule will be unending.
  - The Messiah will be the Son of God.

Samuel: Samuel is considered a priest, prophet, and judge (1st Samuel 3:20; 7:15).

God's own heart: For additional information, see "How could David be considered a man after God's own heart?" on the GotQuestions. org website, available at https://www.gotquestions.org/man-after-God-heart.html (accessed October 17, 2019).

Ron Edmonson's comments mentioned above can be found at "10 Reasons David is Called 'A Man After God's Own Heart'" available at biblestudytools.com (https://www.biblestudytools.com/blogs/ron-edmondson/10-reasons-david-is-called-a-man-after-god-s-own-heart.html) accessed October 17, 2019.

Wilde: From the second act of his play, "The Accidental Husband."

21

The Kingdom Divided

The height of Israel's glory occurs under the kingships of David and David's son, Solomon. Israel is **united**, its borders are expanded, her enemies are defeated, and the temple to God is built. You will recall that Moses had warned the people about a king (our previous lesson). God also gives instructions concerning what a king should and should not do:

> The king must not acquire many horses for himself. (Deuteronomy 17:16)

> He must not take many wives for himself, lest his heart go astray. (Deuteronomy 17:17)

> He must not accumulate for himself great amounts of silver and gold. (Deuteronomy 17:17)

Most importantly, the king is to obey God and follow God's instructions:

> He will not turn aside from the commandment, to the right or to the left. (Deuteronomy 17:14–20)

Samuel also warned the people about what happens under the rule of a king:

> "He will take the best of your fields and vineyards and olive groves and give them to his servants. He will take a tenth of your grain and grape harvest and give it to his officials and servants. And he will take your menservants and maidservants and your best cattle and donkeys and put them to his own use.
>
> He will take a tenth of your flocks, and you yourselves will become his slaves. When that day comes, you will beg for relief from the king you have chosen, but the LORD will not answer you on that day." (1st Samuel 8:11–18)

The statements from Moses and Samuel were prophetic. David's son, Solomon, spends seven years building the temple to God (1st Kings 6:38), but thirteen years building his own palace (1st Kings 7:1).

But there is more . . . unfortunately:

> The weight of gold that came to Solomon each year was **666 talents**, not including the revenue from the merchants and traders. And all the Arabian kings and governors of the land also brought gold and silver to Solomon. (2nd Chronicles 9:13, 14)
>
> Additionally, the king made a great throne of ivory and overlaid it with pure gold ... nothing like this had ever been made for any kingdom. (2nd Chronicles 9:17, 19b)
>
> All King Solomon's drinking cups were gold ... King Solomon surpassed all the kings of the earth in riches. (2nd Chronicles 9:20, 22)

Solomon had 4,000 stalls for horses and chariots, and 12,000 horses, which he stationed in the chariot cities and also with him in Jerusalem. (2nd Chronicles 9:25)

King Solomon conscripted a labor force of thirty thousand men from all Israel. (1st Kings 5:13)

King Solomon...loved many foreign women along with the daughter of Pharaoh—women of Moab, Ammon, Edom, and Sidon, as well as Hittite women. These women were from the nations about which the LORD had told the Israelites, "You must not intermarry with them, for surely they will turn your hearts after their gods." Yet Solomon clung to these women in love. He had seven hundred wives of royal birth and three hundred concubines—and his wives turned his heart away. (1st Kings 11:1–3)

The king was supposed to follow God's instructions, not turning "to the right or to the left." Sadly, though,

When Solomon grew old, his wives turned his heart after other gods, and he was not wholeheartedly devoted to the LORD his God, as his father David had been. Solomon followed Ashtoreth the goddess of the Sidonians and Molech the abomination of the Ammonites. So Solomon <u>did evil in the sight of the LORD</u>—and unlike his father David, he did not follow the LORD completely. (1st Kings 11:4–6)

It is fitting that the refrain heard seven times in the book of Judges is repeated here. In Judges, the text reads, "The Israelites did evil in the sight of the LORD" (see lesson 18). Now, it is the king of Israel that does evil in the sight of God.

A righteous God cannot and will not let sin go **unpunished**. God's covenant with Moses was conditional. If God's chosen people remain faithful to the covenant, they would be blessed. But Solomon had abandoned the Mosaic Covenant.

We read in the biblical text,

> Now the LORD grew angry with Solomon, because his heart had turned away from the LORD, the God of Israel, who had appeared to him twice. Although He had warned Solomon explicitly not to follow other gods, Solomon did not keep the LORD's command.
>
> Then the LORD said to Solomon, "Because you have done this and have not kept My covenant and My statutes, which I have commanded you, I will tear the kingdom away from you and give it to your servant. Nevertheless, for the sake of your father David, I will not do it during your lifetime; I will tear it out of the hand of your son. Yet I will not tear the whole kingdom away from him. I will give one tribe to your son for the sake of My servant David and for the sake of Jerusalem, which I have chosen." (1st Kings 11:9–13)

Solomon was the type of king that Moses and Samuel warn about. Following Solomon's reign, Israel will be punished—and will not return to its days of glory. This will remain true for centuries—but not forever. Israel will be diminished until the Messiah returns and establishes his millennial rule.

It is here in the Biblical Story, that we read of problem after problem, disappointment after disappointment. The world of the Israelites falls apart. Eventually, all that they have built up is torn down. The people will suffer through famine and plague and will die by the swords of their adversaries. It is not a pleasant picture. Throughout all of this there are glimmers of hope—but the ultimate hope awaits the arrival of the Messiah.

Upon Solomon's death, Rehoboam, one of his sons, becomes king. And the people look for change:

> The whole assembly of Israel came to Rehoboam and said, "Your father put a heavy yoke on us. But now you should lighten the burden of your father's service and the heavy yoke he put on us, and we will serve you." (1ˢᵗ Kings 12:3, 4)

Rehoboam seeks the advice of the elders, who are men of wisdom. Their counsel is prudent,

> "If you will be a servant to these people and serve them this day, and if you will respond by speaking kind words to them, they will be your servants forever." (1ˢᵗ Kings 12:7)

Does Rehoboam accept the guidance of these statesmen?

> Rehoboam rejected the advice of the elders; instead, he consulted the young men who had grown up with him and served him. He asked them, "What message do you advise that we send back to these people who have spoken to me, saying, 'Lighten the yoke your father put on us'?"

> The young men who had grown up with him replied, "This is how you should answer these people who said to you, 'Your father made our yoke heavy, but you should make it lighter.' This is what you should tell them: 'My little finger is thicker than my father's waist! Whereas my father burdened you with a heavy

yoke, I will add to your yoke. Whereas my father scourged you with whips, I will scourge you with scorpions'." (1st Kings 12:8–11)

In one of the Bible's few understatements, we read,

The king did not listen to the people. (1st Kings 12:15)

Rehoboam listens to the younger men. He tells the people he will increase the burdens placed upon them—scourging them with scorpions.

The people revolt against this harsh rule and Israel is split into two, ushering in the period of the divided kingdom. Ten tribes occupy the Northern Kingdom, which is called "Israel." The tribes of Benjamin and Judah remain as the Southern Kingdom, which is called "Judah."

The division of the nation prevents those residing in the Northern Kingdom from having access to the temple in Jerusalem. Jeroboam, the Northern Kingdom's first king (Israel's first king), provides the solution. He simply steers the people into violating the first two of the Ten Commandments:

After seeking advice, the king made two golden calves and said to the people, "Going to Jerusalem is too much for you. Here, O Israel, are your gods, who brought you up out of the land of Egypt." (1st Kings 12:28)

The people have come full circle. The exodus generation had experienced the power of God and His continuing providence. But they fabricate a golden calf at the foot of Mt. Sinai for their worship. Now, hundreds of years later, the people once again turn their backs on God. Once again, a golden calf becomes an object of worship.

We need to put this in perspective. God had been faithful to Abraham, Isaac, and Jacob. He had delivered the people from Egyptian slavery. He had protected the Israelites and provided for them throughout their forty years in the wilderness. He had brought them into the Promised Land and had defeated their enemies. Time after time he had raised up judges to return peace to the people. He had allowed the people to have their king.

Marcion had it all wrong. We continually see a God showing abundant love to His people—a God that repeatedly forgives them, showing both grace and mercy. And time after time, the people walk away and rebel. The first chance they get they are falling down in worship to Baal or constructing Asherah poles and even golden calves as objects of their worship.

It is here that we might ask, "Will God's people ever learn?"

The answer is "no."

All of this is evidence of the brokenness after the fall. No one is righteous. No one seeks God. As the Biblical Story continues, we will be shown the continual and complete failure of God's people.

We see Jeroboam rebelling against God. God tells Jeroboam,

> "You have flung Me behind your back." (1st Kings 14:9)

And then God continues:

> "I am bringing disaster on the house of Jeroboam." (1st Kings 14:10)

The nation of Israel will be destroyed. Judah will crumble.

From lesson 21: What do we learn about God?

- A righteous God cannot and will not let sin go unpunished.

---

united: After Saul's death, the kingdom became temporarily divided, with Saul's son Ishbosheth ruling eleven of the tribes for two years, while David ruled Judah. After Ishbosheth was assassinated, David became king over all twelve tribes.

666 talents: This is about 23 metric tons of gold. Many might think this is simply an exaggeration written into the biblical text. However, archeologists have discovered evidences of large amounts of gold given to ancient kings of this region. They have uncovered, for example, ruins of the non-biblical city of Ebla that included a great royal palace. The ruins date back to the time of the patriarchs—Abraham, Isaac, and Jacob. Among the ruins, were over fifteen thousand tablets and fragments containing writings. One writing describes 880 pounds of gold given to the king on a single occasion. This is a far cry from 23 metric tons associated with Solomon—but what Solomon received was submitted from all of his empire over the period of a year. Paying large sums of gold and silver to a ruler was not unheard of.

unpunished: Sin must be punished, but the Christian *cannot* be punished. Our sins were imputed to Christ. Peter writes,

> He Himself bore our sins in His body on the tree. (1st Peter 2:24)

Christ took the punishment we deserve through his suffering and death on the cross. John tells us:

The blood of Jesus His Son cleanses us from all sin. (1ˢᵗ John 1:7)

He Himself is the atoning sacrifice for our sins. (1ˢᵗ John 2:2)

Because of the cross and the shedding of the blood of Christ, those who put their faith in God's salvation have peace with God. Paul writes,

Since we have been justified through faith, we have peace with God through our Lord Jesus Christ. (Romans 5:1)

There is no condemnation for the Christian. Again, from Paul:

There is now no condemnation for those who are in Christ Jesus. (Romans 8:1)

The Christian cannot and will not be punished. However, the Bible teaches those whom God loves, He disciplines (Revelation 3:19).

Aren't punishment and discipline the same thing?

No. There are at least three major differences:

1. The sentence of punishment is the act of a judge. Discipline is the act of a father.
2. The recipients of punishment are those who go against God—those who are His enemies. Those who receive God's discipline are members of God's household—they are the children of God.
3. Punishment is retributive. Discipline is remedial.

22

The Kings: Evil in the Sight of the LORD

On his deathbed, King David tells Solomon, his son and heir to the throne:

> "I am about to go the way of all the earth. So be strong and prove yourself a man. And keep the charge of the LORD your God to walk in His ways and to keep His statutes, commandments, ordinances, and decrees, as is written in the Law of Moses, so that you may prosper in all you do and wherever you turn." (1st Kings 2:2, 3)

After the completion and dedication of the temple, God appears to Solomon and tells him:

> "If you walk before Me as your father David walked, with a heart of integrity and uprightness, doing all I have commanded you, and if you keep My statutes and ordinances, then I will establish your royal throne over Israel forever, as I promised your father

David when I said, 'You will never fail to have a man on the throne of Israel.'

But if indeed you or your sons turn away from following Me and do not keep the commandments and statutes I have set before you, and if you go off to serve and worship other gods, then I will cut off Israel from the land that I have given them, and this temple that I have sanctified for My Name I will banish from My presence. Then Israel will become an object of scorn and ridicule among all peoples.

And though this temple is now exalted, all who pass by it will be appalled and will hiss and say, 'Why has the LORD done such a thing to this land and to this temple?' And others will answer, 'Because they have forsaken the LORD their God who brought their fathers out of the land of Egypt, and have embraced other gods, worshiping and serving them. Because of this, the LORD has brought all this disaster upon them'." (1st Kings 9:4–9)

We saw in our previous lesson how Solomon completely falls away from God. And we hear that same refrain that was repeated seven times in the book of Judges—only now it is referring to Israel's king:

So Solomon did evil in the sight of the LORD. (1st Kings 11:6)

Tragically, throughout the Biblical Story, the people's devotion to God continually vacillates. God does bring disaster upon the people. The nation is divided, with a succession of kings that continually distance themselves from reliance upon God and faithfulness to the Mosaic Covenant.

Under king Rehoboam of Judah:

> Judah did evil in the sight of the LORD. (1st Kings 14:22)

Under king Abijam of Judah:

> Abijam walked in all the sins that his father before him had committed, and his heart was not as fully devoted to the LORD his God as the heart of David his forefather had been. (1st Kings 15:3)

Under king Nadab of Israel:

> And he did evil in the sight of the LORD and walked in the way of his father and in his sin, which he had caused Israel to commit. (1st Kings 15:26)

Under king Baasha of Israel:

> And Baasha did evil in the sight of the LORD and walked in the way of Jeroboam and in his sin, which he had caused Israel to commit. (1st Kings 15:34)

Baasha's son becomes king of Israel, but he and all of Baasha's family are struck down:

> This happened because of all the sins Baasha and his son Elah had committed and had caused Israel to commit, provoking the LORD, the God of Israel, to anger with their worthless idols. (1st Kings 16:13)

Zimri destroys the household of Baasha and takes reign as king of Israel. But Zimri died...

... because of the sins he had committed, doing evil in the sight of the LORD and following the example of Jeroboam and the sin he had committed and had caused Israel to commit. (1st Kings 16:19)

Omri replaces Zimri in Israel:

> But Omri did evil in the sight of the LORD and acted more wickedly than all who were before him. (1st Kings 16:25)

Ahaz replaces Omri:

> Ahab son of Omri did evil in the sight of the LORD, more than all who were before him. And as if it were not enough for him to walk in the sins of Jeroboam son of Nebat, he even married Jezebel the daughter of Ethbaal king of the Sidonians, and he then proceeded to serve and worship Baal. (1st Kings 16:30, 31)

The list could be continued, but the pattern simply repeats itself. A string of **corrupt kings** turns both Israel and Judah toward evil and idolatry.

Throughout this history, a good king will occasionally appear. But even then, we see flaws in his allegiance to God.

One of Judah's most honorable kings is King Hezekiah. About 300 years after King David's rule, Hezekiah becomes king of Judah (the Southern Kingdom). The main accounts of his reign are found in 2nd Kings 18–20, Isaiah 36–39, and 2nd Chronicles 29–32. Hezekiah is a reformer and rids Judah of idolatry.

> ... he did what was right in the eyes of the LORD, just as his father David had done. He removed the high places, shattered the sacred pillars, and cut down the

Asherah poles. He also demolished the bronze snake called Nehushtan that Moses had made, for up to that time the Israelites had burned incense to it.

Hezekiah trusted in the LORD, the God of Israel. No king of Judah was like him, either before him or after him. He remained faithful to the LORD and did not turn from following Him; he kept the commandments that the LORD had given Moses. (2nd Kings 18:3–6)

And God honors Hezekiah.

The LORD was with Hezekiah, and he prospered wherever he went. (2nd Kings 18:7)

Despite attacks on Judah by the Assyrians (which we will discuss in lesson 24), Jerusalem remains safe under Hezekiah. Remnants of the defenses Hezekiah built against Assyrian invasion can be seen in today's Jerusalem. One structure still in existence is Hezekiah's Tunnel—built to protect Jerusalem's water obtained from the Gihon Spring. Though constructed almost three thousand years ago, tourists visiting the Holy Land can traverse the tunnel in an easy, twenty-minute walk. This is a favorite experience for those who are not claustrophobic and who enjoy wet feet. The building of this tunnel is described in 2nd Chronicles 32:1–5, 30 and 2nd Kings 20:20.

Another easily seen remnant from Hezekiah's rule and his efforts to thwart Assyria is a portion of the "Broad Wall" in Jerusalem. This is a stone structure twenty-three feet thick, built to improve Jerusalem's fortifications against attack.

Compared to the kings of Israel, and other kings of Judah, Hezekiah stands apart as a man of God. But there were adverse decisions associated with his reign. During times of conquests and invasions, the kings of Israel and Judah had five options:

- They could surrender.
- They could fight.
- They could form alliances with neighboring countries to oppose a common enemy.
- They could pay financial tribute to the opposing king.
- They could do what God wanted and what the prophets, the spokesmen of God, advocated. They could put their trust in God.

Hezekiah, for the most part, did place his trust in God. But he also relied upon an alliance with Egypt—a pagan nation and a centuries' old adversary. He also provided financial tribute to the Assyrian king in order to buy peace. These payoffs were substantial—ten metric tons of silver and a metric ton of gold. A portion of these riches came from the temple, and in order to obtain the required amount of gold, the gold plating from the temple's doors and doorposts had to be stripped away (2nd Kings 18:15, 16). If this continued, Judah would be slowly robbed of its treasure and wealth—adding financial bankruptcy to its periods of spiritual bankruptcy.

But the true disappointments with Hezekiah came in the latter years of his life. He becomes sick and prays for an extended life (2nd Kings 20:1–11). God responds to his prayer:

> "I will add fifteen years to your life, and I will deliver
> you and this city from the hand of the king of Assyria.
> I will defend this city for My sake and for the sake of
> My servant David." (2nd Kings 20:6)

During the fifteen-year period when Hezekiah's life is prolonged, envoys from Babylon visit. Hezekiah arrogantly shows them all of his riches and the treasures of the temple. He proudly tells the prophet Isaiah, whom we'll learn about shortly, that there was nothing among his treasures that he did not show the Babylonian visitors (2nd Kings 20:15).

Isaiah responds with the voice of prophecy:

> "Hear the word of the LORD: The time will surely come when everything in your palace and all that your fathers have stored up until this day will be carried off to Babylon. Nothing will be left, says the LORD. And some of your descendants, your own flesh and blood, will be taken away to be eunuchs in the palace of the king of Babylon." (2nd Kings 20:16–18)

Later, after Hezekiah's death, all of Judah will be destroyed by the Babylonians. At a great feast in Babylon, the ruler will enjoy wine from the gold and silver vessels taken from the temple (Daniel 5:2).

There is a second tragedy concerning Hezekiah. After his death, his son Manasseh becomes king of Judah. The Bible tells us Manasseh is twelve years old when this occurs. This suggests Manasseh was conceived during the fifteen-year period when Hezekiah's life is extended.

Manasseh overturned all of his father's reforms and returned idolatry to Judah. He is credited (discredited) as being the most corrupt ruler of the Southern Kingdom.

> He did evil in the sight of the LORD by following the abominations of the nations that the LORD had driven out before the Israelites. For he rebuilt the high places that his father Hezekiah had destroyed, and he raised up altars for Baal. He made an Asherah pole, as King Ahab of Israel had done, and he worshiped and served all the host of heaven.
>
> Manasseh also built altars in the house of the LORD, of which the LORD had said, "In Jerusalem I will put My Name." In both courtyards of the house of the

LORD, he built altars to all the host of heaven. He sacrificed his own son in the fire, practiced sorcery and divination, and consulted mediums and spiritists. He did great evil in the sight of the LORD, provoking Him to anger.

Manasseh even took the carved Asherah pole he had made and set it up in the temple, of which the LORD had said to David and his son Solomon, "In this temple and in Jerusalem, which I have chosen out of all the tribes of Israel, I will establish My Name forever. I will never again cause the feet of the Israelites to wander from the land that I gave to their fathers, if only they are careful to do all I have commanded them—the whole Law that My servant Moses commanded them."

But the people did not listen and Manasseh led them astray, so that they did greater evil than the nations that the LORD had destroyed before the Israelites. (2ⁿᵈ Kings 21:2–9)

Manasseh tore down all that Hezekiah had built up, and the nation of Judah will be severely punished:

This is what the LORD, the God of Israel, says: 'Behold, I am bringing such calamity upon Jerusalem and Judah that the news will reverberate in the ears of all who hear it. (2ⁿᵈ Kings 21:12)

Remarkably, the story of Manasseh does not end here, though.

Despite the idolatry, the abominations associated with the temple, Judah adopting the pagan practices of **child sacrifice**, with the shedding of "so much innocent blood that he filled Jerusalem from end to end" (2ⁿᵈ Kings 21:16), Manasseh ultimately turns to God.

And in his distress, Manasseh sought the favor of the LORD his God and earnestly humbled himself before the God of his fathers. And when he prayed to Him, the LORD received his plea and heard his petition; so He brought him back to Jerusalem and to his kingdom. Then Manasseh knew that the LORD is God. (2nd Chronicles 33:12, 13)

Manasseh repents for his wrongdoing, and God receives his plea and hears his petition. Manasseh is forgiven.

Through Manasseh, we recognize that regardless of how sinful we have been and the extent of our rebellion against God, we can always humble ourselves before our God of mercy. And God will not cast us out or turn away.

But there is also a second lesson.

Even though sins can be forgiven, that doesn't mean the consequences of sin are removed.

That's the subject of lesson 24.

But before we get this, there is even more to learn concerning Israel's sin.

That's the subject of our next lesson.

From lesson 22: What do we learn about God?

- In our last lesson, we saw that a righteous God cannot and will not let sin go unpunished.

- In this lesson, we see the patience of God. Ruler after ruler turns from the Mosaic Covenant and brings idolatry into the land, but God withholds His wrath.
- God is a God of grace. He forgives us and gives us the many blessings that we do not deserve.
- And God is a God of mercy. He delays or withholds his punishment that we do deserve.
- Manasseh represents an exceptional example of God's grace and mercy.

---

corrupt kings: After Solomon's reign and the kingdom being divided, there will be 19 kings that rule in the north (Israel), and 19 kings (plus one queen) that will rule in the south (Judah). We see the phrase "did evil in the eyes of the LORD" in the following verses:

1st Kings 11:6	1st Kings 16:30	2nd Kings 13:2	2nd Kings 15:24
1st Kings 14:22	1st Kings 22:52	2nd Kings 13:11	2nd Kings 15:28
1st Kings 14:26	2nd Kings 3:2	2nd Kings 14:24	2nd Kings 16:3
1st Kings 14:34	2nd Kings 8:18	2nd Kings 15:9	2nd Kings 17:2
1st Kings 16:25	2nd Kings 8:27	2nd Kings 15:18	

There is a common, repeated theme here.

child sacrifice: Describing the numerous evils of King Manasseh, 2nd Kings 21:6 says:

He sacrificed his own son in the fire.

We'll discuss this in more detail in our next lesson.

23

The Kings: Idolatry

The first half of Paul's letter to the Romans discusses sin, salvation, and sanctification. Regarding sin, Paul writes,

> Although they know God's righteous decree that those who do such things are worthy of death, they not only continue to do these things, but also approve of those who practice them. (Romans 1:32)

These words can be used to describe the kings of Judah and Israel—kings who did evil in the eyes of God. God's chosen people begin emulating the rituals performed by the Canaanites and Ammonites. The kings not only approve of these things; they are instrumental in introducing and practicing these evils within the land.

One such evil is that of child sacrifice. This was most often associated with the god Molech (also spelled Moloch or Molek), but such sacrifices were also linked to the pagan god Baal. Statues to Molech were normally fashioned out of bronze, with this pagan god typically depicted as having the head of a bull. The figure would have outstretched arms large enough to hold a child. A fire would be built below the arms, heating the bronze metal until it became red-hot. Children would then be placed on the arms of the statue and consumed by the fire.

God's instructions are clear:

> "Tell the Israelites, 'Any Israelite or foreigner living in Israel who gives any of his children to Molech must be put to death. The people of the land are to stone him. And I will set My face against that man and cut him off from his people, because by giving his offspring to Molech, he has defiled My sanctuary and profaned My holy name.
>
> And if the people of the land ever hide their eyes and fail to put to death the man who gives one of his children to Molech, then I will set My face against that man and his family and cut off from their people both him and all who follow him in prostituting themselves with Molech." (Leviticus 20:2–5)

Solomon built a worship site to Molech on a mountain east of Jerusalem (1st Kings 11:7). Hezekiah's son, Manasseh sacrificed his son to Molech (2nd Kings 21:6). Ahaz sacrificed several of his sons to Molech (2nd Chronicles 28:3). These atrocities against God's Word are repeated failures of the kings—and the people. To paraphrase Paul, they not only continued to do those things, they approved of those who practiced them.

Many of the child sacrifices, for example those associated with King Ahaz, occur at a place known as the "**Valley of Hinnom**," or "Gehenna" in the Greek. When Jesus talks about **hell**, he uses the term Gehenna and does so without exception. It is fitting that the betrayer of Jesus, **Judas** Iscariot, kills himself in the Valley of Hinnom.

The "weeping" prophet, Jeremiah refers to this valley and the pagan practices of child sacrifice that the Israelites had introduced into their worship (syncretism):

> For the people of Judah have done evil in My sight, declares the LORD. They have set up their abominations in the house that bears My Name, and so have defiled it. They have built the high places of Topheth in the Valley of Hinnom so they could burn their sons and daughters in the fire—something I did not command, nor did it ever enter My mind. (Jeremiah 7:30, 31)

> They have built high places to Baal on which to burn their children in the fire as offerings to Baal. (Jeremiah 19:5)

> They have built the high places of Baal in the Valley of Hinnom to make their sons and daughters pass through the fire to Molech—something I never commanded them, nor had it ever entered My mind, that they should commit such an abomination and cause Judah to sin. (Jeremiah 32:35)

One of the reasons God orchestrates the invasion and eventual defeat of Judah, including the complete destruction of Jerusalem and the temple by the Babylonians, is because of the Israelite practice of child sacrifice. Ultimately, Jerusalem is delivered to the Babylonian king "by sword and famine and plague" (Jeremiah 32:36). These three terms are brought together and mentioned fifteen times in the book of Jeremiah and eight times in the Book of Ezekiel. Famine represents judgment through nature; sword judgment through men. The people's sins will be judged. Time after time spokesmen from God, His prophets, warn of this.

There are many other sins associated with the Israelites and their kings—but the sacrifice of children is the most hideous. Note God's words to the prophet Jeremiah:

> Go out to the valley of Ben-hinnom ... Proclaim there the words I speak to you, saying, 'Hear the word of the LORD, O kings of Judah and residents of Jerusalem. This is what the LORD of Hosts, the God of Israel, says: I am going to bring such disaster on this place that the ears of all who hear of it will ring, because they have abandoned Me and made this a foreign place. They have burned incense in it to other gods that neither they nor their fathers nor the kings of Judah have ever known. They have filled this place with the blood of the innocent.' (Jeremiah 19:2–4)

We see that Gehenna is mentioned ("the valley of Ben-hinnom"), and the term "blood of the innocent" is referring to the Israelite practice of child sacrifice, in that the next verse adds,

> They have built high places to Baal on which to burn their children in the fire as offerings to Baal. (Jeremiah 19:5)

In these last two lessons, we have seen how the Israelites and their kings have turned away from the God who provides—the God of their salvation. God, though, continues to show His mercy and withholds His wrath.

But this is about to change.

God's words to Solomon, spoken many years prior to this, are instructive. Many of us have read these words—some have memorized them. They are given by God after the dedication of the temple in Jerusalem:

If ... my people who are called by My name humble themselves and pray and seek My face, and turn from their wicked ways, then I will hear from heaven, forgive their sin, and heal their land. (2nd Chronicles 7:14)

In lesson 1, we learned how people purchase tee shirts and coffee mugs stamped with Jeremiah 29:11 ("For I know the plans I have for you..."). But rarely is this placed into context. This is true with this 2nd Chronicles verse as well.

Yes, God has the desire, and certainly the ability, to provide salvation to the people and to heal their land. And this is true for all people at all times and in all places—and we should share this in joy and reassurance. The forgiveness and healing come because of the blood of Christ and final payment of sin for those willing to accept God's plan for redemption. We should always humble ourselves, seek God, pray, and turn from our wicked ways.

At the temple dedication, these are people under the Mosaic Covenant. They, too, are to humble themselves. They are to pray. They are to seek God. They are to turn from their wicked ways. But the part of the story we miss, and the bulk of the text describing the period of the divided kingdom, is one showing the constant failure on the part of the people. This is true with the people, their kings, and even their priests.

And 2nd Chronicles explains God's warning:

"But if you turn away and forsake the statutes and the commandments I have set before you, and if you go off to serve and worship other gods, then I will uproot Israel from the soil I have given them, and this temple that I have sanctified for My Name I will banish from

My presence. I will make it an object of scorn and ridicule among all the peoples.

And though this temple is now exalted, all who pass by it will be appalled and say, 'Why has the LORD done such a thing to this land and to this temple?' And others will answer, 'Because they have forsaken the LORD, the God of their fathers, who brought them out of the land of Egypt, and have embraced other gods, worshiping and serving them. Because of this, He has brought all this disaster upon them.'" (2nd Chronicles 7:19–22)

The people of Israel continue in their unfaithfulness and failure. They did not seek God or obey his commands. History tells us the result.

God punishes them.

Severely.

Their land is not healed—it is broken, burned, and buried. There is sword, famine, and plague. Some survive only by resorting to cannibalism. Others are exiled from the land. The temple is destroyed (we'll learn in lesson 36 that God even removes His presence from the temple).

In our next lesson, we take a temporary detour away from the biblical text and review the history of Judah and Israel and the disasters God brings upon His people.

Disobeying God brings disaster.

We began this lesson with words from Paul:

Although they know God's righteous decree that those who do such things are worthy of death, they

not only continue to do these things, but also approve
of those who practice them. (Romans 1:32)

Paul is writing to a different people at a different time. But the
message endures—and it is valid for America today. We know God's
righteous decree, but we not only continue to do evil in the eyes of
God, we legitimize evil. Practices considered immoral just a few
short years ago are now accepted as the norm. As a nation, we do
not humble ourselves and pray. We do not seek God. We do not turn
from our wicked ways.

Do I need to cite an example?

How about the practice of child sacrifice?

This has certainly not been limited to the ancients. We practice child
sacrifice in America and do so daily.

We call it abortion.

From lesson 23: What do we learn about God?

- This lesson has focused on the repeated failure of God's
  chosen people to obey God—continually violating the first
  and greatest commandment. But God is a God of patience.
- God warns the people on numerous occasions of their
  impending disaster unless they turn from their wicked ways
  and seek the God of salvation.

Valley of Hinnom: This is also called the "Valley of the son of
Hinnom" (see the Jeremiah 19:2 text above) and "Valley of the
children of Hinnom."

For those familiar with Jerusalem, the Valley of Hinnom runs along the western portion of the Old City, opposite the Kidron Valley. On the eastern side there is the Kidron Valley that separates the temple mount from the Mount of Olives. The Valley of Hinnom is on the opposite side of the temple mount and curves down to the southeast section below the ruins of the City of David, and then connects to the Kidron Valley.

Between the two valleys is a third, smaller valley. If you hold up your thumb and first two fingers of your right hand, palm facing out, you get somewhat of a depiction of the three valleys. They also look similar to the Hebrew letter "shin."

hell: Using Matthew's Gospel for our examples, Jesus' use of the term Gehenna is found in Matthew 5:22; 5:29; 5:30; 10:28; 18:9; 23:15; and 23:33. It is interesting that James, the half-brother of Jesus, also uses the term Gehenna (James 3:6).

The term Gehenna *always* refers to hell. In the New Testament, we also see the term "hades." However, this term does not mean "hell," although sometimes it is translated as such. Hades is the grave—but there is a portion of hades that includes what we think of when we talk about "hell." But even this is a bit misleading. When people talk of "hell," they are probably referring to the lake of fire from Revelation 20. This is the final place of torment for those outside of the kingdom of God. Hades itself is thrown into this lake of fire (as the "grave," it has served its purpose since death is thrown into the lake of fire as well).

For a more in-depth treatment of this topic, see lesson 27 in *A Forty-Day Study of the Book of Hebrews: The Superiority of Christ*.

Judas: Judas killed himself at the southeastern section of the Valley of Hinnom (Gehenna)—a place known as the "Field of Blood" (*Akeldama* in Aramaic—also known as the Potter's Field).

child sacrifice: It should be noted that child sacrifice in ancient Israel was not simply dedicating a child to a pagan god. It was truly the killing of children. Archeologists have located a number of sites where charred remains of many children have been uncovered—some found placed in urns. The pagan sacrifice involved placing children into fires.

24

The Punishment of the People

It is beneficial to know **Israel's history** after Solomon and the breakup of the monarchy. This can be supplemented from sources outside of the biblical text—but a portion of it is also described in 1st and 2nd Kings and 1st and 2nd Chronicles. The books of Ezra, Nehemiah, and Esther also describe events in Israel's history—covering events that occur after the exile.

Knowing this history promotes a better understanding of the remainder of the Old Testament, especially the writings of the prophets. And it also points to why we need Jesus—and the New Covenant. Repeatedly we see the failure of God's chosen people to remain faithful to Him. Continually we see their sin. Ultimately, we see the wrath of God and his righteous punishment. This would be our lot had Jesus not come to his earth—or if we were still bound by the Mosaic Covenant.

Let's briefly go through this history.

After King David's reign, Solomon places heavy burdens on his subjects and accumulates great wealth. In many ways, he is the ancient equivalent of "tax and spend"—or perhaps "tax and hoard."

His son and heir, Rehoboam, is no different. The people resist, resulting in a rebellion and the splitting up of the nation into the Northern Kingdom (Israel) and the Southern Kingdom (Judah). The Northern Kingdom establishes its own places of worship—going against the Mosaic Covenant as syncretism is introduced (lessons 22 and 23).

The conditional Mosaic Covenant promised blessings if the people obeyed, but curses if they turned from God. Moses summarized these in some of his last words before his death. This can be found in Deuteronomy 28.

To provide a sampling of the curses:

> The LORD will turn the rain of your land into dust and powder; it will descend on you from the sky until you are destroyed. (Deuteronomy 28:24)

> The LORD will afflict you with the boils of Egypt, with tumors and scabs and itch from which you cannot be cured. (Deuteronomy 28:27)

The curses include invasion by foreigners and total defeat at their hands. There will be plagues. Food will become scarce:

> During the siege and hardship that your enemy will impose on you, you will eat the fruit of your womb, the flesh of the sons and daughters whom the LORD your God has given you. (Deuteronomy 28:53)

For survival, the people will have to resort to cannibalism:

If you remember our brief discussion on Marcion (lesson 17), it is somewhat understandable why he wasn't enamored with God as He is revealed in the Old Testament. We do see an angry God and His wrath. But perhaps we should view events from God's perspective—not ours.

God chose Abraham and his descendants as a set-apart, covenant people that would be special to Him and that would receive unique blessings from Him. As His chosen people, they are to reflect God's image (where have we heard of that before?). In a world of darkness, these people of God are to be God's light. As recipients of God's instructions, they are to present the one true God to the world. They are to bring blessings to all of the nations. Ultimately, the seed of woman—the Redeemer—will be presented to the world through these people.

But time after time, the Israelites show indifference to God and fail to follow God's commands and instructions. God remains faithful—but God's people do not.

Repeatedly in the biblical text, it is said of the people and their kings, "they did evil in the sight of the LORD." In the list of curses, we also read:

> The LORD will cause you to be defeated before your enemies. You will march out against them in one direction but flee from them in seven. You will be an object of horror to all the kingdoms of the earth. Your corpses will be food for all the birds of the air and beasts of the earth, with no one to scare them away. (Deuteronomy 28:25, 26)

> You who were as numerous as the stars in the sky will be left few in number, because you would not obey the voice of the LORD your God. Just as it pleased the LORD to make you prosper and to multiply you, so also it will please Him to exterminate you and destroy

you. And you will be uprooted from the land you are entering to possess. (Deuteronomy 28:62, 63)

And that is what happens.

Assyria (not to be confused with Syria) begins invading the Northern Kingdom around 740 BC. Its capital, Samaria, falls in 722 BC. This siege against the capital takes three years, and throughout this period of invasion, some of the Israelites are deported from the land while Assyrians also migrate into the land (2nd Kings 17:5, 6). It was the subsequent intermarrying between the Israelites in the north and these invaders that led to a mixed race of Israelites known as the "Samaritans"—despised by Judah (the Southern Kingdom) even up through the time of Jesus.

The reason for the Northern Kingdom's destruction centered on the idolatry of the nation:

> All this happened because the people of Israel had sinned against the LORD their God, who had brought them out of the land of Egypt from under the hand of Pharaoh king of Egypt. They had worshiped other gods and walked in the customs of the nations that the LORD had driven out before the Israelites, as well as in the practices introduced by the kings of Israel. (2nd Kings 17:7, 8)

The fall of Samaria left the Southern Kingdom, Judah, vulnerable. To avoid conflict with Assyria, instead of placing their trust in God, they formed alliances with other nations. They also paid an annual tribute to Assyria. During the reigns of King Ahaz and King Hezekiah, there were brief periods of stability. But these would not last.

In 701 BC, Assyrian invaders sweep into Judah and conquer forty-six of its cities. A well-documented battle is the defeat of Lachish—one of the key fortified cities protecting a major route leading into Jerusalem (2nd Kings 18; 2nd Chronicles 32; Micah 1:13). It is during this siege that Hezekiah gives financial tribute to Assyria's king Sennacherib to ward off further attacks (2nd Kings 18:13–16, see lesson 22). Assyria, however, proceeds to send their army to the outskirts of Jerusalem.

This should be put into perspective. Up to this point, nothing was able to stop Assyrian invaders. They had conquered a broad expanse of land running from Babylonia through Syria, and down the coast through Phoenicia and Philistia. The Northern Kingdom and Samaria had been conquered, as well as most of Judah. To the east, the Assyrians had overrun the mighty city of Babylon. And now they were at the walls of Jerusalem. Using today's geographical names, they had conquered Iraq, Iran, Syria, Lebanon, Jordan, and much of Israel, including the Gaza Strip.

The prophet Isaiah lived during the reigns of four of Judah's kings: Uzziah, Jotham, Ahaz, and Hezekiah. He informed the people that Assyria was God's instrument of punishment (see for example, Isaiah 8). But he also announced the Assyrians would also face God's wrath. Jerusalem would ultimately be spared—at least temporarily:

> Therefore, this is what the Lord GOD of Hosts says:
>
> > "O My people who dwell in Zion,
> >   do not fear Assyria,
> > who strikes you with a rod
> >   and lifts his staff against you
> >   as the Egyptians did.
> > For in just a little while
> >   My fury against you will subside,
> >   and My anger will turn to their destruction."
> > (Isaiah 10:24, 25)

So this is what the LORD says about the king of Assyria:

> "He will not enter this city
>   or shoot an arrow into it.
> He will not come before it with a shield
>   or build up a siege ramp against it.
> He will go back the way he came,
>   and he will not enter this city,
>   declares the LORD.
> I will defend this city
>   and save it
> for My own sake
>   and for the sake of My servant David."
>   (Isaiah 37:33–35)

How was Jerusalem spared from the greatest army on earth at that time period? Ancient records from the Assyrian empire do not mention the failure of the Assyrian king (Sennacherib) in his conquest concerning Jerusalem. The records extol his conquests and victories throughout that part of the world—but Jerusalem is omitted. By omission, they affirm Jerusalem was not taken.

So, what happened when the Assyrians were at the walls of Jerusalem?

For some reason, Assyria's forces left Judah. The Assyrian records are silent, but the Biblical Story provides the answer:

> And that very night the angel of the LORD went out and struck down 185,000 men in the camp of the Assyrians. When the people got up the next morning, there were all the dead bodies! So Sennacherib king of Assyria broke camp and withdrew. He returned to Nineveh and stayed there. (2nd Kings 19:35, 36—also

mentioned in 2nd Chronicles 32:20–23 and Isaiah 37:36–38; and alluded to in Isaiah 17:14)

Jerusalem is saved, but as we have said, this would not be not for long.

Before we conclude our brief review of this portion of Israel's history (we'll add to this in our next lesson), something important needs to be shared. This lesson is titled "The Punishment of the People." The invasion by Assyria and the eventual invasion by Babylonia, along with the removal of the people from the land, was God's punishment.

But it was not punishment for punishment's sake.

When the people of God turn from Him, God wants to bring His people to a state of repentance. From their time in the wilderness upon leaving Egypt, throughout the period of the judges, and throughout the monarchy and divided kingdom, the Israelites lived in sin and rebellion, confident in their own strength and in that of the neighboring nations with which they would ally.

God has to intervene and teach His people in a dramatic way. The Mosaic Covenant clearly spelled out the curses the people will experience if they turn from Him. And to this, God adds the voices of the prophets. These messages were also very clear—continual warnings of His impending judgment. He persistently tells the people of His reasons for this judgment and destruction. Included in the prophetic word was God's expressed desires for the people that, if followed, would prevent His wrath.

But the people do not listen or change their ways.

And it should also be noted that God, through His prophets, always promises protection for a remnant of the people. He assures the eventual return of this remnant to the land. Most importantly, God's word through the prophets also provide numerous glimpses of a future King—a King of Righteousness.

But before the light of hope would appear, there would be many seasons of darkness.

From lesson 24: What do we learn about God?

- God uses the pagan nation of Assyria to punish Israel and Judah. But He spares Jerusalem.
- The punishment was deserved and predicted. It should not have come as a surprise.
- God's use of pagans to punish His people does not mean pagan nations escape God's wrath.

Israel's history: Appendix B contains important dates and events in the history of Israel. It is recommended that you briefly scan this listing and occasionally refer to it as the lessons discuss the prophets and events in Israel's history.

25

The Exile

The prophet Isaiah foresaw the Assyrian conquest and defeat of Israel and Judah. These events were no accident; these were part of God's punishment upon the people:

> Because this people has rejected
>   the gently flowing waters of Shiloah
> and rejoiced in Rezin
>   and the son of Remaliah,
> the Lord will surely bring against them
>   the mighty floodwaters of the Euphrates —
>   the king of Assyria and all his pomp. (Isaiah 8:6, 7)

> The LORD will bring on you and on your people and on the house of your father a time unlike any since the day Ephraim separated from Judah—He will bring the king of Assyria. (Isaiah 7:17)

In the words of the prophet,

> They have brought disaster upon themselves.
> Jerusalem staggers. Judah is fallen. (Isaiah 3:8, 9)

As we saw in our last lesson, Assyria was God's tool to punish **Israel**. But Assyria, in turn, will also be punished. Again, from Isaiah:

> Woe to Assyria, the rod of My anger;
>   the staff in their hands is My wrath. (Isaiah 10:5)

> When the Lord has completed all His work against Mount Zion and Jerusalem, He will say, "I will punish the king of Assyria for the fruit of his arrogant heart and the proud look in his eyes." (Isaiah 10:12)

Assyria had been the dominant empire for over two centuries. But this ended.

God's punishment of Assyria came at the hands of the **Babylonians**, who captured Nineveh, Assyria's capital, in 612 BC. While this was foretold by Isaiah; the book of **Nahum**, written by the prophet of that name, is an oracle specifically describing God's anger toward Nineveh. The book of Jonah is the story of the individual sent to warn Nineveh against its eventual destruction.

The Babylonian conquest did not stop at Nineveh. The armies of Egypt had been allied with remnant soldiers from Assyria. They, too, are attacked. Their defeat at the hands of the Babylonians came in 605 BC at the Battle of Carchemish.

During this time period, Jehoiakim is the king of Judah. He allies the Southern Kingdom with Egypt and begins to pay tribute to the new Babylonian king, Nebuchadnezzar. Some of the nobility of Judah are taken to Babylon—including young Daniel, the author of the book by his name (we'll discuss the book of Daniel in lesson 37).

In 601 BC, though, Jehoiakim discontinues paying tribute to Nebuchadnezzar and revolts against Babylon. This leads to a three-month siege of Jerusalem (598 BC). You will recall how, many years prior to this, King Hezekiah had proudly showed visitors from

Babylon the treasures contained at the temple and within his palace (lesson 22). Babylon would now capture these riches.

Jehoiakim dies during this siege and is succeeded by his son, Jehoiachin, who is also called Jeconiah. Jerusalem falls to Nebuchadnezzar, and Jeconiah and officials within his administration, along with prominent citizens of Jerusalem, are taken to Babylon. The prophet Ezekiel is among those exiled.

To replace Jeconiah, Nebuchadnezzar appoints Jeconiah's uncle, Zedekiah, as king.

Another prophet, Jeremiah, predicts the fall of Jerusalem and warns Zedekiah not to rebel against Babylon (we'll study Jeremiah in lesson 35). Judah and Jerusalem (Zion) were experiencing the rightful punishment from God. King Zedekiah, though, does not listen and revolts against Babylon's rule. This leads to Nebuchadnezzar's return and the final devastation of Jerusalem in 587 BC. It was during this siege that the temple is completely destroyed.

Zedekiah would be Judah's last king.

There is an interesting nuance in biblical prophecy concerning what happens to Zedekiah. His fate is mentioned by both Jeremiah and Ezekiel. While the two prophets lived during the same time period, Ezekiel had been taken to Babylon while Jeremiah remained in Jerusalem where he witnessed the destruction of the temple. Jeremiah's prophecy reads,

> This is the word that came to Jeremiah from the LORD in the tenth year of Zedekiah king of Judah, which was the eighteenth year of Nebuchadnezzar. At that time, the army of the king of Babylon was besieging Jerusalem, and Jeremiah the prophet was

imprisoned in the courtyard of the guard, which was in the palace of the king of Judah.

For Zedekiah king of Judah had imprisoned him, saying: "Why are you prophesying that the LORD says: 'Behold, I am about to deliver this city into the hand of the king of Babylon, and he will capture it. Zedekiah king of Judah will not escape from the hands of the Chaldeans, but <u>he will surely be delivered into the hand of the king of Babylon to speak with him face to face and to see him eye to eye</u>. <u>He will take Zedekiah to Babylon</u>, where he will stay until I attend to him, declares the LORD. If you fight against the Chaldeans, you will not succeed'." (Jeremiah 32:1–5)

According to the prophet Jeremiah, Zedekiah would not escape the Babylonians (Chaldeans) and Nebuchadnezzar. He would face Nebuchadnezzar face-to-face and eye-to-eye, and then be taken to Babylon.

Ezekiel's prophecy concerning Zedekiah seems to conflict with this:

I will bring him to Babylon, the land of the Chaldeans; yet <u>he will not see it</u>, and there he will die. (Ezekiel 12:13)

According to the word of God through Ezekiel, somehow Zedekiah will be taken to Babylon, but will not see Babylon.

Which prophet was correct?

Both, of course.

The book of 2ⁿᵈ Kings records the following:

The Chaldeans seized the king and brought him up to the king of Babylon at Riblah, where they pronounced judgment on him. And <u>they slaughtered the sons of Zedekiah before his eyes</u>. <u>Then they put out his eyes</u>, bound him with bronze shackles, and took him to Babylon. (2nd Kings 25:6, 7)

Zedekiah witnessed the execution of his sons, after which he was blinded and taken to Babylon.

Yes, Zedekiah saw Nebuchadnezzar face-to-face and eye-to-eye.

Yes, Zedekiah was taken to Babylon.

And yes, even though Zedekiah was taken to Babylon, Zedekiah never saw Babylon. This was due to his blindness afflicted upon him by the Babylonians.

There is another interesting biblical nuance. God's prophetic word revealed that the Babylonian exile would last seventy years. Jeremiah writes:

For this is what the LORD says: "When Babylon's seventy years are complete, I will attend to you and confirm My promise to restore you to this place."

This is Jeremiah 29:10, the verse right before the one available on tee shirts and coffee mugs.

Daniel, exiled to Babylon, had access to Jeremiah's writings and was aware of this seventy-year period. Daniel writes,

In the first year of Darius son of Xerxes, a Mede by descent, who was made ruler over the kingdom of the Chaldeans — in the first year of his reign, I, Daniel, understood from the sacred books, according to the word of the LORD to Jeremiah the prophet, that the desolation of Jerusalem would last seventy years. So I turned my attention to the Lord God to seek Him by prayer and petition, with fasting, sackcloth, and ashes. (Daniel 9:1–3)

Why did the Babylonian captivity last seventy years?

Earlier, when we discussed why God picked Abraham or Moses or David, our answer was simply, "God chose these men because He wanted to." But there is more to the story concerning the seventy-year period for the exile. To understand this, there are a few items to review.

God had established the concept of the Sabbath day—a day of rest—and also the Sabbath year:

> For six years you may sow your field and prune your vineyard and gather its crops. But in the seventh year there shall be a Sabbath of complete rest for the land—a Sabbath to the LORD.
>
> You are not to sow your field or prune your vineyard. You are not to reap the aftergrowth of your harvest or gather the grapes of your untended vines. The land must have a year of complete rest. (Leviticus 25:3–5)

The Sabbath year was a year where there was to be no planting or harvesting. It was a year of rest for the land.

After seven Sabbath years (seven sevens—there's that number "seven" again), there is the Jubilee Year. And once again, the land is to experience a year where crops are not to be planted:

And you shall count off seven sabbaths of years—
seven times seven years—so that the seven sabbaths
of years amount to forty-nine years.

The fiftieth year will be a jubilee for you; you are not
to sow the land or reap its aftergrowth or harvest the
untended vines. (Leviticus 25:8, 11)

The text includes punishments for disobedience:

I will set My face against you, so that you will be
defeated by your enemies. (Leviticus 26:17)

I will scatter you among the nations and will draw out
a sword after you as your land becomes desolate and
your cities are laid waste. (Leviticus 26:33)

And now, the key part:

Then the land shall enjoy its Sabbaths all the days
it lies desolate, while you are in the land of your
enemies. At that time the land will rest and enjoy its
Sabbaths. As long as it lies desolate, the land will have
the rest it did not receive during the Sabbaths when
you lived in it. (Leviticus 26:34, 35)

Why did the Babylonian captivity last seventy years? The Bible
provides the answer:

Those who escaped the sword were carried by
Nebuchadnezzar into exile in Babylon, and they
became servants to him and his sons until the
kingdom of Persia came to power.

So the land enjoyed its Sabbath rest all the days of
the desolation, until seventy years were completed,

in fulfillment of the word of the LORD through
Jeremiah. (2nd Chronicles 36:20, 21)

The people had violated seventy Sabbath years—seventy years in
which the land was not given the rest as instructed by God. As
punishment, the people would be removed from the land for seventy
years.

Before we leave this section on Israel's history, there is an additional
area of prophecy that we'll introduce here—and we will also come
back to it. The people have disobeyed God. They have repeatedly
broken God's covenant with Moses, particularly through their idolatry,
and this leads to God's punishment through the Assyrian invasion
and the Babylonian captivity. But both Ezekiel and Jeremiah hint at a
covenant that replaces the Mosaic Covenant (as we saw earlier).

> When they return to it, they will remove from it all
> its detestable things and all its abominations. And I
> will give them singleness of heart and put a new spirit
> within them; I will remove their heart of stone and
> give them a heart of flesh, so that they may follow
> My statutes, keep My ordinances, and practice them.
> Then they will be My people, and I will be their God.
> (Ezekiel 11:18–20)

Ezekiel foresees a time when the people will be returned to the land
and will be given "a new spirit within them." He repeats this later
in his writing:

> For I will take you from among the nations and gather
> you out of all the countries, and I will bring you back
> into your own land. I will also sprinkle clean water
> on you, and you will be clean. I will cleanse you from
> all your impurities and all your idols. I will give you
> a new heart and put a new spirit within you; I will

remove your heart of stone and give you a heart of flesh. And I will put My Spirit within you and cause you to walk in My statutes and to carefully observe My ordinances. (Ezekiel 36:24–27)

Jeremiah also foresees this:

> "Behold, the days are coming, declares the LORD,
>   when I will make a new covenant
> with the house of Israel
>   and with the house of Judah.
> It will not be like the covenant
>   I made with their fathers
> when I took them by the hand
>   to lead them out of the land of Egypt—
> a covenant they broke,
>   though I was a husband to them,"
>   declares the LORD.

> "But this is the covenant I will make with the house of Israel
>   after those days, declares the LORD.
> I will put My law in their minds
>   and inscribe it on their hearts.
> And I will be their God,
>   and they will be My people.
> No longer will each man teach his neighbor or his brother,
>   saying, 'Know the LORD,'
> because they will all know Me,
>   from the least of them to the greatest, declares the LORD.
> For I will forgive their iniquities
>   and will remember their sins no more." (Jeremiah 31:31–34)

The people will return to the land. They will rebuild the temple. They will await this new covenant.

That there will be a new covenant is supremely important. It means that someday God's covenant with the people, the Mosaic Covenant, would be replaced. Remember, God's covenant with Abraham is unconditional and everlasting, as is his covenant with David. But the Mosaic Covenant was both conditional and temporary. It will be replaced by the New Covenant. We've mentioned the New Covenant in lessons 15, 16, and 24—and now, here in lesson 25. It deserves frequent mentioning. You and I live under the New Covenant.

We're getting ahead of ourselves, but Jesus will announce the New Covenant at the Passover meal before his crucifixion. It is his blood—his sacrifice on the cross—that completes the fulfillment of the Mosaic law, obsoletes the temporary Mosaic covenant, and ushers in the everlasting New Covenant of God. We will devote a lesson to the New Covenant in volume 2.

I can't think of a greater gift from God, than his coming to earth, dying for us, and then forming a new covenant that we can be a part of. This truly is God's grace.

From lesson 25: What do we learn about God?

- Though we have only reviewed small sections of the Bible, we repeatedly see the accuracy of God's Word.
- We also see the conditions of the Mosaic Covenant played out. When the people obey God, they are blessed. When they disobey, God delays judgment and shows grace and mercy. But ultimately the people face punishment according to the covenant.

Israel: Prior to the division of the monarchy, the nation was called Israel. As discussed, after its division, the Northern Kingdom was called Israel and the Southern Kingdom was called Judah. However, often times the biblical text will use "Israel" to refer to both the north and the south. Context normally suggests what is being meant.

Here, I'm referring to both the Northern Kingdom and the Southern Kingdom—all of "Israel."

Nathan: The prophet Nathan, and others classified as "minor prophets," are discussed in the next two lessons.

Babylonians: Babylonia is located in the southeast portion of Mesopotamia (today's Iraq). In the Bible it is also called Shinar or the land of the Chaldeans.

26

An Introduction to the Minor Prophets:

Prophets addressing the Northern Kingdom

We began this lesson series looking at the first five books of the Bible—the writings of Moses. These are referred to as the Pentateuch and are also called the Torah.

We then proceeded to the next section of the Bible, referred to as the historical books. These include Joshua, Judges, Ruth, 1st and 2nd Samuel, 1st and 2nd Kings, and 1st and 2nd Chronicles. There are three additional books that are in this section—Ezra, Nehemiah, and Esther—but these cover historical events that occur after the exile of God's chosen people, so we will save our review of these for later.

Theologians use the term "post-exilic" when referring to authors or events after the exile, and the term "pre-exilic" when referring to those before the exile. These three remaining historical books are post-exilic.

Before we get to these, though, we will briefly look at some of the books that are in the section of the Bible containing the writings of the prophets. For now, we'll specifically cover those who proclaimed God's word prior to and during the exile of the Israelites.

We should begin, though, by asking, "What is a prophet?" In lesson 1, we briefly covered the numerous ways God reveals Himself. As one example, God's great acts in the history of Abraham and his descendants are part of God's revelation. God reveals himself through history ("His Story"). These events have been written down, and these recordings (the Hebrew Scriptures) are used by God to reveal Himself. This is His written word.

These writings include God's revelation through the use of His spokespeople—prophets and prophetesses. They bring God's word to His people. These are also part of God's written word.

We've already discussed some of the prophets of God. God calls Abraham a prophet (Genesis 20:7). Moses is a prophet (Deuteronomy 18:15). In the book of Judges, Deborah is described as a prophetess (Judges 4:4). The last judge, Samuel, is a prophet (1st Samuel 3:20). Throughout the Biblical Story, we are introduced to other prophets of God, such as Nathan (during the time of David) and Elijah and his successor, Elisha (during the time of King Ahab).

A prophet speaks the word of God to the people. They proclaim God's will or explain God's purposes. Most often, the covenant people of God are in need of repentance. God raises up a prophet to draw the people's attention to their evil ways, compelling them to turn back to God and to be obedient to His instructions.

The prophetic voice is also used to warn the covenant people of the consequences of their failure to do so. Accordingly, much of this not only includes admonitions against the sins of the people and their leaders, they contain visions of God's wrath poured out among the people. The prophets are given glimpses into the future, and their proclamations help place what will happen into the perspective of God's will and His acts in history.

When the prophet writes about future events, context helps us determine when that "future" occurs. For example, the prophet may share visions predicting events that occur during the prophet's lifetime. This is known as the prophecy's "primary fulfilment." But the fulfillment may also await some time off into the future—beyond the prophet's lifetime. This is known as the prophecy's secondary fulfillment. And the prophecy may even relate to end times—usually the second coming of Christ and his millennial rule, or sometimes the period of the new heaven and new earth. This is referred to as the prophecy's final fulfillment.

A prophecy can also have more than one fulfillment. It can have a secondary fulfillment and a final fulfillment. As an example, the prophet Daniel foresees a detestable act associated with desecration of the temple, that is, the "abomination of desolation" of Daniel 9:27. This has occurred historically. Antiochus IV, the king of Syria, desecrates the temple in 167 BC as a statue of Zeus is erected in the temple and a pig is sacrificed as an offering to Zeus (this occurred over 200 years after Daniel lived).

But something similar will occur again. In other words, there will also be a final fulfillment. This will occur when the antichrist desecrates the temple during the end times. We learn this from Jesus, who tells us about this event and relates what he is teaching to Daniel's prophecy (Matthew 24:15).

Several of the prophets have their writings consolidated into "books" and included in the Old Testament. These writings are identified by the prophet's name. These are the prophets and their writings that we will be looking at.

It's important to note, in that a prophet brings God's word to the people, all Christians are prophets. This does not mean we can foresee future events—other than sharing what the Bible teaches about future events—but it does mean we can bring God's word to people. We are equipped to do this because we possess God's Word—the Bible. Paul tells Christians in Rome:

> Faith comes by hearing, and hearing by the word of Christ. (Romans 10:17)

> How then can they call on the One in whom they have not believed? And how can they believe in the One of whom they have not heard? And how can they hear without someone to preach? And how can they preach unless they are sent? As it is written: "How beautiful are the feet of those who bring good news!" (Romans 10:14, 15)

We bring God's Word, particularly the good news, to those around us through the sharing of the Bible and what it teaches. This activity is not a suggestion—it is a command (Mark 16:15; Matthew 28:19, 20).

We will now review several of the prophets, basing this on chronology—the time the prophet lived—not on where the prophet's writing appears in the Bible or when the events being described occur. In this lesson, we'll briefly cover two of the prophets with messages addressed to the Northern Kingdom, or Israel, plus a prophet who brings God's message to Israel's enemy—the Assyrians. In lesson 27, we will cover several of the prophets who address Judah—the Southern Kingdom.

For now, we will be looking at writings from the "**minor prophets**." This term has nothing to do with the prophet's age, height, or relative importance. They are categorized this way simply because their writings are short in length. Longer writings fall under the term "**major prophets**." We've already looked at some of the writings of the major prophets, such as those of Isaiah and Jeremiah, but these will be addressed in much more detail later.

To set the stage, let's review where we are historically in the Biblical Story. The kingdom, united under the reigns of King David and King Solomon, is now divided. Israel, the Northern Kingdom, immediately builds worship sites away from Jerusalem in violation of the Mosaic Law. Syncretism is introduced as the gods of the pagan nations are worshipped alongside the God of the Bible.

The first of the minor prophets we will discuss is Amos, a shepherd from the Southern Kingdom (Judah) called to prophesy to Israel. He goes to the temple in the Northern Kingdom at Bethel and proclaims God will punish Israel for her idolatry and the corruption and evil deeds of her aristocracy and rulers. He tells the people:

> Surely the Sovereign LORD does nothing
>   without revealing his plan
>   to his servants the prophets. (Amos 3:7)

> "You only have I chosen
>   of all the families of the earth;
>   therefore I will punish you
>   for all your sins." (Amos 3:2)

> "I will destroy the altars of Bethel." (Amos 3:14)

> "I will stir up a nation against you, O house of Israel,
>   that will oppress you." (Amos 7:14)

> "Jeroboam [Israel's king] will die by the sword,
>   and Israel will surely go into exile,
>   away from her homeland." (Amos 7:11)

Five times in Amos 4 we see the phrase "you did not return to Me," and finally,

"Prepare to meet your God, O Israel!" (Amos 4:12)

The people of the Northern Kingdom, through idolatry and disobeying the Mosaic Law, had left God and refuse to return to Him. They will now meet God—but not as they expect. As covered in lesson 24, Israel experiences the wrath of God as He orchestrates the destruction of the nation by the Assyrians.

Through the prophet Amos, God's message to the people is summarized:

"Seek good, not evil,
  so that you may live.
And the LORD, the God of Hosts,
  will be with you, as you have claimed.
Hate evil and love good;
  establish justice in the gate.
Perhaps the LORD, the God of Hosts,
  will be gracious to the remnant of Joseph." (Amos 5:14, 15)

Hosea is a second prophet addressing the north. God's Word continues to address the people's idolatry and syncretism. At the time of Hosea's writing, the people of God are visiting shrine prostitutes and have adopted the worship practices associated with fertility cults. Hosea depicts these practices as spiritual prostitution—unfaithfulness to God. Through Hosea, God tells the people:

"This land is flagrantly prostituting itself by departing from the LORD." (Hosea 1:2)

"My people consult their wooden idols,
  and their divining rods inform them.

For a spirit of prostitution leads them astray
　　and they have played the harlot against their God.
They sacrifice on the mountaintops
　　and burn offerings on the hills." (Hosea 4:12, 13)

"My people are destroyed for lack of knowledge.
　　Because you have rejected knowledge,
I will also reject you as My priests.
Since you have forgotten the law of your God,
　　I will also forget your children." (Hosea 4:6)

"I will put an end to the kingdom of Israel." (Hosea 1:2)

We could view Israel's history through the eyes of Marcion and see God as being unjust. But time after time, God has warned His people and has made clear His expectations.

In the fifth chapter of the book of Amos, we see the **repeated phrase**, *"Seek me and live."* This is the desire of God. It is an echo of the words of God to Solomon after the dedication of the temple that we looked at earlier:

> If ... My people who are called by My name humble themselves and pray and seek My face, and turn from their wicked ways, then I will hear from heaven, forgive their sin, and heal their land. (2nd Chronicles 7:14)

God wants His people to seek Him. This has always been the case. And God will always seek out His people. This, too, has always been the case.

But time after time, the people fail to seek God. They fail to place their trust in His promises. They fail to obey His instruction. They show indifference to God.

So God brings His righteous judgment and wrath upon the people.

But God also continually promises, and ultimately provides, an eventual restoration. Yes, the prophets declare God's judgment. But they also pronounce hope. There will be a remnant of the people that return to the land after its destruction and after their exile.

As we read these words of hope, we should realize that the prophet's visions of restoration don't always relate to the healing of the land after the Assyrian conquest or the Babylonian exile. Sometimes they do refer to this—especially when their words specifically describe the eventual defeat of the Assyrians, the defeat of the Babylonians, or the return of exiled captives to Judah and Jerusalem. But these prophetic visions can also look further into the future and refer to a time when the Righteous King will rule over God's people—the millennial rule of Christ.

And sometimes the visions will look even further into the future and point us to the ultimate destiny of God's people: our eternal existence in the new earth of Revelation 21. Usually, context and the details in what is being described can help us understand the time period associated with the revelation (and whether events that occur relate to primary, secondary, or final fulfillment, as discussed).

The foundational truth, though, regardless of the specific time period being described, is that *God is faithful*. Despite the repeated failures of His people, God promises restoration and redemption. There will always be a remnant that receives the blessings of God.

So, through the prophet Amos, God tells His people:

> I will restore My people Israel from captivity;
>   they will rebuild and inhabit the ruined cities.
> They will plant vineyards and drink their wine;
>   they will make gardens and eat their fruit.
> I will firmly plant them in their own land. (Amos 9:14)

And through the prophet Hosea, God tells His people:

> The number of the Israelites will be like the sand of
> the sea, which cannot be measured or counted. And
> it will happen that in the very place where it was said
> to them, 'You are not My people,' they will be called
> 'sons of the living God.' Then the people of Judah and
> of Israel will be gathered together. (Hosea 1:10, 11)

> I will betroth you to Me forever;
>   I will betroth you in righteousness and justice,
>   in loving devotion and compassion.
> And I will betroth you in faithfulness,
>   and you will know the LORD. (Hosea 2:19, 20)

While Amos and Hosea address the Northern Kingdom, there is a
third prophet we should briefly mention: Jonah. Though he came
from Galilee (2nd Kings 14:25) and lived in the Northern Kingdom,
his message from God does not address Israel but instead focuses on
Assyria and its capital, Nineveh.

While considered a prophet, we find only one verse of prophecy in
Jonah's writing—just five words in the Hebrew:

> "Forty more days and Nineveh will be overturned!"
> (Jonah 3:4)

That's the extent of Jonah's prophecy. The rest of this writing depicts
Jonah's reluctance to bring God's message to the enemies of Israel.

But we mustn't overlook the importance of Jonah. He is the only
minor prophet mentioned by Jesus and is the only prophet to whom
Jesus compares himself (Matthew 12:29–41). The "sign of Jonah"—
resurrection—is the Messiah's final sign to the people of Israel and
its importance to God's plan of redemption cannot be overstated (a
full lesson is devoted to this one topic in volume 2). The sign of Jonah

will occur three times: the resurrection of Lazarus, the resurrection of Christ himself, and the resurrection of the two witnesses in Revelation 11—one of the last signs given to Israel prior to Christ's return as Lord of Lords and King of Kings.

In our next lesson, we will briefly look at the minor prophets who address the Southern Kingdom (Judah). Their voices are clear—but go unheeded.

God does not turn His back on His people. He brings forth His prophets to tell His people of His expectations and what they will experience when they turn their backs on Him and violate the covenant.

But the people do not listen. And they do turn their backs on God.

From lesson 26: What do we learn about God?

- God speaks through prophets and prophetesses.
- God points out the sins of the people and warns them of impending punishment.
- God's desire is that we seek Him.
- God will always protect a remnant and provide restoration.

Five times: Amos 4:6, 8, 9, 10, 11.

minor prophets: These include Hosea, Joel, Amos, Obadiah, Jonah, Micah, Nahum, Habakkuk, Zephaniah, Haggai, Zechariah, and Malachi. In the Hebrew Bible, this section is known as the "Book of the Twelve."

major prophets: Five books are considered to fall within those of the "major prophets": Isaiah, Jeremiah, Lamentations, Ezekiel, and Daniel.

repeated phrase: Amos 5:4, 6, 18.

27

Prophets addressing the Southern Kingdom

From our earlier lessons, we know the Assyrians attack and eventually conquer the Northern Kingdom. They then orchestrate a series of attacks on the Southern Kingdom. However, Jerusalem does not fall until it faces Nebuchadnezzar and the Babylonians—events that do not happen until a century later. While Amos and Hosea spoke to the peoples of the Northern Kingdom, and the prophet Jonah eventually takes God's words of warning to the Assyrians, a number of prophets address the Southern Kingdom (Judah).

The prophet Micah speaks God's voice during the reigns of three of Judah's kings: Jotham, Ahaz, and Hezekiah. Idolatry and corruption persist, and Micah foresees the destruction of Samaria, the capital of the north, and Jerusalem, the capital of Judah. This occurs not because God has turned His back on His people. These are orchestrated by God's sovereign will as divine acts of punishment. The words of God through Micah are similar to those spoken through Amos and Hosea:

Woe to those who devise iniquity
   and plot evil. (Micah 2:1)

I am planning against this nation a disaster
   from which you cannot free your necks.
Then you will not walk so proudly,
   for it will be a time of calamity (Micah 2:3)

I will make Samaria a heap of rubble. (Micah 1:6)

All her carved images will be smashed to pieces.
(Micah 1:7)

Zion will be plowed like a field,
Jerusalem will become a heap of rubble,
   and the temple mount a wooded ridge. (Micah 3:12)

These are God's words of judgment on Judah and Israel. And just like we saw with Amos and Hosea, God also declares His desires for His people:

He has shown you, O mankind, what is good.
   And what does the LORD require of you
but to act justly, to love mercy,
   and to walk humbly with your God? (Micah 6:8)

And, also like we saw with Amos and Hosea, God promises restoration:

"On that day," declares the LORD,
   "I will gather the lame;
I will assemble the outcast,
   even those whom I have afflicted.
And I will make the lame into a remnant,
   and the outcast into a strong nation." (Micah 4:6, 7)

In our previous lesson, we mentioned that the prophetic visions will sometimes extend beyond the glimpse of the eventual defeat of the Assyrians and the Babylonians. The prophetic word will look further out into the future. We see this with Micah:

> But you, Bethlehem Ephrathah,
>   who are small among the clans of Judah,
> out of you will come forth for Me
>   One to be ruler over Israel,
> whose origins are of old,
>   from the days of eternity. (Micah 5:2)

God's promises include a future ruler over Israel "whose origins are of old, from the days of eternity." This is a prophecy concerning God's Anointed, the Messiah, who will truly bring redemption to God's people. He will one day reign upon this earth—reflecting God's faithfulness to His covenant with King David. And through God's Messiah, all the peoples of the earth will be blessed—reflecting God's faithfulness to His covenant with Abraham.

And here, the prophet Micah provides another clue concerning the Messiah (the Son of God, King, Son of David, Greater Prophet, and Genesis 3:15 seed of woman). He will come from the small town of Bethlehem.

The prophet Nahum follows Micah and speaks God's word during the time of King Hezekiah. Here, though, the focus is on the Assyrians and their capital, Nineveh. Nathan's message: God rules over *all* the kingdoms of the earth. Even though God uses the Assyrians in His judgment against Israel and Judah, because of her pride, Assyria will not escape God's wrath.

> This is the burden against Nineveh, the book of the vision of Nahum the Elkoshite:

The LORD is a jealous and avenging God;
   the LORD is avenging and full of wrath.
The LORD takes vengeance on His foes
   and reserves wrath for His enemies.
(Nahum 1:1, 2)

The LORD has issued a command concerning you,
O Nineveh:

"There will be no descendants
   to carry on your name.
I will cut off the carved image and cast idol
   from the house of your gods;
I will prepare your grave,
   for you are contemptible." (Nahum 1:14)

God reminds the people of Judah that the Assyrians will ultimately be judged. And these words of eventual destruction promised for Nineveh alternate with His words of encouragement to Judah. Nahum reminds the people:

The LORD is good,
   a stronghold in the day of distress;
   He cares for those who trust in Him. (Nahum 1:7)

Nahum's prophecies are realized historically when Babylonia conquers the Assyrians and Nineveh is destroyed. We might add, today there is no Nineveh, no Assyria, no Babylon, no Babylonia—but there is an Israel!

During the time period of the transition between the rule of the Assyrians and the rule of the Babylonians, God brings forth the prophet Habakkuk. If we envision all that Judah and Israel have gone through, we can understand Habakkuk's pleas to God:

How long, O LORD, must I call for help
    but You do not hear,
or cry out to You, "Violence!"
    but You do not save?
Why do You make me see iniquity?
    Why do You tolerate wrongdoing?
Destruction and violence are before me.
    Strife is ongoing, and conflict abounds.
Therefore the law is paralyzed,
    and justice never goes forth.
For the wicked hem in the righteous,
    so that justice is perverted. (Habakkuk 1:2–4)

Habakkuk sees the destruction of God's chosen people by the pagan Assyrians. Where is God's justice? Why does God allow the wicked to defeat the "righteous"?

God responds to Habakkuk by announcing that the Babylonians (Chaldeans) will be His instrument against the Assyrians, but the story won't end here. The Babylonians, themselves, will also suffer His wrath.

With this assurance of God's justice, Habakkuk ends by praising God and His righteousness,

I will exult in the LORD;
    I will rejoice in the God of my salvation!
GOD the Lord is my strength. (Habakkuk 3:18, 19)

There are two passages in Habakkuk that we should not skip over. The first addresses the absolute foolishness of idolatry:

What use is an idol,
    that a craftsman should carve it—
or an image,

a teacher of lies?
For its maker trusts in his own creation;
    he makes idols that cannot speak.
Woe to him who says to wood, 'Awake!'
    or to silent stone, 'Arise!'
    Can it give guidance?
Behold, it is overlaid with gold and silver,
    yet there is no breath in it at all. (Habakkuk 2:18, 19)

Lifeless idols can do nothing. Habakkuk ends this portion of his oracle simply stating a foundational truth:

But the LORD is in His holy temple;
    let all the earth be silent before Him. (Habakkuk 2:20)

While idols have no use, no voice, no value—God *is* present. All are to show reverence to our Creator God. We hear echoes of Psalm 2.

The second important passage to review is because of its significance in changing the history of the entire world—recognizing, of course, that all of scripture has changed the world.

The passage is Habakkuk 2:4, cited in Romans 1:17, Galatians 3:11, and Hebrews 10:38:

The righteous will live by faith. (Habakkuk 2:4)

This verse was foundational to the "protesters" who wanted to reform the church: Roman Catholicism (that is, it was foundational to the Protestant Reformation). A key principle of the Reformation is *"sola fide"*— a Latin term that means "faith alone."

Martin Luther and the other reformers recognized that we become righteous in the eyes of God not because of anything we do. As Paul writes in his letter to the Philippians:

> Not having my own righteousness from the law, but
> that which is through faith in Christ, the righteousness
> from God on the basis of faith. (Philippians 3:9)

Note what Paul is saying, and what the reformers recognized. Our righteousness is not something we can achieve. It is not a righteousness that we get by obeying the law. Instead, it is a righteousness we *receive from God*. Our righteousness—our right standing before God—comes from Christ's righteousness **imputed** to the Christian. This happens not because of anything we do, but because of what Christ has done—the blood of Christ. We are judged righteous in the sight of God purely on the basis of what Christ has done. We place our faith in this. "The righteous will live by faith."

As we continue our discussion of the prophets, we now come to the prophet Joel. We said we would discuss the prophets chronologically—but the time period when Joel wrote is difficult to ascertain. His writing does not refer to the reign of any particular king, and scholars have varying opinions as to when this text was written.

Joel describes Judah as a land being overrun by a swarm of locusts—devouring everything in sight. Through Joel, God calls upon the people to repent.

> "Yet even now,"
> > declares the LORD,
> "return to Me with all your heart,
> > with fasting, weeping, and mourning." (Joel 2:12)

Joel tells the people:

> So rend your hearts and not your garments,
> > and return to the LORD your God.
> For He is gracious and compassionate,

slow to anger, abounding in loving devotion.
And He relents from sending disaster. (Joel 2:13)

As we have seen with God's messages through the other prophets, Joel's prophecy also contains words of hope and encouragement, and of restoration and renewal:

"Behold, I will send you
grain, new wine, and oil,
and by them you will be satisfied.
I will never again make you
a reproach among the nations.
The northern army I will drive away from you,
banishing it to a barren and desolate land." (Joel 2:19, 20)

We also see a Messianic reference. God promises a time when He will pour our His Spirit (Joel 2:28, 29). It is a time when,

Everyone who calls
on the name of the LORD will be saved;
for on Mount Zion and in Jerusalem
there will be deliverance, as the LORD has promised,
among the remnant called by the LORD. (Joel 2:32)

The beginning fulfillment of these words came as Christ proclaims a new covenant at the Last Supper (as we've discussed), and as he promises his followers that he will send the Comforter—the Holy Spirit (John 14:15–26; John 16:5–16). Christ's blood initiates this new covenant as God's Spirit indwells His people (Acts 2:14–36). Again, though, a full discussion of the New Covenant must await volume 2.

The remaining two prophets (minor prophets) prior to the people's return from exile are Zephaniah and Obadiah. Zephaniah lived during the time of King Josiah and his reforms. He is connected to the other great reformer of Judah that proceeded Josiah—King Hezekiah. The opening verses of Zephaniah tell us that he is the great-great-grandson of Hezekiah.

Again, we see words similar to God's words through the other prophets:

> "I will stretch out My hand against Judah
>   and against all who dwell in Jerusalem.
> I will cut off from this place
>   every remnant of Baal,
> the names of the idolatrous
>   and pagan priests—
> those who bow on the rooftops
>   to worship the host of heaven,
> those who bow down and swear by the LORD
>   but also swear by Milcom,
> and those who turn back
>   from following the LORD
> and neither seek the LORD
>   nor inquire of Him." (Zephaniah 1:4–6)

Zephaniah describes *the day of the Lord* that is coming against Judah and Jerusalem (this term and references to "day" occur almost two-dozen times in this short book of prophecy). Like the other prophets, he calls for national repentance. He foresees destruction against the Philistines, the Moabites, the Ethiopians (Cushites), the Assyrians—and also Jerusalem itself.

And again, God's word announces hope for His people and a time of future restoration:

> Sing for joy, O Daughter of Zion;
>   shout aloud, O Israel!
> Be glad and rejoice with all your heart,

O Daughter of Jerusalem!
The LORD has taken away your punishment;
    He has turned back your enemy.
Israel's King, the LORD, is among you;
    no longer will you fear any harm.

The LORD your God is among you;
    He is mighty to save.
He will rejoice over you with gladness;
    He will quiet you with His love;
He will rejoice over you with singing. (Zephaniah 3:14,
15, 17)

We also have the short prophecy of Obadiah, an oracle against Edom, the peoples to the east of Judah:

Because of the violence against your brother Jacob,
    you will be covered with shame
    and cut off forever. (Obadiah 1:10)

And again, we see God's promise of deliverance:

But on Mount Zion there will be deliverance,
    and it will be holy,
and the house of Jacob
    will reclaim their possession. (Obadiah 1:17)

This completes a brief review of the prophets found in the Minor Prophets section of the Bible—men who spoke God's word prior to the return of God's people from exile.

We now return to the historical books, looking at those that are post-exilic (after the exile). This will be followed by a discussion of the post-exilic minor prophets and then discussions covering the major prophets.

From lesson 27: What do we learn about God?

This lesson continues a discussion of prophets sent by God to bring His word to the people. As such, what we learn parallels that of lesson 26:

- God speaks through prophets and prophetesses.
- God points out the sins of the people and warns them of impending punishment.
- God's desire is that we seek Him.
- God will always protect a remnant and provide restoration.

---

imputed: While our sins are given over, that is, imputed to Christ, Christ's righteousness is imputed to the Christian. This is an important concept and is discussed in detail in lesson 23 in the book *A Forty-Day Study on Sin, Salvation, and Sanctification: Our Journey in Christ.*

faith: We find the word "faith" 232 times in the New Testament (KJV). However, it is only found twice in all of the Old Testament—here in Habakkuk 2:4 and also in Deuteronomy 32:20 (in Deuteronomy the Hebrew word implies "no faith"—so English translations uses the word "unfaithfulness").

Why is "faith" absent from the Old Testament?

If you are asking this question, you might have missed something along the way. Remember? Noah building a boat (faith), Joshua blowing horns (faith), Gideon whittling down the size of this army (faith), and so forth. We see evidences of faith throughout the Old Testament. Read the eleventh chapter of Hebrews for a good summary showing faith among those written about in the Old Testament.

For a more complete discussion on faith, see lesson 33 in *A Forty-Day Study of the Book of Hebrews: The Superiority of Christ.*

28

Post-exilic Historical Books: Ezra, Nehemiah, and Esther

Before his death, Moses tells the people of God:

> See, I have set before you today life and goodness, as well as death and disaster. For I am commanding you today to love the LORD your God, to walk in His ways, and to keep His commandments, statutes, and ordinances, so that you may live and increase, and the LORD your God may bless you in the land that you are entering to possess.
>
> But if your heart turns away and you do not listen, but are drawn away to bow down to other gods and worship them, I declare to you today that you will surely perish; you shall not prolong your days in the land that you are crossing the Jordan to possess. (Deuteronomy 30:15–18)

In our review of the history of God's people, we see that their hearts did turn away. They did not follow the Mosaic Law—the commandments and instructions from God. They did not listen to the repeated warnings of Moses and warnings through the prophets that came after Moses. God's covenant people—called out by God, blessed by God, protected by God—introduce syncretism into the land. They bow down to Molech and Baal and other pagan gods. And as we saw, this false, idolatrous worship includes child sacrifice, which even some of the kings take part in.

All of this is a tragedy and paints an unflattering picture of the Israelites. But it is not adversaries of the Jewish people that are telling us these things and revealing the on-going, persistent flaws and failures of these people. We learn about this from their writings—the Hebrew Scriptures (the Christian Old Testament). These are the writings of Jewish men called by God.

These writings repeatedly describe the sins of the people and their idolatry. And they show how the ultimate curse associated with the covenant is eventually realized as the covenant people of God experience the wrath of God.

Zion and the walls protecting Jerusalem became mounds of broken rock, dirt, and dust. Pagan armies successfully put many of God's people to the sword, spear, or arrow. Some are burned alive. Others are starved to death or die by plague. Many who escape death are removed from the land—those of the north are taken by the Assyrians, those in the south are taken by the Babylonians. Others escape to Egypt and parts unknown.

What happened to the promised seed of woman that we have talked about?

Or the Psalm 2 Messiah, Son of God and King?

What about the promised Prophet who would be greater than Moses? The one we are supposed to listen to?

Solomon had built the magnificent temple for the God of the Israelites. It no longer exists. This is supposed to be God's dwelling place. Where is God?

What about the Abrahamic covenant? God promised to make these people into a great nation. But now there is no nation. It is gone. Zion is desolate and in ruins.

Of course, on this side of the cross we know how the story continues. But let's pause and put ourselves into the sandals of the Jews who have witnessed the deaths of their friends and families, the destruction of their temple, and their exile from the land. Their world has collapsed. Where *is* their God?

Where is *our* God?

Of course, God never leaves His people. Nor does He ever discontinue His messages of hope and His provisions for an eventual future of promise. Even a half-millennium before the destruction of Israel and Judah, God's servant Moses proclaimed God's eventual restoration of His disobedient people:

> When all these things come upon you—the blessings and curses I have set before you—and you call them to mind in all the nations to which the LORD your God has banished you, and when you and your children return to the LORD your God and obey His voice with all your heart and all your soul according to everything I am giving you today, then He will restore you from captivity and have compassion on you and gather you from all the nations to which the LORD your God has scattered you. Even if you have been banished to the farthest horizon, He will gather you and return you from there. (Deuteronomy 30:1–4)

God promises restoration. And He repeats this time and again through His prophets—as we reviewed previously.

And through the prophet Isaiah, God's word goes a step further. God not only assures restoration and renewal—He provides the name of the specific individual He will use to orchestrate the return of the exiles to Judah:

> I will raise up Cyrus in righteousness,
>   and I will make all his ways straight.
> He will rebuild My city
>   and set My exiles free. (Isaiah 45:13)

We need to put this amazing prophecy into perspective. Isaiah lived around 740 BC. Cyrus wasn't born until 140 years later. And yet, we find his name and his role in God's story within the pages written by Isaiah.

And, as we saw earlier, God had revealed the exact duration of the exile—seventy years—through His prophet Jeremiah. We can now look at Jeremiah's verse that's on the coffee mug:

> For I know the plans I have for you, declares the LORD, plans to prosper you and not to harm you, to give you a future and a hope. (Jeremiah 29:11)

God describes this future, as these verses continue:

> "Then you will call upon Me and come and pray to Me, and I will listen to you. You will seek Me and find Me when you search for Me with all your heart. I will be found by you, declares the LORD, and I will restore you from captivity and gather you from all the nations and places to which I have banished you, declares the LORD. I will restore you to the place from which I sent you into exile." (Jeremiah 29:12–14)

God is faithful to His people. And these words are coming true as Cyrus allows the remnant to leave Babylon and return to the land.

Now when we see "Jer. 29:11" on sweatshirts and the baseball cap, we can put this into context. God *is* faithful. He *will* and *did* restore His people—returning them to the land of the covenant promise. The Abrahamic covenant *is* alive and well. And soon—soon the seed of woman—the Psalm 2 Messiah, King, and Son of God—*will* appear.

But let's not get ahead of ourselves.

The people's return from exile and the post-exilic events are detailed in three books of the Bible: Ezra, Nehemiah, and Esther. Even though Ezra and Nehemiah make up two separate books in the Christian Bible, in the Hebrew Scriptures they are a single book—a unified work. Accordingly, we will discuss Ezra-Nehemiah as a unit.

Ezra and Nehemiah, the individuals for which the books are named, are two Jews that return to Judah from **Babylonia**. The dates of their returns can get a bit confusing in that there were separate waves of returning exiles. The first group of Israelites returned in **538 BC** under the decree from the Persian King Cyrus in fulfilment of Isaiah's prophecy. Ezra did not return until 458 BC. Nehemiah did not arrive to Jerusalem until 14 years after that—although he and Ezra were contemporaries.

The book of Esther is also post-exilic and describes a community of Jews staying in Persia. Although they were free to return to their homeland, Judah and Jerusalem had been completely destroyed and many of the Jewish people saw nothing desirous about returning to a war-torn land. Esther's story covers the period between 483 BC and 473 BC and takes place in Persia.

These three writings conclude the section of the Bible known as the **historical books** of the Old Testament.

As to this period in history, the Assyrians have been defeated by Babylon. And Babylon, in turn, has been defeated by the Persians. The king of Persia, Cyrus, removes from his treasury the items taken from the Jerusalem temple by Nebuchadnezzar and presents these to the Israelites (Ezra 1:9, 10). He then allows the Israelites living in Babylonia to return to Judah to rebuild their temple.

Why would a Persian King do such a thing? Why should he care about this small band of people?

The actions of Cyrus are in obedience to God:

> This is what Cyrus king of Persia says:
>
> 'The LORD, the God of heaven, who has given me all the kingdoms of the earth, has appointed me to build a house for Him at Jerusalem in Judah.' (Ezra 1:2)

An Israelite named Zerubbabel, a descendant of David, is in the first wave of those returning and is appointed governor over Judah. Under his leadership, and the authority given to him by King Cyrus, the foundations of the temple are laid, and reconstruction of the temple begins. An individual accompanying Zerubbabel from Persia is an Israelite named Joshua, who functions as priest.

But all is not well. There are Assyrians who have remained in the land—as well as Samaritans. These are the Jews who had intermarried with the Assyrians. **They want to take part** in rebuilding the temple, but Zerubbabel does not allow this. This leads to continual friction and opposition to the work being done by the returned exiles. Ultimately, Persia withdraws its support for the project, and for seventeen years the temple sits unfinished (Ezra 4:21–24).

In our next lesson, we will learn about the post-exilic prophets. But here, it is beneficial to mention that two of them, Haggai and Zechariah, are sent by God to provide encouragement to Zerubbabel and the Israelites (Ezra 5:1, 2). Their words from God lead to resumption in construction and the temple is completed **four years later** (Ezra 6:16).

About sixty years after this, a second important individual returns from exile: Ezra. Ezra is knowledgeable in the Mosaic Law (Torah) and is anxious to bring and teach God's word to the people. We saw how the pagan king Cyrus sent Zerubbabel to Jerusalem with the gold and silver taken from the temple by Nebuchadnezzar. The then-present king of Persia, Artaxerxes, blesses Ezra similarly. He tells Ezra,

> You are to take with you the silver and gold that the king and his counselors have freely offered to the God of Israel, whose dwelling is in Jerusalem, together with all the silver and gold you may find in all the province of Babylon, as well as the freewill offerings of the people and priests to the house of their God in Jerusalem. (Ezra 7:15, 16)

> I, King Artaxerxes, decree to all the treasurers west of the Euphrates: Whatever Ezra the priest, the scribe of the Law of the God of heaven, may require of you, it must be provided promptly, up to a hundred talents of silver, a hundred cors of wheat, a hundred baths of wine, a hundred baths of olive oil, and salt without limit. Whatever is commanded by the God of heaven must be done diligently for His house. (Ezra 7:21–23)

God is orchestrating the plans He has for His people—plans to prosper them and give them a future and a hope, as Jeremiah prophesied and as the phrase on the coffee cup proclaims.

But we continue to see problems in the land. With Zerubbabel, it was associated with the non-Jews in the land and the friction and mistrust created around the rebuilding of the temple. With Ezra, a different, though related problem is prominent. Returning exiles had intermarried with non-Jews and neighboring peoples—a violation of the Mosaic Law (Deuteronomy 7:3). Ezra's solution: the marriages are to be annulled and the women and children are to be sent away.

Why couldn't non-Jews help in building a temple to God? And why couldn't those returning into the land marry those outside Judaism?

The actions of Zerubbabel and Ezra should be put into perspective. When God brought His chosen people to the Promised Land (about seven hundred years prior to the events described in the book of Ezra), He was forming a holy (set apart) people. They were not to worship pagan gods, and they were to refrain from intermarriage with non-Jews, who would corrupt Israel and ultimately lead the people into idolatry and the adding of pagan gods to their worship (syncretism). As we saw, this idolatry continually happens—not just with the people, but also with the priests and the kings.

Throughout this period, intermarriage was not uncommon. Solomon married foreign wives, as did other kings, such as King Ahab who married the Phoenician Jezebel (lesson 22). But the Bible clearly teaches how these wives are corrupt and lead their husbands away from the covenant. Separate from these kings, many people in the Northern Kingdom intermarried with Assyrians.

And this trend continues among the returning exiles. This brings considerable distress to Ezra, who confesses to God:

> "O my God, I am ashamed and embarrassed to lift up my face to You, my God, because our iniquities are higher than our heads, and our guilt has reached the heavens. From the days of our fathers to this day, our guilt has been great. Because of our iniquities, we and our kings and our priests have been delivered

into the hands of the kings of the earth and put to the sword and captivity, to pillage and humiliation, as we are this day.

But now, for a brief moment, grace has come from the LORD our God to preserve for us a remnant and to give us a stake in His holy place. Even in our bondage, our God has given us new life and light to our eyes. Though we are slaves, our God has not forsaken us in our bondage, but He has extended to us grace in the sight of the kings of Persia, giving us new life to rebuild the house of our God and repair its ruins, and giving us a wall of protection in Judah and Jerusalem." (Ezra 9:6–9)

The fear is justified. The sinful practices—their failure to obey the Mosaic Law and remain faithful to God's covenant—led to God's wrath. No one wanted to undergo a repeat of God's punishment. Ezra and Zerubbabel (and others—such as the Pharisees at the time of Christ) were adamant that the people turn back toward God and live according to His commands, decrees, and laws.

There's more to add, which comes to us from the book of Nehemiah. Nehemiah was cupbearer to King Artaxerxes. When he learns about the condition of Jerusalem, he asks the Persian king for permission to return to his homeland and rebuild the city, including its walls. He is given approval to do this by way of a decree, signed by Artaxerxes on March 14, 445 BC (we'll get to the importance of this date later in our lessons). Again, we see favor toward the Jews from a pagan king, as Nehemiah travels under the king's authority and is provided army officers and men to accompany him on his journey to Jerusalem.

Nehemiah becomes governor of Judah—and under his leadership the walls around Jerusalem are rebuilt.

But again, there is opposition. Three regional governors representing groups of people originally driven from the land (including the Ammonites and the Samaritans) do not want the walls of Jerusalem to be rebuilt. Nehemiah is forced to divide the Israelites into two groups, with one group armed and protecting the rebuilding process from this opposition, while the other does the reconstruction work on the wall.

Upon the completion of this work, there is a joyous celebration. Ezra reads the words of Moses. The people confess their sins, renew their commitment to God, and worship the God of their salvation. In renewing the covenant, the people agree to:

> ... commit themselves with a sworn oath to follow the Law of God given through His servant Moses and to carefully obey all the commandments, ordinances, and statutes of the LORD our Lord. (Nehemiah 10:29)

They also proclaim:

> We will not neglect the house of our God. (Nehemiah 10:39b)

But as we saw with Zerubbabel and with Ezra, all is not right in the land.

Nehemiah leaves Jerusalem, briefly spending time back in Persia. When he returns, he finds the people are once again violating God's commands. Tithing to support the temple has ceased and the temple itself is being defiled.

In addition, work is being done on the Sabbath. Intermarriage is also occurring throughout the land. In the words of Nehemiah:

> In those days I also saw Jews who had married women from Ashdod, Ammon, and Moab. Half of

their children spoke the language of Ashdod or of the other peoples but could not speak the language of Judah. I rebuked them and called down curses on them. I beat some of these men and pulled out their hair. (Nehemiah 13:23–25)

Despite all that the people had gone through, they are back where they started. Perhaps a suitable question to ask is, "Will God's chosen people ever learn to obey Him?"

The answer is "no."

If this question and answer sound familiar, we asked this same question in lesson 21—referring to the period long before the invasions and the exile. Despite all that the people had experienced nothing has changed.

The people need righteousness. And though they repeatedly renew their oath to God and the Mosaic Covenant—they continually fail. They need some form of new covenant—a covenant where God's laws are written on their hearts, not on stone tablets. They need a Savior. They need the presence of God's Spirit within them. But, once again, we are getting ahead of ourselves.

We'll conclude this lesson with comments on the last of the historical books of the Protestant Bible: Esther. Many Jews remain in the lands of their captors, and the book of Esther describes one such community. These are Jews living in Susa, the capital of Persia. The book occurs during the first half of the reign of King Xerxes—the father of Artaxerxes.

It is the story of a Jewish woman, Esther, and her uncle Mordechai. Esther is an orphan and is raised by her uncle (Ezra 2:7). In an interesting turn of events, the king **marries Esther**, but, in another turn of events, **Haman**, the king's second-in-command and an adversary to the Jewish people, creates a plot designed to lead to the extermination of all Jews who have remained in the land (this has been repeated, historically, as seen in the last century and the holocaust).

A day is determined for the implementation of Hamon's plot to extinguish the Jews. When this is to occur is established by the casting of lots (Esther 3:7–9). A lot that is cast is called a *"pur"* in Hebrew, or *"purim"* for its plural ("lots").

Haman's scheme is thwarted through the bravery of Esther, and the Jewish people are delivered from Haman's plot. This deliverance is celebrated through the Jewish feast of Purim, named after the lots that were cast (Esther 9:18–28). This is still celebrated today in commemoration of what Esther had done to save her people.

Esther is the only book in the Bible where God is not mentioned. It is interesting that it is also the only book of the Old Testament where fragments were not found as part of the Dead Sea Scrolls.

But we see the hand of God throughout this book. By this point in history, we have seen how God delivers His people, whether bringing them out of Egyptian bondage and into the land of promise, or bringing the exiles back into the land after the Babylonian captivity. In the story of Esther, we see how God protects even those living outside the land.

But we learn even more. Esther is an individual of great faith. She confronts the king and risks her life to save her people. She is the heroine of the story.

But perhaps her uncle, Mordechai, shows even greater faith. Initially, Esther hesitates to confront the king on behalf of the Jewish people, and Mordechai tells her,

"If you remain silent at this time, relief and deliverance for the Jews will arise from another place, but you and your father's house will perish. And who knows if perhaps you have come to the kingdom for such a time as this?" (Esther 4:14)

Mordechai believes God has placed Esther where she is, precisely in order to do God's work in the salvation of His people. But more importantly, Mordechai tells her that if she does not do God's work, "relief and deliverance for the Jews will arise from another place."

Mordechai is so sure of God's faithfulness, that even if Esther fails, he knows God will provide another deliverer.

Yes, the word "faith" only occurs twice in the Old Testament—but we see displays of faith continually through people like Esther and Mordechai.

Every time I read stories like this, I am reminded of the words of Jesus:

"When the Son of Man comes, will He find faith on earth?" (Luke 18:8)

From lesson 28: What do we learn about God?

- God works providentially by all means—including working through pagan rulers to bring about His greater purposes.
- Though the people doing God's work face obstacles, opposition, hostility, and even threats of annihilation, God never leaves them.

Babylonia: Babylonia is the name of the region; Babylon is the name of its major city. The ruins of Babylon are in present-day Iraq. Often "Babylon" is used to represent the entire area under rule, just like the term "Rome" can be used to designate the Roman empire.

538 BC: Ezra arrived in Jerusalem in the seventh year of king Artaxerxes (Ezra 7:8), while Nehemiah arrived in Artaxerxes' twentieth year (Nehemiah 2:1–9). If this was Artaxerxes I (465–424 BC), then Ezra arrived in 458 BC and Nehemiah in 445 BC.

historical books: The book of Esther closes out the historical books in the Protestant Old Testament. The Bible used by the Catholic Church includes additional books: Tobit, Judith, Wisdom (also called Wisdom of Solomon), Sirach (also called Ecclesiasticus), Baruch, and 1st and 2nd Maccabees. The Catholic Church also contains expanded versions of the books of Daniel and Esther. It is important to note, while the Jews found these writings to be highly regarded, they never considered them to be the inspired word of God. To provide an analogy, these might be considered, in today's parlance, something written by Dietrich Bonhoeffer or C. S. Lewis. They were widely read and held in high esteem—but they were never considered scripture.

The Catholic New Testament consists of the same writings as that used by Protestants.

They want to take part: Zerubbabel's decision not to allow the adversaries to take part in the rebuilding of the temple seems harsh. Note the text:

> They approached Zerubbabel and the heads of the families, saying, "Let us build with you because, like you, we seek your God and have been sacrificing to Him since the time of King Esar-haddon of Assyria, who brought us here." (Ezra 4:2)

This suggests these are converts to Judaism. However, note what we learn in 2nd Kings in describing these people:

> They worshiped the LORD, but they also served their own gods according to the customs of the nations from which they had been carried away . . . they persisted in their former customs. So these nations worshiped the LORD but also served their idols, and to this day their children and grandchildren continue to do as their fathers did. (2nd Kings 17:33, 41)

four years later: After the completion of the temple, and the resulting celebration by the people (Ezra 6), Zerubbabel's name is not mentioned. For this reason, this temple is referred to as the "second temple" and not "Zerubbabel's temple" (contrasting it with the first temple—recognized as "Solomon's temple"). Centuries later, King Herod will expand the temple mount and the temple itself. And in 70 AD, this temple is destroyed, fulfilling Jesus' prophecy.

marries Esther: This is not a love story. When the king decided he no longer wanted his wife, Queen Vashti, he decrees that young women be captured and brought to the palace as his harem. Esther was a part of this edict (Esther 2:8).

Haman: Haman was a descendant of Agag, king of the Amalekites, who were ancient enemies of God's people (Esther 3:1; 1st Samuel 15:8).

29

Post-exilic Prophets – Haggai

If we assume the prophet Joel wrote before the exile (as stated earlier, it is uncertain when Joel lived and prophesied), there are just three post-exilic prophets found within the writings of the Minor Prophets section of the Bible:

- Haggai, prophesying around 520 BC.
- Zechariah, a contemporary of Haggai, though much younger in age.
- Malachi, prophesying much later—around 400 BC.

To put this into perspective, the first wave of exiles returned to Judah under Zerubbabel around 538 BC.

As we noted earlier, Haggai and Zechariah are mentioned in the book of Ezra:

> Later, the prophets Haggai and Zechariah son of Iddo prophesied to the Jews in Judah and Jerusalem in the name of the God of Israel, who was over them. Then Zerubbabel son of Shealtiel and Jeshua son of Jozadak rose up and began to rebuild the house of God in

Jerusalem. And the prophets of God were with them, helping them. (Ezra 5:1, 2)

If you will recall, the rebuilding of the temple is halted due to opposition from those surrounding Jerusalem, and the Persian king also withdraws his support for the project. God sends Haggai to the people to encourage them:

> Haggai, the messenger of the LORD, delivered the message of the LORD to the people:
>
> > "I am with you,"
> >   declares the LORD". (Haggai 1:13)

Heartened by the voice of God, construction is resumed, and the temple is completed four years later.

But the reconstructed temple is nowhere near the magnificence of the temple that Solomon built. Haggai recognizes this and asks the people:

> 'Who is left among you who saw this house in its former glory? How does it look to you now? Does it not appear to you like nothing in comparison?' (Haggai 2:3)

But God's word through Haggai promises a future glory for this temple:

> My Spirit remains among you;
>   do not be afraid.
>
> I will fill this house with glory,
>   says the LORD of Hosts.
>
> The latter glory of this house
>   will be greater than the former,

says the LORD of Hosts.
And in this place I will provide peace,
declares the LORD of Hosts. (Haggai 2:5b, 7b, 9)

The second temple will one day have a magnificence that will outshine the glory of Solomon's temple.

Has this occurred?

We know the temple was destroyed in 70 AD. When, if ever, did this temple radiate God's glory?

To answer this, we need a bit of background. One word that relates to God's visible glory is the Hebrew word *"Shekinah."* Though this word is not found in the Bible (Hebrew Scriptures), the Jewish rabbis refer to God's glory using this term. The word means "God's presence" or "God's manifested glory." The Shekinah appears as the Israelites left Egypt and throughout the wilderness journey.

> And the LORD went before them in a pillar of cloud to guide their way by day, and in a pillar of fire to give them light by night, so that they could travel by day or night. Neither the pillar of cloud by day nor the pillar of fire by night left its place before the people. (Exodus 13:21, 22)

As briefly mentioned in lesson 16, during this journey a tent to worship God, called the tabernacle, is constructed under God's instructions. And the Shekinah rested upon the tabernacle.

We also know that God's glory was present in Solomon's temple. At the dedication of the temple,

> When Solomon had finished praying, fire came down from heaven and consumed the burnt offering and the sacrifices, and the glory of the LORD filled the

temple. The priests were unable to enter the house of the LORD, because the glory of the LORD had filled it. (2nd Chronicles 2:1, 2)

As to additional background, God also commanded the Israelites to observe a number of feasts—or celebrations of remembrance (Leviticus 23). Three were given special importance. All able-bodied males living in the land were to journey to Jerusalem for their observance, hence the three are referred to as the "pilgrim" feasts.

The first of the pilgrim feasts is the Passover, which we've discussed. From the perspective of the Israelites, this commemorates release from Egyptian bondage. By placing the blood of a slain lamb on the doorposts of their dwellings, the angel of death passes over them. This event is God's final sign to Pharaoh to release the Israelites. For Christians, Christ's Last Supper occurs during the Passover, followed by his crucifixion. Jesus is the Passover Lamb that protects God's people from His wrath—the Lamb of God that takes away the sins of the world.

The second feast of special importance is **Pentecost**, or the feast of Weeks. In Hebrew, it is also known as Shavuot, the word meaning "weeks." For the Jew, it marks the wheat harvest in Israel and also commemorates the anniversary of the day when God gave the Torah to the nation of Israel at Mt. Sinai. From the Christian perspective, Pentecost relates to the giving of the Holy Spirit and the "harvest" associated with God bringing believers into His family.

The third pilgrim feast is the feast of Tabernacles, or Sukkot. It is also known as the Festival of Ingathering or the Festival of Shelters. We will discuss the remaining Jewish feasts later.

For now, let's return to this word "Shekinah" and see how it connects to this third pilgrim feast, the feast of Tabernacles and fulfilment of Haggai's prophecy.

As mentioned above, at the dedication of Solomon's temple, the Shekinah appears. This occurs during the feast of Tabernacles.

> And when the priests came out of the Holy Place, the cloud filled the house of the LORD so that the priests could not stand there to minister because of the cloud; for the glory of the LORD filled the house of the LORD. (1st Kings 8:10, 11)

> Fire came down from heaven and consumed the burnt offering and the sacrifices, and the glory of the LORD filled the temple. The priests were unable to enter the house of the LORD, because the glory of the LORD had filled it.

> When all the Israelites saw the fire coming down and the glory of the LORD above the temple, they bowed down on the pavement with their faces to the ground, and they worshiped and gave thanks to the LORD. (2nd Chronicles 7:1–3)

It was also at the feast of Tabernacles that the Israelites, who had returned to rebuild the temple, gather together to hear Ezra proclaim the Word of God (Nehemiah 8).

But note what has happened. The second temple has been rebuilt, *but there is no Shekinah*. This second temple fell far short of the magnificence of the temple Solomon built, as Haggai reminds the people. Solomon's temple housed the Ark of the Covenant and experienced God's glory—the light of God. But this was not the case with the second temple. This remained true even after King Herod added to the temple many years later.

But let's again note what God has proclaimed through Haggai:

The latter glory of this house
will be greater than the former,
says the LORD of Hosts. (Haggai 2:9)

When would God's glory fill the temple? The temple no longer exists, so when did this occur?

We can now make a number of connections.

During the feast of Tabernacles, there was a daily ceremony called the "illumination of the temple." Within the temple, in the section known as the Court of the Women, there were four very large, oil-fed **menorahs**— each seventy-five feet in height. During this celebration, and with much fanfare, these giant menorahs are lighted at night to remind the people of the pillar of fire that had guided Israel in their wilderness journey. The brightness of these lights illuminated all of Jerusalem.

It was during this celebration, the feast of Tabernacles, that Jesus journeys to Jerusalem and enters the temple. He stands before the people and proclaims,

"I am the light of the world. Whoever follows Me will never walk in the darkness but will have the light of life." (John 8:12)

It is the presence of Jesus that places God's glory into the temple—a glory much greater than anything witnessed in Solomon's temple. Jesus, the light of the world, has come to God's temple. Haggai's prophecy is fulfilled.

The words of God through Haggai also promised,

... in this place, I will provide peace. (Haggai 2:9)

Was this also fulfilled?

Yes.

Just outside the walls of Jerusalem, not far from where Jesus stood when he proclaimed that he is the light of the world, there is darkness. This is Golgotha—the place of the skull. Seven hundred years before this event, God's words through Isaiah foretold of what would happen there. In describing the Messiah as Suffering Servant, Isaiah writes:

> He was pierced for our transgressions,
>> He was crushed for our iniquities;
> the punishment that brought us peace was upon Him,
>> and by His stripes we are healed. (Isaiah 53:5)

Jesus' sacrifice on the cross is the "punishment that brought us peace." For those who have accepted what Jesus has done, we have been reconciled to God and have been granted God's peace. It is the blood of Christ, the one pierced for our transgressions and crushed for our iniquities, that brings us our peace. Paul writes,

> Therefore, since we have been justified through faith, we have peace with God through our Lord Jesus Christ. (Romans 5:1)

Haggai's prophecy comes true as Christ, the Light of the World, enters the temple.

Haggai's prophecy comes true as Christ, the sacrificial Lamb, brings peace to the believer through his death and resurrection.

There is another proclamation of God's glory that occurs when Jesus is at the temple during this feast of Tabernacles. In addition to the lighting of the giant menorahs and the illumination of the temple (and Jerusalem), the feast included a ceremony called the "rite of the water libation."

On the first morning of the feast, priests would form a procession and walk down the steep terrain to the pool of Siloam. There, golden containers are dipped into the water and are brought back to the temple.

As the procession returns to the temple, rams' horns are blown and words from the Psalms are recited. A priest then pours the contents out of two silver bowls: one holding water from the pool of Siloam, and the other containing wine. This is to remind the people of their dependence upon God, as they trust Him to pour out His blessings of rain upon the earth so that the earth will produce and provide for the people's sustenance.

The Gospel writer John tells us:

> On the last and greatest day of the feast, Jesus stood up and called out in a loud voice, "If anyone is thirsty, let him come to Me and drink. Whoever believes in Me, as the Scripture has said: 'Streams of living water will flow from within him.'" He was speaking about the Spirit, whom those who believed in Him were later to receive. (John 7:37–39)

Jesus, God incarnate, fills the temple with God's glory as he proclaims that he is the light of the world. And he tells the people of God, if they come to him, God's Spirit will be poured out upon them. This is one of the promises of the New Covenant that we have discussed numerous times before—the covenant we live under.

We said this feast was also known as the Festival of Ingathering or the Festival of Shelters. Jesus *is* the light of the world. He gathers those to him who are in darkness. Jesus *is* their shelter—our shelter—as we take refuge in him. We are reminded once again of Psalm 2: "Blessed are all who take refuge in Him" (Psalm 2:12).

Much more could be said here, but we'll save this for another **lesson series**.

With the second temple, the *only* time God's glory would be present is when Jesus stands within its walls and proclaims to those present, and to all of us, that *he* is the light of the world.

Before we leave this, I find it interesting that God commands the Israelite males to attend all three of the pilgrim feasts, including this feast of Tabernacles. Why is this important to God?

The Bible doesn't answer this—but from our side of the cross we know that **all three** directly relate to God's Messiah.

For those living during the time of Christ, being present in Jerusalem provided them the opportunity to witness Christ's proclamation in the temple (feast of Tabernacles). Being present at Passover (feast of Firstfruits) allowed them to witness his sacrifice and resurrection. Being present at the first Pentecost after the resurrection allowed them to hear the disciples preach, and for many, to receive the Holy Spirit as the Church Age begins.

The entire Bible is about Jesus.

From lesson 29: What do we learn about God?

- God's glory, the Shekinah, is present in the wilderness tabernacle and in Solomon's temple. But His glory does not appear in the second temple. This remains the case until the Light of the World—Jesus of Nazareth—appears in the temple.

Pentecost: The feast of weeks takes place exactly 50 days after the feast of Firstfruits, celebrating Passover. "Pentecost" means fifty.

lesson series: This will be covered in greater detail in *A Forty-Day Study of the Book of John: Who is Christ?* For additional information on the illumination of the temple during the feast of Tabernacles, see: https://www.jewishroots.net/library/holiday-articles/illumination-of-the-temple-ceremony.html (accessed November 18, 2019).

There is another nuance that I find interesting. The opening words of John's Gospel include:

> The true Light who gives light to every man was coming into the world. (John 1:9)

and

> The Word became flesh and made His dwelling among us. (John 1:14)

The word translated "dwelling" is also "tabernacle." Some believe Jesus might have been born on the day commemorating the feast of Tabernacles. We know Jesus was most probably not born on December 25th. This date was set by Roman Catholicism in the fourth century AD.

Another interesting nuance is that Jesus says, "*I* am the light of the world" (John 8:12). But Jesus also says, "*You* are the light of the world" (Matthew 5:14).

Which is it?

Both, of course. Jesus is the light of the world, but through the Holy Spirit we receive the light of Christ and are called to bring this light into the world of spiritual darkness.

menorahs: A menorah is a sacred lampstand with seven branches used in the temple (see Exodus 37:17–24). The large menorahs associated with the feast of Tabernacles were so enormous that their huge wicks were made from the garments used by the Levitical priests.

30

Post-exilic Prophets – Zechariah

Zechariah was a contemporary of Haggai, though much younger in age. His prophecy begins with words shared by other prophets: a call to repentance.

> "Return to Me," declares the LORD of Hosts. (Zechariah 1:3a)

As seen consistently when God speaks through His prophets, His words through Zechariah also include encouragement:

> "... and I will return to you," says the LORD of Hosts. (Zechariah 1:3b)

> Therefore, this is what the LORD says: "I will return to Jerusalem with mercy, and there My house will be rebuilt, declares the LORD of Hosts ... 'My cities will again overflow with prosperity; the LORD will again comfort Zion and choose Jerusalem." (Zechariah 1:16, 17)

> This is what the LORD says: "I will return to Zion and dwell in Jerusalem. Then Jerusalem will be called the

City of Truth, and the mountain of the LORD of Hosts
will be called the Holy Mountain." (Zechariah 8:3)

"Zechariah" means "God remembers" (Yahweh remembers)—an
appropriate name in that God's word through Zechariah shows that
He has remembered His people and that, despite the miserable state
of post-war Jerusalem and Judah, they are destined for a future glory.

As we saw with the prophet Haggai, Zechariah is also sent to encourage
Zerubbabel to resume work on the temple. Zechariah tells the people:

> The hands of Zerubbabel have laid the foundation of
> this house, and his hands will complete it. Then you
> will know that the LORD of Hosts has sent me to you.
> (Zechariah 4:9)

And as seen in God's word through the other prophets, God's desires
for the people are repeated:

> This is what the LORD of Hosts says: "Administer true
> justice. Show loving devotion and compassion to one
> another. Do not oppress the widow or the fatherless,
> the foreigner or the poor. And do not plot evil in your
> hearts against one another." (Zechariah 7:9, 10)

Earlier, it was mentioned that sometimes the prophetic vision
describes events occurring in the relative near-term. But many times,
the visions look further out—to the time of the Messiah. This is true
with God's revelations to Zechariah as well.

Two of these messianic passages might be familiar:

> Rejoice greatly, O Daughter of Zion!
>   Shout in triumph, O Daughter of Jerusalem!
> See, your King comes to you,
>   righteous and victorious,

humble and riding on a donkey,
     on a colt, the foal of a donkey. (Zechariah 9:9)

Then I will pour out on the house of David and on the people of Jerusalem a spirit of grace and prayer, and they will look on Me, the One they have pierced. They will mourn for Him as one mourns an only child, and weep bitterly for Him as one grieves a firstborn son. (Zechariah 12:10)

But there is far more in Zechariah's writing concerning the Messiah. We won't quote the passages but will provide background information to help add perspective as you read Zechariah on your own. This will also be beneficial when we look at the books found in the Major Prophets section of the Old Testament.

Part of this background is becoming familiar. Jesus came to earth as the seed of woman that would crush Satan. But he, himself, would have to suffer and die. Through the shedding of his blood, he received God's wrath—God's righteous punishment. Jesus was without sin—the punishment he took upon himself was for our sins. He was our substitute on the cross.

After the resurrection, Jesus appears before the disciples, and as we saw earlier, he commissions them (sends them) to be his witnesses in Jerusalem, and in all of Judea and Samaria, and to the ends of the earth (Acts 1:8). At the great feast of Weeks festival (Pentecost), when Jewish people throughout the land pilgrim to Jerusalem, the Apostle Peter shares the Good News concerning Christ—and three thousand embrace his message and are brought from spiritual death to life through the Holy Spirit (Acts 2:41).

This launches the Church Age—when many Gentiles will be brought into God's family and become participants in His kingdom plans.

Jesus, as the true Light, had come into the world. But many in the world did not recognize him. The Apostle John tells us:

> He came to His own, and His own did not receive Him. (John 1:11)

"His own" references the Jewish people. Most did not receive Jesus as the Messiah. John continues, though:

> But to all who did receive Him, to those who believed in His name, He gave the right to become children of God— children born not of blood, nor of the desire or will of man, but born of God. (John 1:12, 13)

The Church Age is made up of those who receive Christ and are brought into the family of God. These are individuals born of the Spirit of God (John 3). But very early in its history, the body of believers consisted mainly of Gentiles. Paul addresses this in his letter to the believers in Rome—a mixed group of both Jewish and Gentile believers. He is distraught:

> I have deep sorrow and unceasing anguish in my heart. For I could wish that I myself were cursed and cut off from Christ for the sake of my brothers, my own flesh and blood, the people of Israel. (Romans 9:2–4)

Paul sees that more and more Gentiles are coming to Christ but is grieved because many (most) of his Jewish brothers and sisters are not. He devotes three chapters to this (Romans 9, 10, and 11), explaining why this is the case. And he concludes:

> I do not want you to be ignorant of this mystery, brothers, so that you will not be conceited: A hardening in part has come to Israel, until the

full number of the Gentiles has come in. (Romans 11:25)

God has certainly not forgotten Israel—nor will He ever forget Israel. The Jews remain the chosen people of God and He has magnificent plans in store for them as they come to Jesus ("Yeshua") the Messiah. There are also glorious plans for Jerusalem.

Many of the prophets are given visions of this future. But these are not visions of Christ's first coming. Israel's glory happens when Christ returns as King of Kings and Lord of Lords for his millennial rule. And there will be an even more glorified Jerusalem when the New Jerusalem is placed upon the new earth (Revelation 21).

But much happens between now and then. God will build His Church, the Bride of Christ, during the age you and I are living in—the Church Age. Despite this, the world will draw further and further away from God. A great suffering will occur, leading to the appearance of what many will assume to be the Messiah. But this is a false messiah—a false Christ (antichrist). Prior to this, though, the Church will be **raptured**. This false messiah, or anti-Christ, will appear as a man of peace, and many will give their allegiance to him.

When the antichrist is finally revealed for who he is, many of the Jewish people will rebel against him and will call upon the name of the Lord for their salvation and deliverance. It is at this time that Jesus, and the raptured Church, will return. This is known as the Second Coming of Christ—which leads to his millennial rule. Our Lord will establish his rule in Zion—today's Jerusalem. Satan will be bound, and the reign of Jesus on earth will last a thousand years (Revelation 20).

Zechariah describes this period in much of his writing. He pictures Christ in his first coming (Zechariah 9:9, that we looked at above), but also sees Christ's second coming and millennial rule. In God's words through Zechariah:

> And on that day living water will flow out from Jerusalem, half of it toward the Eastern Sea and the other half toward the Western Sea, in summer and winter alike. On that day the LORD will become King over all the earth—the LORD alone, and His name alone. (Zechariah 14:8, 9)

There is one additional minor prophet to discuss.

About 120 years after Haggai and Zechariah were speaking to Zerubbabel and the other exiles who had returned to Jerusalem, Malachi appears—the last of the prophets and whose writing is the last book of the Old Testament. Once again, the people, particularly the priests, are showing indifference to God. Because his text is a fitting introduction to the New Testament and the arrival of the Messiah, we will save our review of this until later in this lesson series (lesson 38).

Also, you probably have noticed, interspersed throughout our discussion of the historical books and the minor prophets, our lessons have included texts from the prophets Isaiah, Jeremiah, Ezekiel, and Daniel. Writings from these prophets fall into the section of the Old Testament labeled as the Major Prophets—which we've yet to address in detail. We'll also get to these.

For now, though, there is a section in the Bible that precedes the prophetic writings. It is known as the "Wisdom Literature" (or "Poetry and Wisdom"). The book of **Job** falls into this category, as do Proverbs, Ecclesiastes, and Song of Songs. But for purposes of our journey through the Biblical Story, we're going to focus on Psalms, a compilation of writings also contained within the Wisdom Literature.

And we'll narrow this focus to the "Messianic Psalms"—writings that pertain to Jesus. After this, we'll then address the major prophets. Once this has been completed, it should be apparent why our lessons have been ordered in this way.

From lesson 30: What do we learn about God?

- Through His prophets, we repeatedly see God communicating His wishes to His chosen people.
- This includes words announcing warnings and punishments, when needed, and words of hope and encouragement.

raptured: This description is that of a "pre-tribulation" view, or "pre-trib" view of the rapture. In this understanding, Christians are removed from the earth prior to the great tribulation. The Bible supports this view. However, one can also interpret text to suggest the rapture does not happen until after the tribulation (a "post-tribulation," or "post-trib" view). There is a third view that holds to Christians not being raptured until halfway through the tribulation (a "mid-tribulation" or "mid-trib" view).

My studies favor a pre-trib view, which to me is the most biblically sound. In discussions with those holding to a post-tribulation view, I find sometimes they mistakenly take text focused toward Israel and apply it to the Church. Regardless, there is room in our interpretive grid to show tolerance to those that have a different perspective concerning the time of the rapture.

Job: Job is the oldest book in the Bible. Even here we see words relating to the Messiah:

> But I know that my Redeemer lives,
>   and in the end, He will stand upon the earth.

Even after my skin has been destroyed,
>   yet in my flesh I will see God.
I will see Him for myself;
>   my eyes will behold Him, and not as a stranger.
>   How my heart yearns within me! (Job 19:25–27)

31

Psalms and the Messiah (Part 1)

If you will recall, lesson 3 is a verse-by-verse look at Psalm 2. This Psalm covers the panorama of history, particularly in anticipation of the end times and the rule of Jesus, who we find from this Psalm has the titles Messiah, Son of God, and King.

This is one of one hundred and fifty writings that are a collection of Israelite song lyrics and poems. These have been grouped together and are found in the Bible as the "book of Psalms." Like songs of today, these reflect upon events in the lives of the writers of the Psalms and the experiences of the community. Used in worship, they include remembrances and celebrations of the work of God in Israel's history.

Psalms can be segmented into **five parts**, also called "books," with each part marked off by the phrase, "Blessed be the LORD ... Amen and Amen" (some translation use "praise" instead of the word "blessed"). They are also placed in an order reflecting the three-part story of Israel's history: the period of the monarchy, the time of the exile, and the return to the land.

For those interested in Bible trivia, Psalms is the **largest book** in the Bible. We also find the Bible's shortest chapter in the book of Psalms (Psalm 117), which is also the middle chapter found within the Bible (keeping in mind, chapter and verse designations were not in the original Hebrew or Greek texts). The Bible's longest chapter is also found in Psalms—Psalm 119.

The New Testament authors quote from Psalms sixty-eight times—more than any of the other writings found in the Old Testament. For what it's worth, Isaiah comes next, quoted fifty-five times, followed by Deuteronomy, quoted forty-four times.

The Psalms include instruction and encouragement. Here is a short example:

> Blessed is the man
>> who does not walk in the counsel of the wicked,
> or set foot on the path of sinners,
>> or sit in the seat of mockers.
> But his delight is in the law of the LORD,
>> and on His law he meditates day and night.
> He is like a tree planted by streams of water,
>> yielding its fruit in season,
> whose leaf does not wither,
>> and who prospers in all he does. (Psalm 1:1–3)

The Psalms also recognize the power, glory, and magnificence of God:

> The heavens declare the glory of God;
>> the skies proclaim the work of His hands. (Psalm 19:1)

They also express the psalmist's love and praise toward God:

I love You, O LORD, my strength.

The LORD is my rock, my fortress, and my deliverer.
    My God is my rock, in whom I take refuge,
my shield, and the horn of my salvation,
    my stronghold. (Psalm 18:1, 2)

Many of the Psalms relate to Jesus and tell us something about him.
For the purposes of our journey through the Biblical Story, these are
the Psalms we will look at.

We also should note that Jesus quotes from the Psalms, and does so
more than any other portion of the Hebrew Scriptures.

- He **quotes the Psalms** in discussions with the Pharisees, the
  chief priests, and the elders (as examples, Psalm 8:2; Psalm
  110:1; and Psalm 118:22–23—see Matthew 21:16; 21:42; and
  22:44).
- When the people want to stone Jesus for claiming to be God, he
  responds with a verse from a Psalm (Psalm 82:6, see John 10:34).
- He references the Psalms when describing Jerusalem's future
  destruction (Psalm 118:26, see Matthew 23:39).
- He quotes from a Psalm when announcing his betrayal (Psalm
  41:9, see John 13:18).
- He quotes a Psalm when asked by Pilate if he is the Son of
  God (Psalm 110:1, see Matthew 26:64).
- He uses words from a Psalm while dying on the cross (Psalm
  22:1, see Matthew 27:46).
- His very last words before his death come from a Psalm, as he
  commits his spirit to the Father (Psalm 31:5, see Luke 23:46).

While Jesus quotes the Psalms and uses them in his teachings, the
Psalms also reveal a great deal about Jesus—even though they were
written hundreds of years before his birth.

We have already seen an example of this in lesson 2 and the discussion on Psalm 2. This is a short song, containing just twelve verses. But from Psalm 2, we learn:

- The titles Messiah (Anointed), the Son of God, and King (2:2, 6, 7).
- Political and religious leaders will conspire against the Messiah (2:1–3).
- The Messiah will ask God for his inheritance (2:8).
- He will have authority over all things (2:8, 9).
- He will destroy those who do not honor him (2:12).
- We are to seek refuge in him (2:12).

Psalms containing references to Jesus, the Messiah, are referred to as "Messianic Psalms." In this lesson, we will look at one of these—Psalm 22. In our next lesson, we will briefly review other references to Jesus that are contained in the Psalms.

Psalm 22:1, 2 -

> My God, my God, why have You forsaken me?
>> Why are You so far from saving me,
>> so far from my words of groaning?
> I cry out by day, O my God,
>> but You do not answer,
>> and by night,
> but I have no rest.

The beginning words of this Psalm are cried out by Jesus while he is on the cross (Matthew 27:46). The phrases "cry out," "by day," "by night," and "I have no rest" possibly reference his prayer for the disciples and the people as described in John's Gospel (chapter 17), as well as his prayers at the garden of Gethsemane as found in Matthew's Gospel (Matthew 26:36–46).

Psalm 22:3–8 -

> Yet You are holy,
>> enthroned on the praises of Israel.
> In You our fathers trusted;
>> they trusted and You delivered them.
> They cried out to You and were set free;
>> they trusted in You and were not disappointed.
> But I am a worm and not a man,
>> scorned by men and despised by the people.
> All who see me mock me;
>> they sneer and shake their heads:
> "He trusts in the LORD,
>> let the LORD deliver him;
> let the LORD rescue him,
>> since He delights in him."

The Messiah was despised and rejected by his own. Some mocked Jesus, telling him to save himself if he was truly God. Matthew records the bystanders sneering at Jesus:

> And those who passed by heaped abuse on Him, shaking their heads and saying, "You who are going to destroy the temple and rebuild it in three days, save Yourself! If You are the Son of God, come down from the cross!"

> In the same way, the chief priests, scribes, and elders mocked Him, saying, "He saved others, but He cannot save Himself. He is the King of Israel! Let Him come down now from the cross, and we will believe in Him. He trusts in God. Let God deliver Him now if He wants Him. For He said, 'I am the Son of God.'"

In the same way, even the robbers who were crucified with Him berated Him. (Matthew 27:39–43)

In Psalm 22, note the phrase, "But I am a worm and not a man." It is interesting that the Messianic reference is one of a "**worm**" (Psalm 22:6). Like a worm, the Messiah was deemed lowly and insignificant. But the Hebrew word translated "worm" references a particular worm that dies to give life (see the end-of-lesson notes).

Psalm 22:9, 10 -

> Yet You brought me forth from the womb;
>> You made me secure at my mother's breast.
> From birth I was cast upon You;
>> from my mother's womb You have been my God.

The Messiah's intimate connection with God the Father is a continuum, even while Jesus is in the womb.

Psalm 22:11 –

> Be not far from me,
>> for trouble is near
>> and there is no one to help.

The Messiah was abandoned by those around him. Even his disciples fled before the crucifixion.

Psalm 22:12, 13 -

> Many bulls surround me;
>> strong bulls of Bashan encircle me.
> They open their jaws against me
>> like lions that roar and maul.

The Messiah will be surrounded by wicked beings. Throughout his ministry, the religious leaders oppose him—to the extent that they desire to have him killed.

Psalm 22:14 -

> I am poured out like water,
>   and all my bones are disjointed.
> My heart is like wax;
>   it melts away within me.

In Roman crucifixion, the victim's weight pulls upon the bones until they became disjointed. Death occurs as the weakened body can no longer hold itself up. When this happens, air cannot be pulled into the condemned person's lungs—and the person dies.

Many of those condemned to crucifixion never made it to the cross, though. They died of the beatings that occurred prior to this. The biblical record tells us that Jesus was also beaten before his crucifixion. It might be noted that, in obeying the Mosaic Law (Deuteronomy 25:3), Jews would never strike their condemned with more than forty lashes. Actually, so as to not accidentally break the Law, they would only strike the victim 39 times. In 2nd Corinthians 11:24, Paul talks about being beaten through the Jewish punishment system five times, where he "received from the Jews the forty lashes minus one." However, Jesus' punishment was given over to the Romans, and they had no such limits on how many times they could strike the victim.

During the crucifixion, Jesus' side was pierced by a spear. John, an eyewitness to the event, tells us blood and water flowed from the open wound (John 19:34). This must have appeared strange to John—so much so that he draws our attention to it. He probably had no idea what it meant. But with today's knowledge of medicine, we do.

During crucifixion, the condemned experience a rapid heartbeat—leading to hypovolemic shock. This causes fluid to gather in the sack around the heart and around the lungs. In medical terms, the condemned is experiencing pericardial effusion (fluid gathering in the membrane around the heart) and pleural effusion (fluid gathering around the lungs).

The Roman spear must have pierced both the heart and lungs of Jesus, resulting in the flow of both blood and water from this wound, as John has recorded.

Psalm 22:15 -

> My strength is dried up like a potsherd,
>> and my tongue sticks to the roof of my mouth.
>> You lay me in the dust of death.

The Messiah will thirst while dying. John writes,

> After this, knowing that everything had now been accomplished, and to fulfill the Scripture, Jesus said, "I am thirsty." (John 19:28)

Note that John tells us the thirst was "to fulfill the Scriptures"—a reference to the Psalms.

Here, we might interject a verse from Psalm 69,

> They poisoned my food with gall
>> and gave me vinegar to quench my thirst. (Psalm 69:21)

This, too, was fulfilled (see Matthew 27:23, 24).

Continuing with Psalm 22,

Psalm 22:16 -

> For dogs surround me;
>> a band of evil men encircles me;
>> they have pierced my hands and feet.

It is suggested that the two references, "dogs" and "band of evil men," refer to the Gentiles (dogs) and to Jews (band of evil men) present at the crucifixion. The piercing of the Messiah's hands and feet describe the crucifixion process. These words were written more than five hundred years before crucifixion was invented.

Psalm 22:17, 18 -

> I can count all my bones;
>> they stare and gloat over me.
> They divide my garments among them
>> and cast lots for my clothing.

John records that soldiers at the foot of the cross placed Jesus' clothing into four piles and cast lots to determine who would take possession (John 19:23, 24).

Psalm 22:19–21 -

> But You, O LORD, be not far off;
>> O my strength, come quickly to help.
> Deliver my soul from the sword,
>> my precious life from the power of wild dogs.
> Save me from the mouth of the lion;
>> at the horns of the wild oxen You have answered Me!

God remains faithful to the Messiah.

Psalm 22:22 –

> I will proclaim Your name to my brothers;
>> I will praise You in the assembly.

The Messiah will suffer greatly. But he will remain faithful to his Father.

Psalm 22:23–31 –

> You who fear the LORD, praise Him!
>> All descendants of Jacob, honor Him!
>> All offspring of Israel, revere Him!
> For He has not despised or detested
>> the torment of the afflicted.
> He has not hidden His face from him,
>> but has attended to his cry for help.
> From You comes my praise in the great assembly;
>> before those who fear You I will fulfill my vows.
> The poor will eat and be satisfied;
>> those who seek the LORD will praise Him.
>> May your hearts live forever!
> All the ends of the earth
>> will remember and turn to the LORD.
> All the families of the nations
>> will bow down before Him.
> For dominion belongs to the LORD
>> and He rules over the nations.
> All the rich of the earth will feast and worship;
>> all who go down to the dust will kneel before Him—
>> even those unable to preserve their lives.
> Posterity will serve Him;
>> they will declare the Lord to a new generation.
> They will come and proclaim His righteousness
>> to a people yet unborn—

all that He has done.

The Messiah will bring many people into the family of God. The Psalm ends with the exaltation of the Messiah—despised and rejected by the people for whom he died but honored by the Father. The ending of this Psalm might remind us of words from the apostle Paul:

> And being found in appearance as a man,
>   He humbled Himself
> and became obedient to death—
>
> even death on a cross.
>
> Therefore, God exalted Him to the highest place
>   and gave Him the name above all names,
> that at the name of Jesus every knee should bow,
>   in heaven and on earth and under the earth,
> and every tongue confess that Jesus Christ is Lord,
>   to the glory of God the Father. (Philippians 2:8–11)

Jesus humbled himself to death—even death on a cross. But the grave could not hold him. He has been exalted by God the Father to the highest place and given a name above all names.

Numerous additional revelations from God concerning Jesus can be found throughout the Psalms. We'll look at several more of these in our next lesson.

From lesson 31: What do we learn about God?

- The word of God is not just the words spoken by the prophets. The entire Bible is the word of God, and the Psalms, as part of the Bible, also speak God's words.

- The Psalms contain additional revelations from God about Jesus—the Messiah, Son of God, and King.
- These include startling descriptions of Jesus' suffering and death. And also, his glorification.

---

five parts: The "books" found in the Psalms are as follow:

Book 1: Psalm 1 – 41
Book 2: Psalm 42 – 72
Book 3: Psalm 73 – 89
Book 4: Psalm 90 – 106
Book 5: Psalm 107 – 150

largest book: I've stated that Psalms is the largest book in the Bible, and some might question this. If the ranking is based on numbers of verses, Psalms wins this title (2,527 verses, followed by Genesis with a distant 1,533 verses). But verse count can be misleading. If we count the actual words in the Hebrew, Jeremiah becomes the longest book (22,285 words versus the Psalms' 19,662 words).

You might be asking, why would I take the time to count the verses and the Hebrew words?

I wouldn't and I didn't.

I simply read "What is the Longest Book in the Bible? (Hint: It's Not the Psalms)" by Justin Taylor, dated September 6, 2016 and available at https://www.thegospelcoalition.org/blogs/justin-taylor/what-is-the-longest-book-in-the-bible-hint-its-not-the-psalms/ (accessed November 20, 2019).

How on earth did I find this article? That's where Google comes in.

quotes the Psalms: Jesus quotes the Psalms eleven times, including parallels. These can be found as follows:

Matthew 21:16	Mark 12:10	Luke 13:35	John 6:31
Matthew 21:42	Mark 12:36	Luke 20:17	John 10:34
Matthew 22:44	Mark 14:62	Luke 20:42, 43	John 13:18
Matthew 23:39	Mark 15:34	Luke 23:46	John 15:25
Matthew 26:64			
Matthew 27:46			

worm: The word translated "worm" is the Hebrew word *"tola."* This word is found in various forms over twenty times in the book of Exodus—almost always implying the color scarlet or crimson.

"Tola" relates to a type of worm used in antiquity to make scarlet dye—the color of royalty. The female worm, when ready to lay its eggs, attaches itself to the side of a tree. After laying the eggs—giving life—the worm dies, staining the side of the tree crimson. In ancient times, these dead worms were collected and used in the making of the dye.

A portion of the curtains in the tabernacle were dyed scarlet, as was the veil separating the Holy of Holies (Exodus 26:1, 31). Priestly garments also contained scarlet (Exodus 28:5, 6).

To have this Messianic Psalm mention this worm allows us to connect the concept of death, crimson and scarlet, and new life: The Messiah's death on the cross; his crimson blood but ultimate resurrection and royalty; and his death and resurrection allowing us new life through spiritual rebirth and eventual bodily resurrection.

> and they will be passed on.
> But You remain the same,
> and Your years will never end. (Psalm
> 102:25–27)

- He will teach in parables:

  > I will open my mouth in parables;
  >> I will utter things hidden from the beginning. (Psalm 78:2)

- The Messiah will calm the stormy sea:

  > Then they cried out to the LORD in their trouble,
  >> and He brought them out of their distress.
  > He calmed the storm to a whisper,
  >> and the waves of the sea were hushed. (Psalm 107:28, 29)

- He comes in the name of the LORD (God the Father):

  > Blessed is he who comes in the name of the LORD.
  >> From the house of the LORD we bless you. (Psalm 118:26)

- Despite this, he will be rejected by many:

  > The stone the builders rejected
  >> has become the cornerstone. (Psalm 118:22)

- The Messiah will be scorned and attacked. He will be accused by false witnesses and hated without reason. There will be numerous attempts to kill the Messiah.

  > Let not my enemies gloat over me without cause,
  >> nor those who hate me without reason
  >> wink in malice.
  > (Psalm 35:19)

Do not hand me over to the will of my foes,
for false witnesses rise up against me,
breathing out violence. (Psalm 27:12)

Those who hate me without cause
outnumber the hairs of my head;
many are those who would destroy me—
my enemies for no reason. (Psalm 69:4)

For I hear the slander of many;
there is terror on every side.
They conspire against me
and plot to take my life. (Psalm 31:13)

- He will be betrayed by a friend:

Even my close friend whom I trusted,
the one who shared my bread,
has lifted his heel against me. (Psalm 41:9)

- He will be rejected by the Jews—and his own family:

I have become a stranger to my brothers
and a foreigner to my mother's sons.
(Psalm 69:8)

- He is a man of sorrows:

Insults have broken my heart,
and I am in despair.
I looked for sympathy, but there was none,
for comforters, but I found no one. (Psalm
69:20)

- When the Messiah is crucified, none of his bones will be broken:

> He protects all his bones;
>> not one of them will be broken. (Psalm 34:20)

There's more to this than may be readily apparent. God commanded that none of the bones of the Passover lamb could be broken. Note Exodus 12:46,

> ... you may not break any of the bones.

The Passover instructions repeat this in Numbers 9:12,

> ... they may not ... break any of its bones. They must observe the Passover according to all its statutes.

Although Roman crucifixion involved breaking the legs of the condemned to ensure they had died, this was not done on Jesus, our Passover Lamb. At the end of his crucifixion, and before his body was removed from the cross, he had already died when the Roman soldiers approached. To assure of his death, a spear was thrust into the side of Jesus.

- He will cry out to God (see Luke 23:46):

> Into Your hands I commit my spirit. (Psalm 31:5)

- The Messiah will not suffer decay in death, nor will he be abandoned to the grave.

> For You will not abandon my soul to Sheol,
>> nor will You let Your Holy One see decay.
> (Psalm 16:10)

- The Messiah will be resurrected and glorified, ascending to the right hand of God the Father. The Messiah triumphs.

The LORD said to my Lord:
    "Sit at My right hand
until I make Your enemies
    a footstool for Your feet."

The LORD will extend Your mighty scepter
from Zion...
(Psalm 110:1, 2)

You have made known to me the path of life;
    You will fill me with joy in Your presence,
with eternal pleasures at Your right hand.
(Psalm 16:10, 11)

Let Your hand be upon the man at Your right
hand,
    on the son of man You have raised up for
    Yourself. (Psalm 80:17)

"You are a priest forever
    in the order of Melchizedek." (Psalm 110:4)

There are one hundred and fifty psalms, so what is shared above and in our previous lessons leave much that we have not explored. But we do see how God uses His word through the psalmists to inform the world concerning the Messiah, and to prepare the world for his arrival.

From lesson 32: What do we learn about God?

- God uses His word through the psalmists to encourage and to inform—and also to prepare the world for the Messiah.

32

Psalms - Songs of the Messiah (Part 2)

Psalm 22, discussed during our last lesson, is just one of many references to Jesus contained in the book of Psalms. Let's piece together what we learn from other Psalms.

- Scripture is about the Messiah, who does the will of the Father:

> Then I said, "Here I am, I have come—
> it is written about me in the scroll:
> I delight to do Your will, O my God;
> Your law is within my heart."
>
> I proclaim righteousness in the great assembly;
> behold, I do not seal my lips,
> as You, O LORD, do know.
> I have not covered up Your righteousness in
> my heart;
> I have declared Your faithfulness and
> salvation;
> I have not concealed Your loving devotion and
> faithfulness
> from the great assembly. (Psalm 40:7–10)

- The Messiah will come from the lineage of David. He will call God his Father and will be God's only begotten Son. However, the Messiah is also pre-existent, eternal, and the creator of all things:

> You said, "I have made a covenant with My chosen one,
>> I have sworn to David My servant:
> 'I will establish your offspring forever
>> and build up your throne for all generations'." (Psalm 89:3, 4)

> He will call to Me, 'You are my Father,
>> my God, the rock of my salvation.'
> I will indeed appoint him as My firstborn,
>> the highest of the kings of the earth.
>> (Psalm 89:26, 27)

> In the beginning You laid the foundations of the earth,
>> and the heavens are the work of Your hands.
> They will perish, but You remain;
>> they will all wear out like a garment.
> Like clothing You will change them,
>> and they will be passed on.
> But You remain the same,
>> and Your years will never end.
>> (Psalm 102:25–27)

- He will teach in parables:

> I will open my mouth in parables;
>> I will utter things hidden from the beginning. (Psalm 78:2)

- The Messiah will calm the stormy sea:

    > Then they cried out to the LORD in their
    > trouble,
    >> and He brought them out of their distress.
    >
    > He calmed the storm to a whisper,
    >> and the waves of the sea were hushed.
    >
    > (Psalm 107:28, 29)

- He comes in the name of the LORD (God the Father):

    > Blessed is he who comes in the name of the
    > LORD.
    >> From the house of the LORD we bless
    >> you. (Psalm 118:26)

- Despite this, he will be rejected by many:

    > The stone the builders rejected
    >> has become the cornerstone. (Psalm
    >> 118:22)

- The Messiah will be scorned and attacked. He will be accused
  by false witnesses and hated without reason. There will be
  numerous attempts to kill the Messiah.

    > Let not my enemies gloat over me without
    > cause,
    >> nor those who hate me without reason
    >> wink in malice. (Psalm 35:19)

    > Do not hand me over to the will of my foes,
    >> for false witnesses rise up against me,
    > breathing out violence. (Psalm 27:12)

Those who hate me without cause
   outnumber the hairs of my head;
many are those who would destroy me—
   my enemies for no reason. (Psalm 69:4)

For I hear the slander of many;
   there is terror on every side.
They conspire against me
   and plot to take my life. (Psalm 31:13)

- He will be betrayed by a friend:

   Even my close friend whom I trusted,
      the one who shared my bread,
      has lifted his heel against me. (Psalm 41:9)

- He will be rejected by the Jews—and his own family:

   I have become a stranger to my brothers
      and a foreigner to my mother's sons.
   (Psalm 69:8)

- He is a man of sorrows:

   Insults have broken my heart,
      and I am in despair.
   I looked for sympathy, but there was none,
      for comforters, but I found no one.
   (Psalm 69:20)

- When the Messiah is crucified, none of his bones will be broken:

   He protects all his bones;
      not one of them will be broken.
   (Psalm 34:20)

There's more to this than may be readily apparent. God commanded that none of the bones of the Passover lamb could be broken. Note Exodus 12:46,

> ... you may not break any of the bones.

The Passover instructions repeat this in Numbers 9:12,

> ... they may not ... break any of its bones. They must observe the Passover according to all its statutes.

Although Roman crucifixion involved breaking the legs of the condemned to ensure they had died, this was not done on Jesus, our Passover Lamb. At the end of his crucifixion, and before his body was removed from the cross, he had already died when the Roman soldiers approached. To assure of his death, a spear was thrust into the side of Jesus.

- He will cry out to God (see Luke 23:46):

> Into Your hands I commit my spirit. (Psalm 31:5)

- The Messiah will not suffer decay in death, nor will he be abandoned to the grave.

> For You will not abandon my soul to Sheol,
> nor will You let Your Holy One see decay.
> (Psalm 16:10)

- The Messiah will be resurrected and glorified, ascending to the right hand of God the Father. The Messiah triumphs.

> The LORD said to my Lord:
> "Sit at My right hand

until I make Your enemies
a footstool for Your feet."

The LORD will extend Your mighty scepter
from Zion... **(Psalm 110:1, 2)**

You have made known to me the path of life;
You will fill me with joy in Your presence,
with eternal pleasures at Your right hand.
(Psalm 16:10, 11)

Let Your hand be upon the man at Your right
hand,
on the son of man You have raised up for
Yourself. (Psalm 80:17)

"You are a priest forever
in the order of Melchizedek." (Psalm 110:4)

There are one hundred and fifty psalms, so what is shared above and in our previous lessons leave much that we have not explored. But we do see how God uses His word through the psalmists to inform the world concerning the Messiah, and to prepare the world for his arrival.

From lesson 32: What do we learn about God?

- God uses His word through the psalmists to encourage and to inform—and also to prepare the world for the Messiah.

33

The Major Prophets: Isaiah

We are now ready to address the major prophets, particularly from the perspective of the Messiah. We've reviewed the history of the Israelites and saw their suffering and destruction under the Assyrians and Babylonians. Over and over again the people had been warned:

> ... through all His prophets and seers, the LORD warned Israel and Judah, saying, "Turn from your wicked ways and keep My commandments and statutes, according to the entire Law that I commanded your fathers and delivered to you through My servants the prophets." (2nd Kings 17:13)

Isaiah was one of the prophets used by God for these warnings. He prophesized in Judah during the reigns of Uzziah, Jotham, Ahaz, and Hezekiah—four of Judah's kings. In that much of the warnings (and promises) echo those of the prophetic word from the prophets discussed earlier, our review of Isaiah's text will only focus on God's words relating to the Messiah.

There is a part of me that would like to suggest Isaiah is the greatest prophet who ever lived. Of course, we know this can be questioned, especially when we place his life alongside that of Moses—or when we add in **Jesus**. But there are a number of reasons why Isaiah's writings might place him high on such a list:

- Of the seventeen prophetic books in the Bible, Isaiah's comes **second in length**—only slightly shorter than Jeremiah's writing.
- Isaiah's visions cover a great expanse of time—from roughly 700 BC all the way to the new heaven and new earth of Revelation 21. Many of John's apocalyptic visions recorded in the book of Revelation echo words from Isaiah's text.
- Isaiah is the prophet most quoted by the New Testament authors. Jesus quotes from Isaiah more than he does any of the other prophets (eight times—we'll look at these below).
- The book of Isaiah provides the most comprehensive prophetic picture of Jesus found in the entire Old Testament. It includes:
  - the announcement of his coming (Isaiah 40:3–5).
  - his virgin birth (Isaiah 7:14).
  - his ministry and proclamation of the good news (Isaiah 61:1–2).
  - his sacrificial death for the forgiveness of our sins (Isaiah 52:13–53:12).
  - his future return to establish his earthly kingdom (Isaiah 60:2–3).

Much of Isaiah's text focuses on the cataclysmic events surrounding God's people. He foresees the Assyrian invasion of both Israel and Judah, as well as the Babylonian invasion. His visions include the exile and God's protection of a remnant and their eventual return to the land. He sees Israel's failure as God's servant—and a Messiah who is God's perfect Servant.

You will recall, through the other prophets we have reviewed, God continually warns His people concerning punishment and destruction. But He also provides encouragement and hope (remember the Jeremiah coffee mug?). And this is no different with His words through Isaiah. The prophet sees the ultimate glorification of Zion and the Jewish people through Christ's messianic reign.

Along the way, Isaiah sees God's wrath against each of Israel's adversaries—described opponent by opponent and in detail. And he foresees the end-times destruction of the entire world (the event of Revelation 20 that occurs *after* the millennial reign of Christ).

The Isaiah text will be reviewed in a similar fashion we used in looking at the Psalms. We will first look at how Jesus uses text from Isaiah, and then we'll discuss what Isaiah's writings tell us about Jesus.

- Jesus begins his ministry in the synagogue in Nazareth, and the very first words recorded are his quoting of the first two verses of Isaiah 61 (see Luke 4:16–21—discussed in lesson 3). Jesus is declaring to those within the synagogue that he is the one Isaiah wrote about some seven hundred years earlier (and, through the Apostolic witness, Jesus makes this declaration to us).

  And he doesn't just make this declaration by word. As we learn about his ministry, we see that he fulfills Isaiah's prophecy in both word and deed.

  Note the Isaiah text:

  > The Spirit of the Lord GOD is on Me,
  > because the LORD has anointed Me
  > to preach good news to the poor.
  >
  > He has sent Me to bind up the brokenhearted,
  > to proclaim liberty to the captives
  > and release from darkness to the prisoners,

to proclaim the year of the LORD's favor ...

When Jesus is baptized, the Spirit, in visible form, descends upon him. Jesus is anointed as the voice from heaven declares him to be the Son of God. This is not an appointment—it is an announcement.

Jesus brings the good news message of God's salvation to both the physically poor and those spiritually impoverished. Jesus provides "liberty to the captives"—freedom from Satan's grip and the power of sin. "Release from darkness to the prisoners" is Jesus bringing light to a world living in darkness—prisoners in bondage to Satan.

The Apostle John tells us, "The true Light who gives light to every man was coming into the world" (John 1:9).

- Another use of the Isaiah text occurs in Matthew 13. In the chapter before this, the religious leaders accuse Jesus of performing his miracles through the power of Satan. From this point on, Jesus will distance himself from this "brood of vipers" and will begin teaching in parables. He explains why he is doing this by quoting Isaiah:

  "This is why I speak to them in parables:

  'Though seeing, they do not see; though
  hearing, they do not hear or understand'."
  (Matthew 13:13, quoting Isaiah 42.20)

He continues, "In them the prophecy of Isaiah is fulfilled" and quotes Isaiah 6:9, 10 (see Matthew 13:14, 15).

- Later Jesus once again confronts the religious leaders and calls them out for their hollow words and hypocrisy. He quotes Isaiah 29:13,

You nullify the word of God for the sake
of your tradition. You hypocrites! Isaiah
prophesied correctly about you:

'These people honor Me with their lips,
  but their hearts are far from Me.
They worship Me in vain;
  they teach as doctrine the precepts of
  men.' (Matthew 15:6–9)

- When Jesus turns over the tables in the temple, he explains
  his actions by quoting Isaiah:

  It is written: 'My house will be called a house
  of prayer.' But you are making it 'a den of
  robbers.' (Matthew 21:13, quoting Isaiah 56:7)

- When John the Baptist is imprisoned and wants encouragement
  that Jesus is truly the Messiah, Jesus answers those sent by
  John in words echoing the Messianic description found in
  Isaiah 35:5–6,

  Go back and report to John what you hear and
  see: The blind receive sight, the lame walk,
  the lepers are cleansed, the deaf hear, the dead
  are raised, and good news is preached to the
  poor. Blessed is the one who does not fall
  away on account of Me. (Matthew 11:4–6)

- In one of his last parables before the cross, Jesus alludes to
  Isaiah when he shares the parable of the vineyard (Matthew
  21:33–47, alluding to Isaiah 5).

- At his Last Supper, Jesus explains what is about to happen—
  that he must die a sinner's death. He quotes Isaiah:

For I tell you that this Scripture must be fulfilled in Me: 'And He was numbered with the transgressors.' For what is written about Me is reaching its fulfillment. (Luke 22:37, quoting Isaiah 53:12)

- Throughout John's Gospel, we are repeatedly reminded that Jesus is the Messiah, the Son of God. Early in his ministry, Jesus quotes Isaiah and tells the people:

    It is written in the Prophets: 'And they will all be taught by God.' Everyone who has heard the Father and learned from Him comes to Me—not that anyone has seen the Father except the One who is from God; only He has seen the Father.

    Truly, truly, I tell you, he who believes has eternal life. I am the bread of life. (John 6:45–48)

The phrase "And they will all be taught by God" is a quote of Isaiah 54:13.

Every time we learn about Christ and his teachings, we are being taught by God. Every word Jesus spoke that is recorded in scripture are teachings from God. Jesus is the bread of life—we are nourished by his life and by his words.

We've reviewed how Jesus uses the Isaiah text, now let's look at what God reveals about Jesus through the prophet Isaiah:

- The Messiah's arrival will be preceded by someone coming before him:

A voice of one calling:

"Prepare the way for the LORD in the wilderness; make a straight highway for our God in the desert." (Isaiah 40:3)

- He will experience virgin birth and will be called "Immanuel"—meaning God with us.

   Therefore, the Lord Himself will give you a sign: Behold, the virgin will be with child and will give birth to a son, and she will call Him Immanuel. (Isaiah 7:14)

- Isaiah 9:6–7 tells us quite a bit about the Messiah. A child will be born, but he will be the Son of God given to mankind:

   For unto us a child is born,
   unto us a son is given ...

The child that is to be born is the seed of woman of Genesis 3:15. The son who is to be given is the Psalm 2 Son of God.

- He will reign,

   ... the government will be upon His shoulders.

- And we are presented various titles for this Anointed One from God:

   And He will be called
   Wonderful Counselor, Mighty God,
   Everlasting Father, Prince of Peace.

- He will rule and bring peace:

> Of the increase of His government and peace
>> there will be no end.

- He fulfills the Davidic Covenant and will rule on David's throne:

> He will reign on the throne of David
>> and over his kingdom,
> to establish and sustain it
>> with justice and righteousness
>> from that time and forevermore.

- We can be absolutely, 100% certain that this will occur:

> The zeal of the LORD of Hosts will accomplish
> this.

- The eleventh chapter of Isaiah also tells us much about the Messiah. He will come from the line of David (David's father, Jesse is mentioned, Isaiah 11:1). God's Spirit will rest upon him (Isaiah 11:2). **The nations** will seek him (Isaiah 11:10). And he will rule the nations in righteousness (11:4, 5). We will only quote a portion of Isaiah 11. It begins:

> Then a shoot will spring up from the stump
> of Jesse,
>> and a Branch from his roots will bear fruit.
> The Spirit of the LORD will rest on Him—
>> the Spirit of wisdom and understanding,
>> the Spirit of counsel and strength,
>> the Spirit of knowledge and fear of the
>> LORD.
> And He will delight in the fear of the LORD.
>
> He will not judge by what His eyes see,

and He will not decide by what His ears hear,

but with righteousness He will judge the poor,
and with equity He will decide for the lowly of the earth.

He will strike the earth with the rod of His mouth
and slay the wicked with the breath of His lips.

Righteousness will be the belt around His hips,
and faithfulness the sash around His waist.
(Isaiah 11:1–5, however, all of chapter 11 is about the Messiah)

- The Messiah will begin his ministry in Galilee:

There will be no more gloom for those in distress. In the past He humbled the land of Zebulun and the land of Naphtali, but in the future, He will honor the Way of the Sea, beyond the Jordan, Galilee of the Gentiles:

The people walking in darkness
have seen a great light;
on those living in the land of the shadow of death,
a light has dawned. (Isaiah 9:1, 2)

- His ministry is described:

Here is My Servant, whom I uphold,
My Chosen One, in whom My soul delights.
I will put My Spirit on Him,
and He will bring justice to the nations.

He will not cry out or raise His voice,
nor make His voice heard in the streets.
A bruised reed He will not break
and a smoldering wick He will not extinguish;
He will faithfully bring forth justice.
He will not grow weak or discouraged
before He has established justice on the earth.
In His law the coastlands will put their hope. (Isaiah 42:1–4)

- The Messiah will have authority over all judgment:

I will place on his shoulder the key of the house of David. What he opens, no one can shut; what he shuts, no one can open. (Isaiah 22:22)

- He will judge in righteousness:

But with righteousness He will judge the poor,
and with equity He will decide for the lowly of the earth.
He will strike the earth with the rod of His mouth
and slay the wicked with the breath of His lips.
Righteousness will be the belt around His hips,
and faithfulness the sash around His waist. (Isaiah 11:4, 5)

- Through the Messiah, the Spirit will be poured out among the people. God's words through Isaiah tell us:

I will pour out My Spirit on your descendants,
and My blessing on your offspring. (Isaiah 44:3)

This relates to the New Covenant and the teaching of the necessity of being born again, as Jesus imparted to Nicodemus in John 3. It is Jesus' proclamation in the temple during the feast of Tabernacles that we looked at earlier (lesson 29). Jesus tells those around him, if they are thirsty, come to him—and we are told that what Jesus is referring to and what he provides is the Holy Spirit (John 7:37). The Holy Spirit is given through Jesus and allows belief in Jesus as we go from spiritual death to rebirth and spiritual life.

- Though not what any contemporary of Isaiah's would expect (how could they?), the Messiah will be spit upon and beaten:

  I offered My back to those who struck Me,
      and My cheeks to those who tore out My
      beard.
  I did not hide My face from scorn and
      spittle. (Isaiah 50:6)

- Also not expected, the Messiah will suffer and die. Isaiah's detailed description of this is powerful and amazingly accurate. We will devote our next lesson to this: Isaiah words associated with the crucifixion of Jesus as found in Isaiah 52:13–53:12.

- But the story does not end with the Messiah's death. He will conquer death:

  On this mountain He will swallow up
      the shroud that enfolds all peoples,
      the sheet that covers all nations;
  He will swallow up death forever.

> The Lord GOD will wipe away the tears
> from every face
> and remove the disgrace of His people
> from the whole earth. (Isaiah 25:7, 8)

Isaiah has shared much concerning God's Anointed, the Psalm 2 Messiah, Son of God and King.

Going all the way back to Genesis 3:15, we are told that the seed of woman would be struck by Satan and die. On this side of the cross, we understand why this had to occur. But seven hundred years before the event, Isaiah provided the reasons as well.

This amazing prophecy from the text of Isaiah is the subject of our next lesson.

From lesson 33: What do we learn about God?

- God's words through the prophet Isaiah include many references to the Messiah.
- We are given the announcement of his coming (Isaiah 40:3–5), his virgin birth (Isaiah 7:14), his ministry and proclamation of the good news (Isaiah 61:1–2), his sacrificial death for our forgiveness (Isaiah 52:13–53:12), and his future return to establish his earthly kingdom (Isaiah 60:2–3).

Jesus: In his deity, Jesus is outside the "dimensionality of time." Per Einstein, the creation of the universe involved the creation of all matter and time itself. Deity is outside the creation—so it is not material (God is Spirit) and it is outside of time (God is eternal). But Deity can appear in the material and can be present within the creation (as seen in the incarnation of Jesus). As such, Jesus, as Deity, is outside of time and knows "the end from the beginning." God's word through Isaiah tells us:

> I declare the end from the beginning and ancient times from what is still to come. (Isaiah 46:10)

This sheds light on Jesus' prayers in the garden of Gethsemane. Jesus clearly foresees the pain that awaits him—hence the agony he went through in preparation for, and in anticipation of, what would soon be happening.

Perhaps an easily understood example of Jesus knowing of future events relates to his conversation with Peter at the Last Supper.

- Jesus knew precisely that a disciple would deny knowing him.
- He knew precisely which of the twelve it would be.
- He knew exactly how many times this disciple would deny him.
- And Jesus knew precisely the time frame in which the denials would occur.

These were not guesses. Jesus could foresee these events because, in his deity, he is outside the dimensionality of time.

Skeptics, though, might question whether this was truly fulfilled prophecy. Perhaps Jesus, as God, simply made sure these events happened so that his predictions would be shown to be true.

But this cannot be the case.

He could not have orchestrated Peter doing this, because this would mean he is causing Peter to sin (Peter's denial of knowing Jesus)—an impossibility for God.

What we see is Jesus, as Deity, knowing the future in the smallest of details.

second in length: Based on number of verses. Ezekiel has a greater word count, based on the Hebrew, and both fall short of Jeremiah's word count.

The nations: Israel is God's chosen people—the Jewish people. When scripture refers to "the nations," such as in Isaiah 11:10, it is saying there will come a time when "us Gentiles" will seek Jesus.

We see this in scripture. A Gentile (Roman) centurion seeks out Jesus to cure his servant (Luke 7:1–10). A Canaanite (Syrophoenician) woman seeks out Jesus for a curing of her daughter (Mark 7:24–30). Note the Pharisee's complaint at the raising of Lazarus:

> The Pharisees said to one another, "You can see that this is doing you no good. <u>Look how the whole world has gone after Him</u>!"
>
> <u>Now there were some Greeks among those who went up to worship at the feast</u>. They came to Philip, who was from Bethsaida in Galilee, and requested of him, "<u>Sir, we want to see Jesus</u>." Philip relayed this appeal to Andrew, and both of them went and told Jesus. (John 12:19–22)

For now, Christianity is mainly composed of Gentiles. If you are curious as to why, our best scholar to explain this is the Apostle Paul. See Romans 9, 10, and 11.

34

The Suffering Servant
(Isaiah 52:13-53:12)

What are we to make of Isaiah 53?

The passage actually begins at Isaiah 52:13, and our English translations are relatively easy to understand. The words of God seem to paint a picture of His Suffering Servant—the Messiah. Though written seven hundred years before his birth, they seem to depict what Jesus of Nazareth experienced through his crucifixion.

But is that truly the case?

Today's rabbis tell us the words have nothing to do with a man named Jesus—nor any person for that matter. These are Hebrew writings—not Christian writings—and, according to today's rabbinical teachings, the words of Isaiah are referencing Israel.

Are they right about this? Are Christians simply reading things into the text to help build the case for Jesus?

Let's look at the text in its entirety, then we will break it down verse by verse and address its message. We'll ascertain whether the Jewish rabbis *of today* have the correct interpretation. You will be the judge.

> **52:13** Behold, My Servant will prosper;
>   He will be raised and lifted up and highly exalted.
> **14** Just as many were appalled at Him —
>   His appearance was disfigured beyond that of any man,
>   and His form was marred beyond human likeness—
> **15** so He will sprinkle many nations.
>   Kings will shut their mouths because of Him.
> For they will see what they have not been told,
>   and they will understand what they have not heard.
>
> **53:1** Who has believed our message?
>   And to whom has the arm of the LORD been revealed?
> **2** He grew up before Him like a tender shoot,
>   and like a root out of dry ground.
> He had no stately form or majesty to attract us,
>   no beauty that we should desire Him.
> **3** He was despised and rejected by men,
>   a man of sorrows, acquainted with grief.
> Like one from whom men hide their faces,
>   He was despised, and we esteemed Him not.
>
> **4** Surely He took on our infirmities
>   and carried our sorrows;
> yet we considered Him stricken by God,
>   struck down and afflicted.
> **5** But He was pierced for our transgressions,
>   He was crushed for our iniquities;

the punishment that brought us peace was upon Him,
and by His stripes we are healed.
6 We all like sheep have gone astray,
each one has turned to his own way;
and the LORD has laid on Him
the iniquity of us all.

7 He was oppressed and afflicted,
yet He did not open His mouth.
He was led like a lamb to the slaughter,
and as a sheep before her shearers is silent,
so He did not open His mouth.
8 By oppression and judgment He was taken away,
and who can recount His descendants?
For He was cut off from the land of the living;
He was stricken for the transgression of My people.

9 He was assigned a grave with the wicked,
and with a rich man in His death,
although He had done no violence,
nor was any deceit in His mouth.

10 Yet it was the LORD's will to crush Him
and to cause Him to suffer;
and when His soul is made a guilt offering,
He will see His offspring, He will prolong His days,
and the good pleasure of the LORD will prosper
in His hand.
11 After the anguish of His soul,
He will see the light of life and be satisfied.
By His knowledge My righteous Servant will justify
many,
and He will bear their iniquities.
12 Therefore I will allot Him a portion with the great,
and He will divide the spoils with the strong,

because He has poured out His life unto death,
>and He was numbered with the transgressors.
Yet He bore the sin of many
>and made intercession for the transgressors.

Now let's look at what these verses are telling us—focusing on Isaiah 53. For this analysis, we will assume the text refers to the Messiah. I have to make this assumption in that, if I try to mold this into somehow referencing Israel, it will make no sense. But again, you be the judge.

>Who has believed our message?
>>And to whom has the arm of the LORD been revealed? (Isaiah 53:1)

Isaiah is telling us that not many will understand this Anointed One from God. But for some, God will reveal who he is.

>He grew up before Him like a tender shoot,
>>and like a root out of dry ground.
>He had no stately form or majesty to attract us,
>>no beauty that we should desire Him. (Isaiah 53:2)

There is nothing about the Messiah that **sets him apart** from other Israelites. You might remember, when Judas betrayed Jesus, he had to show the temple guards which of the men in the garden of Gethsemane was Jesus (Mark 14:44). There apparently was nothing in Jesus' appearance that made him look any different than any of his disciples.

>He was despised and rejected by men,
>>a man of sorrows, acquainted with grief.
>Like one from whom men hide their faces,
>>He was despised, and we esteemed Him not.
>>(Isaiah 53:3)

Many would reject him—nothing outwardly would draw people to him.

> Surely He took on our infirmities
>   and carried our sorrows;
> yet we considered Him stricken by God,
>   struck down and afflicted. (Isaiah 53:4)

Our sins were placed upon the Messiah, and God punished him accordingly. On this side of the cross, and with the Apostolic witness, we understand why this happened. But this was not what the Jewish people were expecting. At least not for their Messiah. And because this rebellious rabbi from Galilee was being nailed to a Roman cross, many felt he must have deserved what he was getting. From their perspective, surely he was stricken by God because of *his* sins. But that is *not* what Isaiah is telling us, as Isaiah's text continues:

> But He was pierced for our transgressions,
>   He was crushed for our iniquities. (Isaiah 53:5)

The punishment meted out by God was not because of the Messiah's sins—the Messiah was without sin and lived in complete obedience to God the Father. Jesus, and only Jesus, was able to keep the Mosaic Law. He will tell those gathered on a mountainside to hear him,

> "Do not think that I have come to abolish the Law or
> the Prophets. I have not come to abolish them, but to
> fulfill them." (Matthew 5:17)

He was pierced and crushed for *our* sins, *our* failures, *our* rebellion against God and *our* indifference toward God.

> The punishment that brought us peace was upon Him,
>   and by His stripes we are healed. (Isaiah 53:5)

God's punishment upon Jesus brings you and I peace.

Why? How?

We have peace because we escape the wrath of God. Sin must be punished—and Jesus took upon himself our sin, accepting God's punishment in our place. It is the blood of Christ that allows our justification (being pronounced "not guilty" before God). We have peace because we have been reconciled to our Creator. We've seen this verse before, but it's worth repeating. Paul tells us,

> Since we have been justified through faith, we have peace with God through our Lord Jesus Christ. (Romans 5:1)

> There is now no condemnation for those who are in Christ Jesus. (Romans 8:1)

This is the Good News message of Christianity: our reconciliation with God that brings us peace due to the blood of Christ and the price *he* paid for our redemption.

The Isaiah text continues:

> We all like sheep have gone astray,
>   each one has turned to his own way;
> and the LORD has laid on Him
>   the iniquity of us all. (Isaiah 53:6)

All have gone astray. Paul will write, "all have sinned." Sin is universal.

> Just as many were appalled at Him —
>   His appearance was disfigured beyond that of any man,
>   and His form was marred beyond human likeness. (Isaiah 52:14)

To pay for our sins, the rejected Messiah undergoes such beatings and sufferings that he is disfigured and unrecognizable.

This brings up something to think about. Will Jesus continue to have the scars of his beatings and those of his crucifixion in his eternal kingdom? I'll address my thinking on this in the **notes** section of this lesson. What are your thoughts?

Let's return to the Isaiah text . . .

> He was oppressed and afflicted,
>> yet He did not open His mouth.
> He was led like a lamb to the slaughter,
>> and as a sheep before her shearers is silent,
>> so He did not open His mouth. (Isaiah 53:7)

What the Messiah did, he did willingly. He voluntarily accepted the punishment of our sins. Jesus told those close to him:

> I am the good shepherd. The good shepherd lays down His life for the sheep. (John 10:11)

> The reason the Father loves Me is that I lay down My life in order to take it up again. No one takes it from Me, but I lay it down of My own accord. I have authority to lay it down and authority to take it up again. This charge I have received from My Father." (John 10:17, 18)

Jesus will lay down his life for those the Father gives him.

Isaiah continues:

> By oppression and judgment, He was taken away,
>> and who can recount His descendants?
> For He was cut off from the land of the living;

He was stricken for the transgression of My people. (Isaiah 53:8)

The Messiah will suffer death—cut off from the land of the living—stricken for our sins. For rabbis who suggest this passage is referring to Israel, Israel was never cut off from the land of the living. But we will get to their interpretation in a moment.

He was assigned a grave with the wicked,
    and with a rich man in His death. (Isaiah 53:9)

He was numbered with the transgressors. (Isaiah 53:12)

His was a sinner's death—and his grave was with the wicked (plural in the Hebrew) and associated with a rich man (singular in the Hebrew, as it is in the English).

Jesus was crucified with a thief on each side of him. He died among thieves, plural.

And his grave was that of the rich man Joseph of Arimathea, singular.

The accuracy of these words is stunning—an accuracy that is true, of course, with the entire biblical text.

Yet it was the LORD's will to crush Him
    and to cause Him to suffer;
and when His soul is made a guilt offering. (Isaiah 53:10)

What the Messiah suffered was not by accident. The cross was not a mistake, it was God's will, and it was a victory. Everything Jesus went through was **propitiation** associated with God's righteous judgment against sin and rightful punishment of sin.

After the anguish of His soul,

He will see the light of life and be satisfied. (Isaiah 53:11)

The Messiah will suffer and die. But he will see the "light of life." Death is conquered. The Messiah's willing sacrifice leads to his bodily resurrection—and allows for our eventual bodily resurrection. If you are not shouting "amen" right now, either check your pulse or place a mirror under your nose.

> By His knowledge My righteous Servant will justify many,
>> and He will bear their iniquities. (Isaiah 53:11)

All of this will happen to God's Anointed—the Messiah and Suffering Servant—so that you and I can be justified (made right before God, that is, so that we can be pronounced "not guilty"). Our justification is not because of what we have done or promise to do, but because of what Christ has done and the completed work of the cross. As Christ himself said on the cross, "It is finished" (John 19:30).

And in this verse in Isaiah 53, again God reminds us that the Messiah bore our sins. Ravi **Zacharias** writes, "Jesus did not come to make bad people good, but to make dead people alive." We were dead in our sins. We were spiritually dead (remember—death is separation; spiritual death is separation from God). But our sins were given to Christ so that we could be born again and have fulness of life, and eternal life.

We began this lesson asking the question: What are we to make of Isaiah 53? For believers in Christ, these words—as we've said numerous times, words written seven hundred years before the event—seem to clearly reference Jesus of Nazareth and the recorded history (the Gospel record) of his crucifixion and resurrection. Christ taking upon himself the sins of the world and accepting punishment for these sins is foundational to our Christian faith. It is only through the cross that we are made acceptable to God and are invited to participate in His kingdom. The resurrection of Jesus assures us that his offering on the cross and the punishment he received fulfilled God's righteousness.

But how does Judaism view this text? After all, these are words from a Jewish prophet, written to Jewish people, and contained in the Jewish scriptures. They, too, are confronted with the question, "What are we to make of Isaiah 53?"

For almost two thousand years, the Jewish interpretation of Isaiah 53 was not that much different from how Christians began interpreting this text after the resurrection. Judaism recognized these words as a description of the Messiah—though they refused to accept Jesus as the Messiah. This was the most natural reading of the text, and the text made some level of sense.

But it is somewhat confusing in that it depicts the one destined to sit on David's throne as having to suffer and die.

Could there be **two Messiahs**? Could there be a Messiah who suffers—and one who is the victorious King? Some of the rabbis had introduced this way of thinking. But even under this belief, the Isaiah text was still thought to be describing a Messiah.

That the text concerned the Messiah was the rabbinical thinking and the way the text was taught until about 1000 AD. But as Christianity grew, the events foretold in these words appeared to be much too close to the events surrounding Jesus of Nazareth and what the Christians were saying. The rabbis faced a dilemma.

From their perspective, there were two solutions to their predicament. The first, and easiest, was to simply not read or focus on this portion of the book (scroll) of Isaiah. Many rabbis follow this path today.

Isaiah 53 is not read or taught in the synagogue. This text out of Isaiah is simply avoided.

The second solution was to **revise the interpretation of the text**. Instead of Isaiah 53 referring to the Messiah, they would now teach that these words reference the nation and people of Israel. Problem solved.

What do you think?

When you read these words can you envision the nation of Israel?

Or does this read more like the events surrounding Golgotha and a man who was crucified? Do the words seem to relate to the Suffering Servant, Jesus of Nazareth, who died on the cross for the forgiveness of your sins?

You be the judge.

Before we leave this section, it is beneficial to see how many times God reveals from this text *why* the Messiah suffers and dies. I have taken the liberty to rearrange and summarize Isaiah 53, organizing it chronological to the events of the cross:

- Many did not believe Jesus was the Christ. They did not believe the message of the prophets (verse 1).
- There was nothing about him that would attract people to him (verse 2).
- There was no majesty about him (verse 2).
- He was despised and rejected (verse 3).
- And familiar with pain and suffering (verse 3).
- He took up our pain (verse 4).
- He bore our suffering (verse 4).
- Because of this, people thought God was punishing him (verse 4).
- But he was sinless (verse 9).

- God laid upon him the sins of us all (verse 6).
- His life was made an offering for sin (verse 10).
- This allowed Christ to intercede on behalf of sinful humankind (verse 12).
- Christ accepted the cross voluntarily (verse 7).
- He was numbered among sinners (verse 12).
- He bore our sins (verse 11).
- He bore the sins of many (verse 12).
- Consequently, he was stricken for the sins of God's people (verse 8).
- It was God's will to crush him and cause him to suffer (verse 10).
- He was oppressed and afflicted (verse 7).
- He was pierced for our transgressions (verse 5).
- He was crushed for our iniquities (verse 5).
- For the sins of the people he was punished (verse 8).
- By his beatings we are healed (verse 5).
- He was assigned a grave (verse 9).
- He poured out his life unto death (verse 12).
- He died (verse 8).
- But he is resurrected (verse 10).
- He will see the light of life (verse 11).
- He will justify many—those who know him (verse 11).
- He is exalted (verse 12).

It's amazing how thoroughly God's word through Isaiah tells us of the reasons for the crucifixion. Jesus took *our* sins and paid the price for *our* sins.

Only Jesus did this.

And because of this, our justification and forgiveness can *only* come through Jesus. Jesus is the *only* way to God.

And that's why the Bible is all about Jesus.

From lesson 34: What do we learn about God?

- God does not remain silent when it comes to His image-bearers. Through His prophets, He provides instruction, warnings, hope, and encouragement.
- Concerning God's plans for redemption, seven hundred years before Jesus of Nazareth died on the cross, God clearly explains why this would happen and what this meant through the prophet Isaiah.

---

sets him apart: Tall, lean, fair-skinned—quite handsome if not downright striking in appearance. That's normally how those of us in the West picture Jesus. We tend to see him not much different than those around us—except tall, handsome, healthy.

I purchased a painting of Jesus from a Vietnamese artist, and his depiction has Jesus as being Asian. If you visit the Church of the Annunciation in Nazareth, a mosaic given to the church by Chinese believers has both the baby Jesus and Mary depicted as Asians.

And this is understandable. Believers everywhere seem to place Jesus within their culture. He looks like he belongs.

If this is your image of Jesus, you don't need to change this—because none of us know what Jesus really looked like. But, with the advent of the field of forensic anthropology, a group of researchers have created what might be a close approximation of what someone living in the ancient near east at the time of Christ would have looked like.

He would have most probably had short hair, not long. Average height of males at the time was 5 ft. 1 in. Average weight was 110 lbs. Due to diet and health issues, he might have had bowed legs and would probably be missing some teeth. All of this is speculation, of course. But it helps us view Jesus in a much broader, more contextualized sense.

If interested, including seeing an artist's sketch of what Jesus might have looked like, see Mike Fillon, "The Real Face of Jesus: Advances in forensic science reveal the most famous face in history", *Popular Mechanics*, January 13, 2015. Available at https://www. popularmechanics.com/science/health/a234/1282186/ (accessed November 23, 2019).

I believe there was an earlier article published in 2002 that discusses the methods used for the research in greater detail, and contains additional insights concerning what Jesus might have looked like. I have been unable to find this earlier article.

notes: Will Jesus continue to have the scars of his beatings and those of his crucifixion in his eternal kingdom?

We know our resurrected bodies will be "glorified." As Paul teaches,

> So will it be with the resurrection of the dead: What is sown is perishable; it is raised imperishable. It is sown in dishonor; it is raised in glory. It is sown in weakness; it is raised in power. (1st Corinthians 15:42, 43)

Bodies that are scarred and deformed and broken will appear renewed. But will Christ have the scars of the crucifixion throughout eternity?

I don't know the answer. Perhaps we can surmise one. You might recall, after the resurrection, those close to Jesus did not immediately recognize him. And yet, all ultimately did recognize him.

One post-resurrection appearance to the disciples is recorded by the historian Luke:

> While they were describing these events, Jesus Himself stood among them and said, "Peace be with you." But they were startled and frightened, thinking they had seen a spirit. (Luke 24:36, 37)

Note that the disciples were startled and frightened—but this might have been due to not expecting the resurrection, as opposed to being startled concerning something about how Jesus looked.

Also, when Jesus appeared at the Transfiguration (Matthew 17) he apparently has no scars—but this event precedes his death and resurrection.

When Jesus appeared after the resurrection, though, we know his scars *were* visible. Notice, he shows the disciples his hands and feet in the verses which follow the Luke text shared above:

> "Why are you troubled," Jesus asked, "and why do doubts arise in your hearts? Look at My hands and My feet. It is I Myself. Touch Me and see—for a spirit does not have flesh and bones, as you see I have." And when He had said this, He showed them His hands and feet. (Luke 24:38–40)

To doubting Thomas, the post-resurrected Jesus appears:

> Then Jesus said to Thomas, "Put your finger here and look at My hands. Reach out your hand and put it into My side. Stop doubting and believe." (John 20:27)

The nail wounds in his hands and feet seem to be present, as does the scar on his side from the Roman spear.

Also, there is an intriguing passage that's part of John's apocalyptic vision, as recorded in the book of Revelation:

> Then one of the elders said to me, "Do not weep! Behold, the Lion of the tribe of Judah, the Root of David, has triumphed to open the scroll and its seven seals." (Revelation 5:5)

John is going to be able to see Jesus. He anticipates seeing the Lion of the tribe of Judah in triumph. John turns and looks.

What does he see?

> Then I saw a Lamb who appeared to have been slain. (Revelation 5:6)

Much of the book of Revelation and the visions contained in it are symbolic. We shouldn't place too much weight behind a literal interpretation of what is being described. This does at least suggest, though, that Jesus, the Lamb of God, will maintain at least some of his scars—perhaps as an eternal reminder when we are with him as to what he did in order for us to be with him.

propitiation: For additional information, see lesson 21 in *A Forty-Day Study on Sin, Salvation, and Sanctification: Our Journey in Christ.*

Zacharias: From *The Grand Weaver: How God Shapes Us Through the Events of Our Lives.* The quote can be found in a Ravi Zacharias article titled "Threads of a Redeemed Heart" at https://www.rzim.org/read/just-thinking-magazine/threads-of-a-redeemed-heart (accessed November 23, 2019).

two Messiahs: For a more in-depth discussion, see Garrett Smith, "The Returning King: The 'Two Messiahs' in Zechariah" at the www.jewsforjesus.org website. The alternative to two Messiahs, of course, is one Messiah who comes twice—the Messiah of the Bible.

revise the interpretation of the text: Rachmiel Frydland, in an article titled, "The Rabbis' Dilemma: A Look at Isaiah 53" provides the following:

> Rashi (Rabbi Shlomo Itzchaki, 1040-1105) and some of the later rabbis interpreted the passage as referring to Israel. They knew that the older interpretations referred it to Messiah. However, Rashi lived at a time when a degenerate medieval distortion of Christianity was practiced. He wanted to preserve the Jewish people from accepting such a faith and, although his intentions were sincere, other prominent Jewish rabbis and leaders realized the inconsistencies of Rashi's interpretation. They presented a threefold objection to his innovation. First, they showed the consensus of ancient opinion. Secondly, they pointed out that the text is in the singular. Thirdly, they noted verse eight. This verse presented an insurmountable difficulty to those who interpreted this passage as referring to Israel.

His complete article can be found at www.jewsforjesus.org, which is an excellent resource to learn more about scripture and Jesus (Yeshua) from a Messianic Jewish perspective. The article referred to above can be found at https://jewsforjesus.org/publications/issues/issues-v02-n05/the-rabbis-dilemma-a-look-at-isaiah-53/

Messianic Jews believe in Jesus (Yeshua) as Lord and Savior, and they accept the blood of Christ for the forgiveness of their sins. But those outside this small community reject Jesus as the Messiah—and, by necessity, either omit reading Isaiah 53 or, when it is studied, distort the text such that it somehow applies to the nation of Israel. Frydland's reference to verse 8 is informative. Israel, as a nation, has never been cut off from the land of the living—nor, according to scripture, will it ever be!

35

The Major Prophets: Jeremiah

Having reviewed much of Isaiah's prophecies as they relate to the Messiah, this lesson reviews God's words associated with another major prophet, Jeremiah. We will also look at several passages from the book of Lamentations, which scholars believe was also written by Jeremiah.

Like all of the prophets we've read about so far, Jeremiah was called to point out the people's sins and to warn of God's impending judgment. What makes Jeremiah unique, though, is the time period in which he prophesied. He was the last major prophetic voice in Judah during the final decades before its destruction. For four decades he announced God's impending judgment and witnessed the people's repeated rejection of his messages from God.

He lived to see the devastation of Jerusalem and the exile of the people in fulfilment of God's word.

After our brief review of Jeremiah, we will examine text from the book of Ezekiel. Ezekiel's life overlaps that of Jeremiah and he writes from Babylonia during the time of the exile. Much of God's words through Ezekiel parallel those we find in Jeremiah. But there is a significant addition: Ezekiel is given visions of God Himself. We learn that God has left Jerusalem, if not literally, then at least figuratively, and through Ezekiel's writings we learn why.

This will be followed with a review of the book of Daniel, who also writes from exile and lives just long enough to see the Jews allowed to return to Jerusalem.

Daniel's writing differs substantially from those of the other prophets. He is given a detailed vision of the upcoming history of God's people, including an amazing prophecy concerning when the Messiah will come. Why did magi, the **"three kings"** from Persia, travel all the way to Jerusalem looking for the Christ-child? Why did they pick that precise time in history for their journey—and Jerusalem for their destination? The book of Daniel sheds light on this.

One of our remaining lessons, then, will very briefly cover the time period between the testaments. But our main focus will be on Malachi—the last prophet we'll discuss on this side of the New Testament. It is his writing that closes out the Old Testament.

So, let's continue.

This might be a good time to briefly review a timeline of events to put the lives of these prophets in perspective—and also review what we will be covering in these last remaining lessons of this volume.

You will recall that the armies of Assyria approached Jerusalem in 701 BC but failed to attack the city, much less conquer it (lesson 25).

Jeremiah is born about a half century after this (655 BC). Within his lifetime, the Assyrians face defeat by the Babylonians (612 BC). Jehoiakim, the king of Judah, begins paying tribute to the new Babylonian king, Nebuchadnezzar, and some of the nobility of Judah are taken to Babylon. This forced exile includes a teenage boy named Daniel, the author of the book by his name. Throughout this period,

Jeremiah warns the people of Judah of the eventual destruction of Jerusalem.

In 601 BC, Jehoiakim revolts against Babylon, leading to a three-month siege of Jerusalem (598 BC). Jehoiakim dies during this siege and is succeeded by his son, Jehoiachin, also called Jeconiah. Jerusalem falls to Nebuchadnezzar, and Jeconiah and officials within his administration, along with prominent citizens of Jerusalem, are taken to Babylon. The prophet Ezekiel is among those exiled.

To replace Jeconiah, Nebuchadnezzar appoints Jeconiah's uncle, Zedekiah, as king. Jeremiah, who continues to predict the fall of Jerusalem, warns Zedekiah not to rebel against Babylon—that Judah and Jerusalem are experiencing their rightful punishment from God.

Zedekiah, though, does not listen and revolts against Babylon's rule. This leads to Nebuchadnezzar's return and a final devastation of Jerusalem, including the complete destruction of the temple (589-586 BC). Zedekiah would be Judah's last king.

By now we recognize a significant teaching from the Old Testament is that sin must be punished—and will be punished.

With the exception of the cross, perhaps the greatest burden placed upon the heart of God is His punishment of Israel and Judah and the exile of His people. Isaiah calls this God's *"strange work"* and his *"disturbing task"* (Isaiah 28:21). This is God's *"destruction against the whole land"* (Isaiah 28:22). As any loving parent knows, when a child is to be disciplined, the pain experienced by the parent greatly exceeds that of the child.

When you read the examples below, see if you get a glimpse into the heart of God and His distress over the people's attitude toward Him—and the judgment His righteousness requires:

I remember the devotion of your youth,
    your love as a bride,
how you followed me. (Jeremiah 2:2)

What fault did your fathers find in Me
    that they strayed so far from Me,
and followed worthless idols. (Jeremiah 2:5)

They did not ask, 'Where is the LORD ...' (Jeremiah 2:6)

The priests did not ask, 'Where is the LORD?'
(Jeremiah 2:8).

My people have forgotten Me for days without number.
(Jeremiah 2:22)

My anguish, my anguish! I writhe in pain! (**Jeremiah 4:19a**)

Earlier it was mentioned that the opposite of love is not hate, it is indifference (lesson 16). Words like those above, though, suggest the opposite of love is also unfaithfulness. And the opposite of love can also be abandonment.

God has experienced the people's indifference. He has seen their unfaithfulness and how they have turned from Him. Over and over again, the people worship useless, lifeless, powerless idols. They forsake God and they forsake the covenant.

For forty years, Jeremiah chastises the people for these sins and this idolatry. He uses the metaphor of adultery, and the language of promiscuity and prostitution, to describe the people's unfaithfulness.

Through Jeremiah, God reminds His people, once again, what He wants from them:

"Return, O faithless children,
  and I will heal your faithlessness." (Jeremiah 3:22)

"If you will return, O Israel,
  return to Me," declares the LORD.

"If you will remove your detestable idols from My
sight
  and no longer waver,
and if you can swear, 'As surely as the LORD lives,'
  in truth, in justice, and in righteousness,
then the nations will be blessed by Him,
  and in Him they will glory." (Jeremiah 4:1, 2)

"Circumcise yourselves to the LORD." (Jeremiah 4:4)

Wash the evil from your heart, O Jerusalem,
  so that you may be saved. (Jeremiah 4:14)

Hear the word of the LORD, O king of Judah, who
sits on the throne of David—you and your officials
and your people who enter these gates. This is what
the LORD says: Administer justice and righteousness.
Rescue the victim of robbery from the hand of his
oppressor. Do no wrong or violence to the foreigner,
the fatherless, or the widow. Do not shed innocent
blood in this place. (Jeremiah 22:2, 3)

As stated earlier, the reference to "innocent blood" is that of child
sacrifice, as the chosen people of God incorporate within their
worship the practices associated with the enemies of Israel and as
they offer children to the pagan gods.

God describes the Israelites accordingly:

"My people are fools;
    they have not known Me.
They are foolish children,
    without understanding.
They are skilled in doing evil,
    but they know not how to do good." (Jeremiah 4:22)

God tells Jeremiah:

"Go up and down the streets of Jerusalem.
    Look now and take note; search her squares.
If you can find a single person,
    anyone who acts justly,
anyone who seeks the truth,
    then I will forgive the city." (Jeremiah 5:1)

"The house of Israel and the house of Judah
    have been utterly unfaithful to Me." (Jeremiah 5:11)

"I will pronounce My judgments against them
    for all their wickedness,
because they have forsaken Me
    to burn incense to other gods
    and to worship the works of their own hands."
    (Jeremiah 1:16)

"My people have exchanged their Glory for idols that
are useless." (Jeremiah 2:11)

"... the stain of your guilt is still before Me." (Jeremiah
2:32)

"Behold, I will judge you, because you say, 'I have not
sinned'." (Jeremiah 2:35)

"Your own evil will discipline you;

your own apostasies will reprimand you."
(Jeremiah 2:19)

As Jeremiah brings God's word to the people—words they refuse to accept—false prophets actively oppose his message. The false prophets deceive the people by offering the untrue assurance that there is nothing to fear. These deceivers spew forth **what the people want to hear**—that there will be peace. They repeat the false message that God will not let Jerusalem fall to an adversary. Didn't God save the city and the temple during the time of Hezekiah?

Jeremiah addresses these false prophets and their words of deception:

> They have lied about the LORD and said:
> "He will not do anything; harm will not come to us;
>   we will not see sword or famine.
> The prophets are but wind,
>   for the LORD's word is not in them." (Jeremiah 5:12, 13)

> "From prophet to priest,
>   all practice deceit.
> They have dressed the wound of My people
>   with very little care,
> saying, 'Peace, peace,'
>   when there is no peace at all." (Jeremiah 6:13, 14)

> The visions of your prophets
>   were empty and deceptive;
> they did not expose your guilt
>   to ward off your captivity.
> The burdens they envisioned for you
>   were empty and misleading. (Lamentations 2:14)

Repeatedly, Jeremiah's message falls on deaf ears, and he laments,

To whom can I give this warning?
    Who will listen to me?
Look, their ears are closed,
    so they cannot hear.
See, the word of the LORD has become offensive to them;
    they find no pleasure in it. (Jeremiah 6:10)

And God's words are clear:

"Their rebellious acts are many,
    and their unfaithful deeds are numerous."
(Jeremiah 5:6)

"I am bringing disaster from the north,
    and terrible destruction." (Jeremiah 4:6)

"Your ways and your deeds
    have brought this upon you.
This is your punishment; how bitter it is,
    because it pierces to the heart!" (Jeremiah 4:18)

"Behold, I am bringing a distant nation against you,
    O house of Israel." (Jeremiah 5:15)

"With the sword they will destroy
    the fortified cities in which you trust." (Jeremiah
    5:17)

"Just as you have forsaken Me and served foreign gods
in your land, so will you serve foreigners in a land
that is not your own." (Jeremiah 5:19)

"Hear, O earth! I am bringing disaster on this people,
    the fruit of their own schemes,
because they have paid no attention to My word
    and have rejected My instruction." (Jeremiah 6:19)

In one of Jeremiah's last acts before Jerusalem's destruction, he sends warnings to King Zedekiah written on a scroll. Zedekiah wants nothing to do with Jeremiah's words of condemnation and despair. The king cuts the scroll into pieces and throws each fragment into a fire (Jeremiah 36). In Zedekiah's eyes, **soon to be blinded** by Nebuchadnezzar, Jeremiah was a troublemaker and traitor.

The king does not listen. The people do not listen. No one listens.

So God must pursue His "strange work"—His "disturbing task":

> "I will hand Judah over to the king of Babylon, and he will carry them away to Babylon and put them to the sword. I will give away all the wealth of this city—all its products and valuables, and all the treasures of the kings of Judah—to their enemies. They will plunder them, seize them, and carry them off to Babylon." (Jeremiah 20:4, 5)

Zedekiah will be Judah's last king. Babylon's destruction of Judah and Jerusalem will be complete.

Note the words describing this event as found in the book of Lamentations:

> Those slain by the sword are better off
>   than those who die of hunger,
> who waste away, pierced with pain
>   because the fields lack produce.
>
> The hands of compassionate women
>   have cooked their own children,
> who became their food
>   in the destruction of the daughter of my people.

> The LORD has exhausted His wrath;
>> He has poured out His fierce anger. (Lamentations
>> 4:9–11)

What befell Jerusalem is appalling. Death came by sword, by plague, and also by famine. Survival required cannibalism. Ultimately, most survivors were taken to Babylon and would never live to see Jerusalem again.

In our lesson on Ruth (lesson 19), it was mentioned that the two most vulnerable people groups in ancient times were the widows and the orphans. Now these terms describe Jerusalem's few remaining survivors:

> We have become fatherless orphans;
>> our mothers are widows. (Lamentations 5:3)

Note the plea that closes out Lamentations:

> You, O LORD, reign forever;
>> Your throne endures from generation to generation.
> Why have You forgotten us forever?
>> Why have You forsaken us for so long?
> Restore us to Yourself, O LORD, so we may return;
>> renew our days as of old,
> unless You have utterly rejected us
>> and remain angry with us beyond measure.
>> (Lamentations 5:19–22)

From Jeremiah's perspective, perhaps God has forgotten His people. He has allowed Jerusalem to be devastated by a pagan king. The temple, the house and presence of God, has been destroyed.

Will God remain angry with His people beyond measure?

All of the prophets we have reviewed warn of God's wrath and depict God's destruction upon His people. The messages from God are clear and cohesive. But nowhere do we see an edict that there will be total annihilation. Messages of judgment and destruction also contain God's words of encouragement and restoration.

God will never abandon His people.

And through Jeremiah, He once again promises protection for a remnant that will be brought back to the land:

> "The whole land will be desolate,
>   but I will not finish its destruction." (Jeremiah 4:27)

> "I will not make a full end of you." (Jeremiah 5:18)

> "I will keep My eyes on them for good and will return them to this land." (Jeremiah 24:6)

> "I will give you shepherds after My own heart, who will feed you with knowledge and understanding." (Jeremiah 3:15)

> For this is what the LORD says: "When Babylon's seventy years are complete, I will attend to you and confirm My promise to restore you to this place. For I know the plans I have for you, declares the LORD, plans to prosper you and not to harm you, to give you a future and a hope." (Jeremiah 29:10, 11)

Note in the above, Jeremiah tells the people the exile will last seventy years (as discussed earlier). And note also, that God promises to prosper the people and to give them a future and a hope—the verse we have on the coffee cups and tee shirts.

Most importantly, God reminds the people of where all of this is headed. All of scripture is about Christ—and much of the Old Testament points toward who the Messiah will be and what he will be like. God's word through Jeremiah adds to what we learn concerning God's Anointed:

> Behold, the days are coming,
>> declares the LORD,
> when I will raise up for David
>> a Righteous Branch,
> and He will reign wisely as king
>> and administer justice and righteousness in the
>> land.
> In His days Judah will be saved,
>> and Israel will dwell securely.
> And this is His name by which He will be called:
>> The LORD Our Righteousness. (Jeremiah 23:5, 6)
> Behold, the days are coming,
>> declares the LORD,
> when I will fulfill the gracious promise
>> that I have spoken
> to the house of Israel
>> and the house of Judah.
> In those days and at that time
>> I will cause to sprout a Righteous Branch of David,
> and He will administer justice
>> and righteousness in the land.
> In those days Judah will be saved,
>> and Jerusalem will dwell securely,
> and this is the name by which it will be called:
>> The LORD Our Righteousness. (Jeremiah
>> 33:14–16)

The people will return to the land and they will be blessed. God does have plans to prosper His people. And He has plans not only to bless

Israel, but to bless all of the nations for those who take refuge in Him. The Abrahamic Covenant will be fulfilled. The promised descendant of David will reign. The Davidic Covenant will be fulfilled.

But this will not happen until God brings forth the seed of woman—the Son of God. The people must await this Redeemer and Righteous King—the Messiah who will fulfill the calling placed upon Israel.

John Mason Neale, an Anglican priest and songwriter, was born some two hundred years ago. Thomas Helmore was a choirmaster and associate of Neale's. We may not know much about these two brothers in Christ, but we do know words that they wrote. These were added to an old Latin tune—something we sing over and over again every Christmas season.

They are words surrounding the exile of God's people and their hope for the Redeemer:

> O come, O come, Emmanuel
> To free your captive Israel
> That mourns in lonely exile here
> Until the Son of God appear.

In our journey through the Biblical Story, we are still several hundreds of years away from the arrival of the Messiah—Emmanuel, God with us. During the time of Jeremiah, God has judged the people and has carried out His "strange work"—His "disturbing task."

But a remnant has been protected.

God will return them to the land.

They await "The LORD Our Righteousness." In the words of John Mason Neale and Thomas Helmore,

Rejoice! Rejoice!
O Israel.
To you shall come Emmanuel.

From lesson 35: What do we learn about God?

- As we saw in our last lesson, God does not remain silent when it comes to His image-bearers. Through His prophets, He provides instruction, warnings, hope, and encouragement. But we see a people who are deaf to the voice of God and blind to His acts of provision and mercy.
- God's righteousness requires sin to be punished.

"**three kings**": The story of visitors from the east traveling to Jerusalem at the time of the birth of Christ is found in Matthew 2. Despite manger scenes and a popular Christmas carol, these are not "three kings" who are "bearing gifts as they traverse afar."

They are magi, which were astrologers and advisers to the king.

Some Bible translations call them "wise men" (for example, the KJV), probably because labeling them as astrologers (or even sorcerers, which the word also implies) might tarnish our Christmas thoughts.

While the Bible only tells us that they came from an easterly direction, we can assume they come from Persia for three reasons:

1. The term "magi" is a Persian term (it is also where we get the word "magistrate" as well as "magician").
2. We find this word in the book of Daniel. Daniel held a position over the Magi during the last years of his life while that region was under Persian rule.

3. How did these Persian Magi know to go to Jerusalem, know that there would be an arrival of an important Jewish king, and that this would happen around this time period? This most likely were words, teachings, and prophecy passed down to them that originated with Daniel (Daniel was told when the Messiah would arrive).

Nowhere is it said that there were only three of these visitors. This tradition stems from there being only three gifts presented to Jesus. Also, contrary to virtually every Christmas card and manger scene out there, the Magi were not present at Jesus' birth. They appear sometime later.

We can ascertain this from at least two directions. Jesus was born in a stable—but the magi visit a house (Matthew 2:11). Also notice that King Herod asks the Magi when the star had appeared, and then proceeds to have male children two years old or younger killed. This could imply the star had appeared two years prior to their visit (that is, Jesus was two years old by the time of the visit of the Magi).

Lastly, and as stated, these are not kings. There is only one king present at the birth of Jesus, and that is Jesus.

Jeremiah 4:19a: There is scholarly disagreement as to whether these words reflect those of God or those of Jeremiah. If you read Jeremiah 4:18–22, it seems the words can be the voice of either. The text is unclear.

For one discussion of this passage, and its ambiguities and possible interpretations, see "Who is Speaking in Jeremiah 4:19–21?" available at https://brendasbiblioblog.wordpress.com/2012/08/23/part-1-who-is-speaking-in-jeremiah-419-21/ (accessed November 28, 2019).

what the people wanted to hear: Isaiah ran into this same situation. The people tell the prophets, in effect, "don't tell us the truth—tell us what we want to hear":

> These are rebellious people, deceitful children,
>> children unwilling to obey the LORD's instruction.
> They say to the seers,
>> "No more visions,"
> and to the prophets,
>> "Do not prophesy to us the truth.
> Speak to us pleasant words;
>> prophesy illusions." (Isaiah 30:9, 10)

soon to be blinded: For those interested in the accuracy of God's prophetic word, you will recall our discussion of prophecies from Jeremiah and Ezekiel concerning King Zedekiah (lesson 25). Zedekiah witnessed the execution of his sons after which he was blinded and taken to Babylon. We saw how the prophetic word from Jeremiah seemed to conflict with that of Ezekiel—but both prophecies were fulfilled precisely as stated.

We see a similar situation in Jeremiah's text containing another prophecy which, on close reading, seems to be in error. To understand this, we need to first go to the New Testament book of Matthew and look at the genealogy from Abraham to Jesus (Matthew 1:1–17). Notice closely verses 11 and 12 and the name "Jeconiah." King Jeconiah is in the family tree of the Messiah.

Now let's look at Jeremiah's prophecy. God pronounces a curse on Judah's King Jeconiah and tells him *none* of his descendants will sit on the throne of David:

> "Enroll this man as childless,
>> a man who will not prosper in his lifetime.
> <u>None of his descendants will prosper</u>

> to sit on the throne of David
> or to rule again in Judah." (Jeremiah 22:30)

Wups. How can none of Jeconiah's descendants sit on the throne of David—and yet the Messiah is in the lineage of Jeconiah? Doesn't this make God's word in Jeremiah conflict with God's word in Matthew and the ancestry of Jesus? Isn't one of the writings incorrect?

Of course not.

Note the genealogy in Matthew specific to how it leads to Jesus:

> ... and Jacob the father of Joseph, the husband of Mary,
> of whom was born Jesus, who is called Christ.
> (Matthew 1:16)

Jeconiah did reign in Jerusalem, but none of his descendants became king. King Zedekiah, who ruled during the Babylonian invasion, was his uncle—not a son and descendant. More importantly, the blood line of Jesus does not come from Jeconiah! Matthew's genealogy goes to Joseph, the husband of Mary. Jesus, conceived by the Spirit of God, did not have a blood relationship with Joseph.

But didn't Jesus have to be a descendant of King David?

Yes. And this happens, but not through Jeconiah (or Joseph). The genealogy in Luke's Gospel clears this up.

Luke traces the blood line from Adam, the first man, through to David (Matthew, writing mainly to the Jews, starts his genealogy with Abraham, the father of the Jews).

From Abraham through David the genealogies in Luke and Matthew are identical.

But when we get to David, the genealogies differ.

Matthew's genealogy leading to Jesus goes through David's son Solomon. This line through Solomon contains Jeconiah—but this only takes us to Joseph, the husband of Mary (who is outside the blood line of the Messiah).

Luke's genealogy, on the other hand, goes through Nathan, the second surviving son of Bathsheba. Jeconiah is *not* in this line. This genealogy takes us down through Heli, the father of Mary and thus Mary is in the blood line of David.

Jeremiah's prophecy (God's curse on the family line of Jeconiah) is historically accurate. None of Jeconiah's descendants will ever sit on David's throne.

36

The Major Prophets: Ezekiel

Because Ezekiel brought God's word to the people during a portion of the time Jeremiah was prophesying, we should expect commonalities in the writings of these two prophets. And that's what we find.

Both Jeremiah and Ezekiel address a disobedient people who continually break their covenant with God. In commissioning Ezekiel, God tells him,

> I am sending you to the Israelites, to a rebellious nation that has rebelled against Me. To this very day they and their fathers have rebelled against Me. They are obstinate and stubborn children. (Ezekiel 2:3–4)

One of the great evils of this rebellious people was their sin of idolatry. Jeremiah repeatedly confronts the people concerning this, which we also see in God's words through Ezekiel:

> These men have set up idols in their hearts. (Ezekiel 14:3)

> ... because of their idols, they are all estranged from Me.' (Ezekiel 14:5)

Repent and turn away from your idols; turn your faces away from all your abominations. (Ezekiel 14:6)

Similarly, like Jeremiah, Ezekiel uses the metaphor of adultery in describing the people's unfaithfulness to God.

"I will make the land desolate, because they have acted unfaithfully, declares the Lord GOD." (Ezekiel 15:8)

"Because of your fame, you trusted in your beauty and played the harlot. You lavished your favors on everyone who passed by, and your beauty was theirs for the asking. You took some of your garments and made colorful high places for yourself, and on them you prostituted yourself. Such things should not have happened; never should they have occurred!" (Ezekiel 16:15, 16)

And, as He did through Jeremiah, God also addresses the abhorrent practice of child sacrifice through Ezekiel:

"You even took the sons and daughters you bore to Me and sacrificed them as food to idols. Was your prostitution not enough? You slaughtered My children and delivered them up through the fire to idols." (Ezekiel 16:20, 21)

God's words through Ezekiel, like His words through Jeremiah, also condemn the false prophets and the people's willingness to place their trust in their deception:

"Prophesy against the prophets of Israel who are now prophesying. Tell those who prophesy out of their own imagination: Hear the word of the LORD! This is what the Lord GOD says: Woe to the foolish prophets who follow their own spirit yet have seen nothing. Your prophets, O Israel, are like foxes among the ruins. You did not go up to the gaps or restore the wall around the house of Israel so that it would stand in the battle on the Day of the LORD."

"They see false visions and speak lying divinations. They claim, 'Thus declares the LORD,' when the LORD did not send them; yet they wait for the fulfillment of their message." (Ezekiel 13:1–6)

"Because you have uttered vain words and seen false visions, I am against you, declares the Lord GOD. My hand will be against the prophets who see false visions and speak lying divinations. They will not belong to the council of My people or be recorded in the register of the house of Israel, nor will they enter the land of Israel. Then you will know that I am the Lord GOD... they have led My people astray, saying, 'Peace,' when there is no peace." (Ezekiel 13:8–11)

Both Jeremiah and Ezekiel provide God's words concerning the judgment of Jerusalem. Both lived there during the first attacks on the city. But Ezekiel was one of the individuals displaced early to Babylon before Jerusalem was destroyed, while Jeremiah remained in Jerusalem throughout its destruction.

Ezekiel does not begin his writings until five years after his exile. But God's "strange work"—his "disturbing task" are yet to be completed, so Ezekiel's warnings are dire and descriptive. Jerusalem and the temple face imminent destruction:

Therefore, this is what the Lord GOD says: 'Behold, I Myself am against you, Jerusalem, and I will execute judgments among you in the sight of the nations. Because of all your abominations, I will do to you what I have never done before and will never do again. As a result, fathers among you will eat their sons, and sons will eat their fathers. I will execute judgments against you and scatter all your remnant to every wind.' (Ezekiel 5:8–10)

Famine is just one display of God's wrath. There will be plagues as well as death from the swords of the Babylonians:

> I will send famine and wild beasts against you, and they will leave you childless. Plague and bloodshed will sweep through you, and I will bring a sword against you. I, the LORD, have spoken. (Ezekiel 5:17)

> He who is far off will die by the plague, he who is near will fall by the sword, and he who remains will die by famine. So I will vent My fury upon them. (Ezekiel 6:12)

Note the three aspects of famine, plague, and sword. As mentioned, in Jeremiah's writing he will group these three terms together fifteen times. Ezekiel will use these same terms together eight times.

While both prophets describe God's wrath and fury, both also include God's promises to protect a remnant and return them to the land. From the Ezekiel text:

> Therefore, declare that this is what the Lord GOD says: 'I will gather you from the peoples and assemble you from the countries to which you have been scattered, and I will give back to you the land of Israel.'

> When they return to it, they will remove from it all its detestable things and all its abominations. And I will give them singleness of heart and put a new spirit within them; I will remove their heart of stone and give them a heart of flesh, so that they may follow

My statutes, keep My ordinances, and practice them. Then they will be My people, and I will be their God. (Ezekiel 11:17–20)

You, O mountains of Israel, will produce branches and bear fruit for My people Israel, for they will soon come home.

For behold, I am on your side; I will turn toward you, and you will be tilled and sown. I will multiply the people upon you—the house of Israel in its entirety. The cities will be inhabited, and the ruins rebuilt. I will fill you with people and animals, and they will increase and be fruitful. I will make you as inhabited as you once were, and I will make you prosper more than before. Then you will know that I am the LORD. (Ezekiel 36:8–11)

While the above show some of the common elements in their prophecies, there are also differences. Ezekiel is not in Jerusalem. He is living among the exiles along the River Kebar, a river or canal located in Babylonia. And he experiences three very unusual visions.

He describes the first as that of "the appearance of the likeness of the glory of the LORD" (Ezekiel 1:28). This is a vision of God. But in this vision, God is not in Jerusalem. He is appearing to Ezekiel in Babylonia.

What is happening? What is the vision suggesting? Why isn't God in Jerusalem?

More specifically, why isn't God's presence in the Holy of Holies within the Temple?

Ezekiel's second vision answers this. It comes a year later when, once again, Ezekiel is given a vision of God. This time, though, Ezekiel is shown the temple in Jerusalem. God tells Ezekiel,

> "Do you see what they are doing—the great abominations that the house of Israel is committing—to drive Me far from My sanctuary?" (Ezekiel 8:6)

Ezekiel sees rampant idolatry, as elders of Israel are worshipping other gods both inside and outside of the temple. Ezekiel sees God depart from the temple and going east toward Babylon. Israel's sins have become so blatant and perverse that God must leave His temple.

It is important to note, though, God has not **abandoned** His people. God says:

> "Although I sent them far away among the nations and scattered them among the countries, yet for a little while <u>I have been a sanctuary for them in the countries to which they have gone.</u>" (Ezekiel 11:16)

God has gone into exile with His people.

And Ezekiel's visions don't end here, with God leaving Jerusalem. A third time Ezekiel is given a vision of God—the glory of the LORD. But God's glory is no longer in Babylon. Nor is it leaving the Jerusalem temple.

Ezekiel sees a new Jerusalem and a *new* temple—with God's glory returning to this temple:

> The vision I saw was like the vision I had seen when He came to destroy the city and like the visions I had seen by the River Kebar. I fell facedown, and the glory of the LORD entered the temple through the gate facing east. Then the Spirit lifted me up and brought

me into the inner court, and the glory of the LORD filled the temple. (Ezekiel 43:3–5)

I looked and saw the glory of the LORD filling His temple, and I fell facedown. (Ezekiel 44:4)

God's "strange work" and his "disturbing task"—God's "destruction against the whole land"—is now over. As Ezekiel's writing comes to a close, Ezekiel foresees God's judgment having ended and God's return to Jerusalem.

There is much more in Ezekiel's prophecies that could be explored, but we will limit our review to two additional sections of his writing. Both foresee the future God has for His people.

The first involves Ezekiel's vision of a valley filled with dry bones (Ezekiel 37). Symbolizing Israel in its captivity, Israel is presented as a valley filled with dry bones—bones that lack flesh and lack life itself. The people are like the skeletons in that valley. They have experienced God's judgment and have felt the brunt of God's wrath. Like many left behind in Jerusalem, with its plagues and starvation, people exist in a state of living death.

Would they remain that way forever, with no end to their judgment?

In the vision, God breathes upon the dry bones and they come to life. The vision makes it clear: God's people will be restored. They will be given new life. This happens through the breath of God, implying their restoration will be both physical and spiritual.

The second section to briefly review involves the two chapters following this, Ezekiel 38 and 39. These refer to the end times and concern an entity called "Gog." This term can reference an individual, or it can be a symbolic name for a group of people.

There will be two times in Israel's future where Gog becomes important.

The first occasion happens when Israel is at peace. Nations under the leadership of Gog attack Israel. Gog and this army are defeated by God Himself, this occurring on the mountains of Israel.

The slaughter associated with this event is massive. A portion of the text reads like what might be expected in a nuclear conflict. The ground shakes and there are collapsing mountains and fire (Ezekiel 38:18–22). The Bible tells us that what remains on the battlefield can be used for fuel for seven years (Ezekiel 39:10). Could this be radioactive materials recovered and used as nuclear fuel for power?

The text also tells us that the dead must be buried, and the land must be cleansed—a process that takes seven months (Ezekiel 39:12, 16). Could this burial and cleansing be necessitated due to remaining radioactivity?

Of course, these are speculations.

Regardless, this portion of Ezekiel's prophecy seems to be describing the tribulation—the presence of the antichrist as God orchestrates a series of events to regather Israel in preparation for the return of Christ and his millennial rule.

God's words through Ezekiel describe this:

> "I will take the Israelites out of the nations to which they have gone, and I will gather them from all around and bring them into their own land. I will make them one nation in the land, on the mountains of Israel, and one king will rule over all of them. Then they will no longer be two nations and will never again be divided into two kingdoms.

They will no longer defile themselves with their idols or detestable images, or with any of their transgressions. I will save them from all their apostasies by which they sinned, and I will cleanse them. Then they will be My people, and I will be their God. My servant David will be king over them, and there will be one shepherd for all of them. They will follow My ordinances and keep and observe My statutes.

They will live in the land that I gave to My servant Jacob, where your fathers lived. They will live there forever with their children and grandchildren, and My servant David will be their prince forever. And I will make a covenant of peace with them; it will be an everlasting covenant. I will establish them and multiply them, and I will set My sanctuary among them forever. My dwelling place will be with them; I will be their God, and they will be My people. Then the nations will know that I the LORD sanctify Israel, when My sanctuary is among them forever." (Ezekiel 37:21–28)

The second, and final time we hear about Gog is at the end of Christ's millennial rule. Nations once again conspire against God and His Anointed (Psalm 2). Here, though, Satan himself is involved.

This is the final battle.

There is no need to bury the dead. The end comes quickly, as fire from heaven destroys the armies opposing God's people. Satan and his followers appear before the great white throne judgment and are cast into the lake of fire (Revelation 20). Those who have opposed God's rule and who have not accepted the blood of the Lamb are also cast into the lake of fire—as is hades itself, and even death. There is no longer any need for hades—hades defined as the grave, as well as its definition as the temporary place for non-believers ("hell").

It is after this event that this earth—the one we are on right now—is completely destroyed and is replaced by our eternal home, the new earth of Revelation 21.

From lesson 36: What do we learn about God?

- Ezekiel's visions include God leaving the temple. But God does not abandon His people. He is with them throughout the exile and will bring them back into the land. His visions also include God returning to a temple in Zion.
- God must judge the sins of the people, but he remains faithful to His people, promising to return them to the land where they will prosper.

abandoned: God has promised never to abandon His people (Deuteronomy 31:6). Of course, for those who have accepted the blood of Christ in payment for our sins, nothing whatsoever can separate us from God and His love (Roman 8:38, 39). There is no condemnation (Romans 8:1) and we have peace with God (Roman 5:1).

Can we be certain of this? Is our salvation secure? This is covered in lesson 37 in volume 2. It is also covered in lesson 28 in *A Forty-Day Study on Sin, Salvation, and Sanctification.*

37

The Major Prophets: Daniel

In my personal studies of the Old Testament, I find only two individuals where nothing negative seems to be said about them. One is Joseph. The other is Daniel.

In this lesson, we will briefly look at the prophet Daniel and his writings. But before we do, let's compare Daniel to Joseph. You will recall, Joseph was sold into slavery and taken to Egypt. He was the favorite son of Jacob, also called Israel.

- The stories of Joseph and Daniel provide "bookends" concerning momentous events in Israel's history. Joseph plays a significant role before the nation of Israel came into being. Daniel's ministry came after Israel's period of glory and while the nation was in ruins.
- When Joseph is in his late teens, he is taken from his homeland and into Egypt. When Daniel was about the same age, he, too, is taken from his homeland. Daniel was taken to Babylon.
- Both find themselves living among a foreign people, who spoke in a foreign language, having foreign customs, and worshipping foreign gods. Neither Joseph nor Daniel were there by desire.

- Despite being given new names, both retain their Hebrew names and, most importantly, both remain faithful to God and do so despite numerous obstacles. Joseph is cast into prison for his faithfulness. Daniel is cast into a den of lions for his.
- But God continually provides both with His protection. Additionally, both are exalted in their respective communities as part of God's plans for His people.
- Perhaps the greatest similarity between the two, both are given unique abilities to interpret dreams and interpret the dreams of kings. Joseph is able to foresee an upcoming famine and prepare Egypt for what happens in its future. Daniel is able to properly interpret the dreams of Nebuchadnezzar and foresee world events on a global scale.
- In both cases, these abilities lead each to be placed into high positions—Joseph within Egypt and Daniel within Babylonia.

While these are a few of the similarities, there is an additional similarity. Both talk about end-of-life issues. But they present an interesting difference.

At the end of Joseph's life, his focus is on his burial. He asks that his bones be taken to the land promised to his forefathers. He has faith that his people will be delivered from Egypt and eventually be in their own land.

Daniel, too, knows that the people of God will be returned to the land of promise after their exile. His focus, though, is not on burial but on resurrection. He is given a vision of the end times, when there will be tribulation but also resurrection:

> There will be a time of distress, the likes of which will not have occurred from the beginning of nations until that time. But at that time your people—everyone

whose name is found written in the book—will be delivered.

And many who sleep in the dust of the earth will awake, some to everlasting life, but others to shame and everlasting contempt. Then the wise will shine like the brightness of the heavens, and those who lead many to righteousness will shine like the stars forever and ever. (Daniel 12:1–3)

As one **theologian** has said, "One man had his mind directed to his burial; the other had his directed to the time when he would be raised from the dead."

Let's now look at Daniel's writing.

The first half of the book of Daniel describes Daniel's life and that of two rulers in that region: the Babylonian king, Nebuchadnezzar, and a subsequent ruler, Belshazzar. It begins by recounting Daniel's situation in Babylon, where he has been taken from the courts of Jerusalem along with three of his friends. His writing describes four major events: An episode involving his three friends and a fiery furnace; a period of madness associated with King Nebuchadnezzar; the fall of Babylon while under the rule of Belshazzar; and lastly, Daniel's salvation from the lion's den.

Of significance, though, are the visions Daniel is given and their interpretation. These should be of interest in that we are included in these visions. All depict the world events that will be orchestrated by God. Although each vision differs in content and the various symbols they use, making them somewhat confusing to interpret, they are all related and connected.

In the first dream King Nebuchadnezzar sees a large statue described as follows:

The head of the statue was pure gold, its chest and arms were silver, its belly and thighs were bronze, its legs were iron, and its feet were part iron and part clay. (Daniel 2:32, 33)

Daniel correctly interprets this as depicting the last four earthly kingdoms. We will put this into perspective shortly.

There is a fifth entity which is also a kingdom. But this kingdom is quite different:

... a stone was cut out, but not by human hands. It struck the statue on its feet of iron and clay and crushed them ...

... the stone that had struck the statue became a great mountain and filled the whole earth. (Daniel 2:34, 35)

There will be four kingdoms from Daniel's time and into the future. Because we live two and a half millennia after Daniel recorded this, we know some of the specifics of the future Daniel saw. But keep in mind, this is the future from Daniel's perspective. He is describing things that didn't come about until hundreds of years after his death.

- The head of the giant statue is made of gold and represents Babylon and Nebuchadnezzar's rule. That this appears as gold is significant. Babylon was known for its wealth and opulence. We see an example of this in the large banquet held by Belshazzar as described in Daniel 5—a banquet attended by a thousand nobles. One of the seven wonders of the ancient world was the beautiful hanging gardens of Babylon.
- Babylon is destroyed by a coalition of two peoples, the Medes and the Persians, which became the Medo-Persian empire. This is depicted by the chest and the two arms of the statue.

These are made of silver. While silver has been used in trade for thousands of years, it was during the Medo-Persian empire that silver coinage became prevalent.

- But this empire, in turn, is destroyed by Alexander the Great and Greece—depicted by the bronze portion of the statue. It was Alexander the Great who introduced brass armor in combat.

- And Greece, in turn, is conquered by Rome—depicted by the statue's legs that are of iron. Iron symbolizes strength. It was the Romans that relied heavily on iron weapons in warfare.

- But Rome, itself, eventually crumbles—easily anticipated by the unwieldy structure of the feet of iron mixed with clay. As the Roman empire grew, instead of the use of force, its influence was spread through various alliances. As a result, Rome became weaker and weaker until its eventual collapse.

- Rome will be the last world empire. There will be no other.

- But the dream includes a cut stone, but not cut through the use of hands and one that grows to fill the whole earth. This is something supernatural. It is the kingdom of God and reflects the presence and supernatural growth of God's **Church**—which today can be found throughout the world.

Daniel is deciphering this vision during Nebuchadnezzar's lifetime—the period of Babylonian rule (~606 BC). Daniel did live to see the rise of the Medo-Persian empire and Babylon's fall. We know the exact date Babylon fell—October 12, 549 BC. But all that follows lie into the future, from Daniel's perspective.

Alexander the Great was not born until 356 BC, and Rome did not defeat Greece until 146 BC.

As to Rome's disintegration, this did not occur until about 500 years after the birth of Christ.

We have only discussed the main theme behind the major portion of Daniel's visions. But they include amazing details. What Daniel describes is so accurate that there was a time when many thought his writing had to have been changed and modified after-the-fact, that is, after the predicted events had already occurred.

However, Daniel's text was translated into Greek around 270 BC—which predates much of the events of his prophecy. Attempts to suggest the accuracy is due to anything other than God's revelation is disingenuous.

The vision ends with the Kingdom of God, not a worldly kingdom. And historically, Rome was the last world empire and was not conquered by a world empire. We might look in a mirror and suggest the United States has replaced Rome, but this is not the case. At present, the United States is a world *power*—but we certainly do not rule the world. The dream and Daniel's subsequent visions suggest there will be not be a world ruler until the time of the antichrist.

Time does not permit an exhaustive review of Daniel's subsequent visions—but each are profoundly accurate, and each provide amazing details (see "**For further study**" below). But let's look at several other items from Daniel.

Daniel places a date on the portion of his writing we call "chapter 9":

> In the first year of Darius son of Xerxes, a Mede by descent, who was made ruler over the kingdom of the Chaldeans —in the first year of his reign, I, Daniel, understood from the sacred books, according to the word of the LORD to Jeremiah the prophet, that the desolation of Jerusalem would last seventy years. (Daniel 9:1–3)

This places the writing around 539 BC. To put this into perspective, Daniel was taken to Babylon in 605 BC, so he has been in Babylon for some sixty-six years (Nebuchadnezzar died around 562 BC). Daniel is reading the sacred books, which include writings from Jeremiah that we looked at earlier. God's word through Jeremiah says the period of exile will last seventy years, allowing Daniel to recognize the period of exile is about to end.

Daniel turns to God in prayer. Time after time, God has asked that His people repent and return to Him. We see Daniel obeying this instruction. Note what Daniel says in his prayer (Daniel 9:4–14):

> O, Lord, the great and awesome God, who keeps His covenant of loving devotion to those who love Him and keep His commandments, we have sinned and done wrong. We have acted wickedly and rebelled. We have turned away from Your commandments and ordinances. We have not listened to Your servants the prophets, who spoke in Your name to our kings, leaders, fathers, and all the people of the land.

Daniel's words are remarkably inclusive concerning the sins of God's people. But Daniel doesn't stop here. He continues:

> To You, O Lord, belongs righteousness, but this day we are covered with shame—the men of Judah, the people of Jerusalem, and all Israel near and far, in all the countries to which You have driven us because of our unfaithfulness to You. O LORD, we are covered with shame—our kings, our leaders, and our fathers—because we have sinned against You.

No attempt is made to justify the people's unfaithfulness. All have sinned against God. Daniel makes no excuses. And in his acknowledgment of sin, Daniel repeatedly uses the term "we."

He includes himself when describing the people's sinfulness and unfaithfulness, though we have no record that Daniel was ever unfaithful to God.

As importantly, he accepts the punishment the Israelites have experienced:

> To the Lord our God belong compassion and forgiveness, even though we have rebelled against Him and have not obeyed the voice of the LORD our God to walk in His laws, which He set before us through His servants the prophets.
>
> All Israel has transgressed Your law and turned away, refusing to obey Your voice; so the oath and the curse written in the Law of Moses, the servant of God, has been poured out on us because we have sinned against You. You have carried out the words spoken against us and against our rulers by bringing upon us a great disaster. For under all of heaven, nothing has ever been done like what has been done to Jerusalem.
>
> Just as it is written in the Law of Moses, all this disaster has come upon us, yet we have not sought the favor of the LORD our God by turning from our iniquities and giving attention to Your truth. Therefore, the LORD has kept the calamity in store and brought it upon us. For the LORD our God is righteous in all He does; yet we have not obeyed His voice.

I've quoted this at length because Daniel has clearly explained the state of God's people and the reason for God's divine judgment. Daniel's confession recognizes Israel's sinful state and he acknowledges guilt. He accepts as being justified the punishment Israel (Israel and Judah) have experienced.

We don't know how Daniel's prayer would have ended because it is interrupted by God.

As Daniel is praying, the angel Gabriel appears. The words spoken to Daniel are weighty, to say the least. Let's first read this in its entirety, and then we will put this into perspective. It is one of most amazing and revealing prophecies of all of the Old Testament.

> **9:24** Seventy weeks are decreed for your people and your holy city to stop their transgression, to put an end to sin, to make atonement for iniquity, to bring in everlasting righteousness, to seal up vision and prophecy, and to anoint the Most Holy Place.
>
> **9:25** Know and understand this: From the issuance of the decree to restore and rebuild Jerusalem, until the Messiah, the Prince, there will be seven weeks and sixty-two weeks. It will be rebuilt with streets and a trench, but in times of distress.
>
> **9:26** Then after the sixty-two weeks, the Messiah will be cut off and will have nothing.
>
> Then the people of the prince who is to come will destroy the city and the sanctuary. The end will come like a flood, and until the end there will be war; desolations have been decreed. **9:27** And he will confirm a covenant with many for one week, but in the middle of the week he will put an end to sacrifice and offering. And on the wing of the temple will come the abomination that causes desolation, until the decreed destruction is poured out upon him.

Daniel is describing the period that includes the arrival of the Messiah, his death, and his eventual return.

We can label these four verses as follows:

Daniel 9:24 – The overall scope of the prophecy.
Daniel 9:25 – The 69 weeks.
Daniel 9:26 – An interval between the 69th and 70th week.
Daniel 9:27 – The 70th week.

If this sounds confusing, that's only because it is confusing. But we'll try to sort it out.

> Seventy weeks are decreed for your people and your holy city to stop their transgression, to put an end to sin, to make atonement for iniquity, to bring in everlasting righteousness, to seal up vision and prophecy, and to anoint the Most Holy Place. (Daniel 9:24)

Note the phrase "your people and your holy city." Gabriel is telling Daniel there are seventy important "weeks" associated with God's people and Jerusalem. The prophecy concerns the Jews and Jerusalem—not the Church.

There is a purpose in God bringing the events of this timeline to pass:

1. "to stop . . . transgression"
2. "to put an end to sin"
3. "to make atonement for iniquity"
4. "to bring in everlasting righteousness"
5. "to seal up vision and prophecy"
6. "to anoint the Most Holy Place"

God's timeline includes the total eradication of sin and its atonement, and the bringing in of everlasting righteousness. From Daniel's perspective, these are future events. From our perspective, while much of this is still in the future, the atonement of sin has already occurred (the crucifixion). The "everlasting righteousness" is the establishment of Christ's millennial rule—something yet to occur.

As to the timeline, the "weeks" mentioned here are not weeks of seven days, they are weeks of seven years. How can a week of seven days refer to a "week" of seven years?

- That's what the scholars tell us—and they have done the research.
- Part of what Gabriel describes has already occurred—and we know the timing of the prophecy's fulfilment is accurate if the "weeks" represents weeks of years (we'll discuss this in detail below).
- Though not common, transitions concerning units of time are not unheard of in scripture. As one example, the prophet Ezekiel is commanded by God to perform a number of visual, symbolic acts among the people as a method of getting their attention:

> "Now you, son of man, take a brick, place it before you, and draw on it the city of Jerusalem. Then lay siege against it: Construct a siege wall, build a ramp to it, set up camps against it, and place battering rams around it on all sides. Then take an iron plate and set it up as an iron wall between yourself and the city. Turn your face toward it so that it is under siege and besiege it. This will be a sign to the house of Israel.
>
> Then lie down on your left side and place the iniquity of the house of Israel upon yourself. You are to bear their iniquity for the number of days you lie on your side. For I have assigned to you 390 days, according to the number of

years of their iniquity. So you shall bear the iniquity of the house of Israel." (Ezekiel 4:1–5)

Ezekiel builds a model to show the people what is about to happen to Jerusalem. He is to lay on his side for 390 days—with each day representing a year in time (the 390 years of the people's iniquity).

Though not as close of a comparison, the seventy years of exile relate to the 490-year period in which the Israelites did not follow God's command concerning the Sabbath rest for the land (Leviticus 25:4, see lesson 25). For 490 years, Israel had failed to observe the land's one-year-in-seven Sabbath rest, so 70 Sabbath rests had been missed. The term of the Babylonian captivity was set at 70 years to make up the deficit (2nd Chronicles 36:21). Here the land enjoys its Sabbath rest—but each year of exile represents seven years of Israel's disobedience.

Gabriel is talking about a unit of time involving seventy weeks, but these are weeks of years.

Let's continue.

> Know and understand this: From the issuance of the decree to restore and rebuild Jerusalem, until the Messiah, the Prince, there will be seven weeks and sixty-two weeks. It will be rebuilt with streets and a trench, but in times of distress. (Daniel 9:25)

Verse 24 mentions seventy weeks. And as we have said, these are weeks of years. This is now broken down into two periods: a period of seven weeks (49 years) and a period of sixty-two weeks (434 years). The "start" of this timeline occurs with the issuance of the decree to restore and rebuild Jerusalem. The Messiah will come 49 plus 434, or 483 years later.

Let's unpack this even further. From the perspective of both Jewish and Babylonian calendars, a year consisted of 360 days. These 483 years, then, represent 173,880 days. Gabriel tells Daniel that the interval between the commandment to rebuild Jerusalem and the time of the Messiah would be 173,880 days. Note that the "start date" is not associated with the rebuilding of the temple—it is associated with the building of the "streets and a trench." It is interesting that the verse continues "but in times of distress." All of this is depicted in the book of Nehemiah where the rebuilding of Jerusalem is described— and as we saw, this was a time of distress.

So, when did this start date, this issuance of this decree, occur? We can pinpoint this precisely: March 14, 445 BC. This is when the commandment to restore and rebuild Jerusalem was given by the Persian king Artaxerxes (a son of King Xerxes—the king over Persia at the time of Esther). We mentioned this date and Artaxerxes in lesson 28.

Hundreds of years after Artaxerxes' decree, Jesus is born. But he is not presented as king until the last time he enters Jerusalem. Actually, the Gospel record shows Jesus going out of his way to avoid this designation. When the people try to make him a king, he withdraws. We see an example of this after Jesus' miraculous feeding the five thousand,

> When the people saw the sign that Jesus had performed, they began to say, "Truly this is the Prophet who is to come into the world."
>
> Then Jesus, realizing that they were about to come and make Him king by force, withdrew again to a mountain by Himself. (John 6:14, 15)

Jesus withdraws so that the people would not make him King. John uses the repeated phrase, "his hour had not yet come" (John 2:4 as an example). We see this phrase six times in John. But it is also mentioned a seventh time, only in the context that Jesus' hour had come.

In lesson 30, we read of a Messianic prophecy from Zechariah:

> Rejoice greatly, O Daughter of Zion!
>   Shout in triumph, O Daughter of Jerusalem!
> See, your King comes to you,
>   righteous and victorious,
> humble and riding on a donkey,
>   on a colt, the foal of a donkey. (Zechariah 9:9)

The King would enter Jerusalem riding on a donkey. It is this specific event where Jesus presents himself as King. The people recognize the significance of this and shout,

> "Blessed is the King who comes in the name of the Lord!" (Luke 19:38)

In hindsight, we can calculate when this occurred. Many put the date at **April 6, 32 AD.** If you do the calculations, correcting for leap years, the period between March 14, 445 BC (the decree) and April 6, 32 AD (Jesus triumphal entry into Jerusalem) totals 173,880 days *exactly*—to the very day! A caution, though. There are those skeptical of this accuracy and present arguments against this precise fulfilment.

But it doesn't matter.

Gabriel's words, recorded by Daniel hundreds of years before the Messiah's triumphal entry into Jerusalem, show a precision that is astonishing—even if we want to quibble over whether the prophecy was meant to give us the exact day of this event.

It is here, though, that we can now conclude our discussion of the magi from lesson 35. As we noted, and as Matthew tells us, around the time Jesus was born, "magi" appear from the "east" (Matthew 2).

The word "Magi" comes from a Latin word that is the translation of the Greek word *"magoi,"* which in turn comes from the transliteration of a Persian word that refers to a select set of priests. Since Daniel was placed in a position over the Magi, perhaps part of his teachings included the expectations concerning the Jewish Messiah. This could explain why, hundreds of years later, Magi from Persia (that is, from the east) travel to Jerusalem at that specific time period to seek the arrival of a specific person—the King of the Jews.

Let's continue our review:

> Then after the sixty-two weeks, the Messiah will be cut off and will have nothing.
>
> Then the people of the prince who is to come will destroy the city and the sanctuary. The end will come like a flood, and until the end there will be war; desolations have been decreed. (Daniel 9:26)

There appears to be a gap between the 69th week (verse 25) and the 70th week (verse 27). Clearly, the Messiah is to be killed ("will be cut off") and Jerusalem and the temple will be destroyed ("will destroy the city and the sanctuary"). Note what we read in Luke:

> As Jesus approached Jerusalem and saw the city, He wept over it and said, "If only you had known on this day what would bring you peace! But now it is hidden from your eyes. For the days will come upon you when your enemies will barricade you and surround you and hem you in on every side. They will level you to the ground—you and the children

within your walls. They will not leave one stone on another, because you did not recognize the time of your visitation from God." (Luke 19:41–44)

In 70 AD, prophecies from Daniel and Jesus are fulfilled as Roman soldiers ransack Jerusalem and destroy the temple. There is much that could be said here. For example, Jesus describes a destruction of the temple that is total:

"Truly I tell you, not one stone here will be left on another; every one will be thrown down." (Matthew 24:2)

This happened literally. Today, along its southwestern wall, tourists in Jerusalem can see some of the stones cast down from the temple mount. Why was the destruction so thorough? When the temple was set on fire, gold melted and ran down between the stones that had been used in the building of the temple. To get access to the gold, the Roman soldiers tore apart the stone structure, casting the stones down off the temple mount. Not one stone was left on another.

But note how the verse in Luke ends:

"They will not leave one stone on another, <u>because you did not recognize the time of your visitation from God.</u>" (Luke 19:44)

One reason for the destruction of the temple is that the people did not recognize Emmanuel—God's presence.

John begins his Gospel telling us about the arrival of the Messiah:

He was in the world, and though the world was made through Him, the world did not recognize Him. He came to His own, and His own did not receive Him. (John 1:10, 11)

The Jewish people did not recognize the time of their visitation from God. He came to them, but they did not know him. Instead of receiving him, they crucified him.

But note the phrase, "the time of your visitation from God." It is possible to see in these words that the people were held accountable as to when the Messiah would arrive as King. They would have known this from Daniel's prophecy.

Let's return to this prophecy. This brings us to the 70th week.

> Then the people of the prince who is to come will destroy the city and the sanctuary. The end will come like a flood, and until the end there will be war; desolations have been decreed. And he will confirm a covenant with many for one week, but in the middle of the week he will put an end to sacrifice and offering. And on the wing of the temple will come the abomination that causes desolation, until the decreed destruction is poured out upon him. (Daniel 9:26, 27)

The 70 AD destruction of Jerusalem is just a precursor to what will eventually occur. The 70th week depicts the time of the antichrist and the tribulation the Jews will experience (if you hold to a rapture of the Church before the tribulation, as I do, the Church does not experience this dreadful and terrible series of events).

Note what we learn concerning the antichrist:

... he will confirm a covenant with many for one week, but in the middle of the week he will put an end to sacrifice and offering. And on the wing of the temple will come the abomination that causes desolation, until the decreed destruction is poured out upon him.

The antichrist will "confirm a covenant with many" and this involves a period of seven years. But halfway through this period, he will put an end to sacrifices and offerings. And then, at the end of the seven years, he will face destruction.

All of this depicts the tribulation and the return of Christ. Much of this will be discussed in our next volume, as we discover what the Biblical Story teaches concerning future events up to and including where we, the redeemed, spend our eternity.

At present, we live in the time period between Daniel's 69th week and the 70th week. This is the period of the Church, or the "Church Age."

When will the Church Age end?

Paul tells us. But this must await volume 2 of our study.

From lesson 37: What do we learn about God?

- God reveals a progression of world empires: that of Babylon, the Medo-Persian empire, Greek rule, and then that of the Roman empire.
- It will be during the Roman empire that the Messiah comes. And it will be during the Church Age that the Messiah will return.
- The Messiah will die and will be cut off from the people, but after a delay and time of tribulation, he will return in glory.

theologian: See Albert McShane, "Links Between Joseph and Daniel", available at http://truthandtidings.com/2002/02/links-between-joseph-and-daniel/ accessed December 19, 2019.

Church: When I capitalize the word "Church," I am referring to the family of God—regardless of church (small "c") affiliation or denomination. While people may attend "church" or belong to a "church" and worship within a "church," the true Church is the family of God—those who are spiritually reborn. They are saved through the blood of Christ and are given spiritual rebirth through the power and presence of the Holy Spirit.

For further study: One key to understanding the book of Daniel is to recognize its structure. King Nebuchadnezzar experiences a significant dream, described in Daniel 2. A different dream occurs, but it references the same things. Only the symbolism changes. The following might be helpful:

Chapter 2: The original dream of a statue with various components:

Head of gold:	Babylonian Empire
Arms, chest of silver:	Medo-Persian Empire
Waist, hips of brass:	Grecian Empire
Legs of iron and feet of iron mixed with clay:	Roman Empire
Stone cut without hands:	Kingdom of God

Chapter 7: The same dream but with different symbols:

Lion:	Babylonian Empire
Bear:	Medo-Persian Empire
Leopard:	Grecian Empire
Beast:	Roman Empire
The "Son of man" and saints:	Kingdom of God

Chapter 8 focuses in on just two empires, the Medo-Persian and Greece. Medo-Persia is depicted as a two-horned ram (a reminder, the Medo-Persian empire was the consolidation of two smaller empires).

Chapter 9, as discussed above, discusses the "70 weeks" which provides a timeline for the various kingdoms.

Chapter 10 discusses Daniel's angelic visitor.

Chapter 11 focuses in on just two empires—what is happening between Greece and Rome. The emphasis is on two regional (versus world) powers: Syria and Egypt.

Chapter 12 focuses in on just two empires—the Roman empire and the Kingdom of God.

April 6, 32 AD: The detailed calculations concerning Daniel's prophecy and the arrival of the King can be found in Robert Anderson's, *The Coming Prince*, Hodder & Stoughton, London, 1894. Excerpts of this can be found via internet searches.

Paul tells us: For those interested, read Romans 9, 10, and 11 and pay close attention to Romans 11:25. This, though, does not replace the need to read volume 2.

38

Malachi and the Time Between the Testaments

Appendix B is a timeline summarizing the major events that occur in Israel from King Saul until the birth of Christ. As we have seen, Daniel's writing includes the fall of Babylon and the introduction of Persian rule, this occurring in 539 BC under Cyrus the Great. The next prophet we hear from, and the last prophet whose writings are contained in the Old Testament, is **Malachi**.

In looking at his writing, it is apparent that temple sacrifices are underway, which means this was written after the temple had been rebuilt, a milestone that occurred in 515 BC.

In Malachi 1:8, there is the term "governor." God tells the people through His messenger, that the offerings being presented in the temple are detestable, and asks, rhetorically, "Why not offer them to your governor!" The term used here and translated "governor" is a word used for a Persian position of authority. So, the writing probably occurs during Persian rule over Judea. Many place the writing around 400 to 440 BC.

We won't spend much time on Malachi, other than to note that he describes a people whose worship practices and dealings with others are corrupt. His portrayal matches the situation in Judea that confronted Nehemiah.

The words of God begin with the people questioning God's love:

> "I have loved you," says the LORD.
> But you ask, "How have You loved us?" (Malachi 1:2)

Worship practices are corrupt and actually dishonor God, who tells the people,

> "A son honors his father, and a servant his master. But if I am a father, where is My honor?" (Malachi 1:6)

Do they even remember who God is? God has to remind them,

> "I am a great King," says the LORD of Hosts, "and My name is to be feared among the nations." (Malachi 1:14)

In Malachi, we find six exchanges, or disputes, between God and His people. They follow a format where God states a problem associated with the corruption of the people. The people then question this or disagree with this. God, then, confronts them and has the last word. These exchanges can be summarized as follows:

1. Malachi begins with God telling His people that He still loves Israel despite their covenant failure. But the people question God's love.

   God reminds them of His love by comparing and contrasting His dealings with Jacob (Israel) versus Esau. God graciously chose Jacob from which to establish His covenant community, instead of Jacob's twin brother Esau, and the people of Edom, Esau's descendants.

2. The second temple has been built, but the people, including the priests, have defiled their worship practices and this new temple. The people question how this is the case.

    God responds by pointing out the unworthiness of the sacrifices they present within the temple, showing that the people are going through the motions but do not truly value or honor God.

3. In the third exchange, God accuses the men of disloyalty against Him (idolatry)—and disloyalty toward their wives. The men deny this.

    God exposes their idolatry and their practices of divorce. We also see, as was the case during the time of Nehemiah, the men are marrying foreign women and are adopting the pagan worship practices of these foreigners (see Nehemiah 13 as a comparison).

4. The people accuse God of neglect—of caring more for those who do evil than for His own people. Where is God's justice?

    God responds by promising a future messenger that will usher forth God's presence among the people:

    > "Behold, I will send My messenger, who will prepare the way before Me. Then the Lord whom you seek will suddenly come to His temple—the Messenger of the covenant, in whom you delight—see, He is coming," says the LORD of Hosts. (Malachi 3:1)

5. God tells the people to turn back to Him, and the people ask, "How?"

    God uses the example of tithing to show how the people have left Him in their selfishness. They are not meeting their financial obligations in support of the temple. One way to show their faithfulness and return to God is through **tithing**. If they do this, God will abundantly bless them.

6. The final dispute may ring true today. From God's perspective, the people complain that it is futile to serve Him. They are questioning what they get from this. From their perspective, it seems the evildoers are the ones that get ahead and prosper (see Malachi 3:14, 15).

God responds by reminding the people where all of this is headed:

> "For behold, the day is coming, burning like a furnace, when all the arrogant and every evildoer will be stubble; the day is coming when I will set them ablaze," says the LORD of Hosts. "Not a root or branch will be left to them."

> "But for you who fear My name, the sun of righteousness will rise with healing in its wings, and you will go out and leap like calves from the stall. Then you will trample the wicked, for they will be ashes under the soles of your feet on the day I am preparing," says the LORD of Hosts. (Malachi 4:1–3)

This "Day of the Lord" is approaching, and God tells His people:

> Behold, I will send you Elijah the prophet before the coming of the great and dreadful Day of the LORD. (Malachi 4:5)

As Malachi's writing ends, and as the Old Testament comes to a close, there is silence. Four centuries will pass before a baptizer named John will walk throughout the Judean wilderness and proclaim,

I am a voice of one calling in the wilderness, 'Make straight the way for the Lord.' (John 1:23)

He will be quoting Isaiah (Isaiah 40:3). He will also see Jesus approaching and announce,

Look, the Lamb of God, who takes away the sin of the world! (John 1:29)

From these last words from God's last prophet of the Old Testament, Israel's condition has remained unchanged. Despite all that Israel has been through, despite the kingdom being torn in two and ravished by pagan invaders, despite their return to the land and a new beginning—nothing has changed. Their unfaithfulness to God continues. Their hearts remain hardened.

But this will not always be the case.

A King will enter Jerusalem. His death will initiate a new covenant between God and all peoples who put their trust in this King.

All of the Old Testament points us to this King and prepares the way for him. We turn to volume 2 for his arrival.

From lesson 38: What we learn about God:

- There is a four-hundred-year period where the voice of God through His prophets falls silent.
- After this a new prophet appears, saying, "Look . . . the Lamb of God who takes away the sins of the world."

Malachi: We cannot be certain that "Malachi" is a name. In Hebrew, the word means "messenger." This writing may simply come from someone referred to as "messenger."

In our English translations, Malachi 1:1 reads,

> This is the burden of the word of the LORD to Israel through <u>Malachi</u>...

The Hebrew text was translated into the Greek around 270 BC (the "Septuagint"). In the Septuagint, translating the Greek into English, Malachi 1:1 reads,

> The burden of the word of the Lord to Israel by the hand of <u>his messenger</u>...

In other words, the Hebrew word for "messenger" is not treated as a name by the Septuagint, but as a description or title.

The Hebrew word "Malachi" is also found in Malachi 3:1, and here the English translation, and the Septuagint, both use the term "messenger" and not a person's name ("Behold, I will send My messenger, who will prepare the way before Me").

The Septuagint was widely used by the New Testament authors when quoting the Hebrew Scriptures and was used by Jesus. For those interested, the Septuagint is available online at websites such as www.ellopos.net.

For the book of Malachi as found in the Septuagint, see https://www.ellopos.net/elpenor/greek-texts/septuagint/chapter.asp?book=42&page=1

For purposes of this study, I use "Malachi" as the name of the author.

tithing: Tithing is an Old Testament practice to provide for the Levitical priesthood. In the New Testament, we are not called to tithe. There is no Levitical priesthood and the temple in Jerusalem no longer stands.

More importantly, the New Testament teaches that *all* that the Christian has belongs to God. We are stewards of what He has entrusted us with (see, for example, the parable of the talents—Matthew 25:14–30).

If we "give" God ten percent, we are really keeping for ourselves ninety percent of what is His. That, to me, sounds a bit greedy. A more thorough discussion on this topic is found in lesson 22 of *A Forty-Day Study of the Book of Hebrews: The Superiority of Christ.* The following comes from this work:

The New Testament does tell us about giving. 1ˢᵗ Corinthians 16:2 is instructive. Paul is writing to the believers in Corinth, discussing a collection to help their fellow brothers and sisters in Jerusalem.

> On the first day of every week, each of you should set aside a portion of his income, saving it up, so that when I come no collections will be needed.

This teaches us:

1. Giving is to be routine and periodic (*"on the first day of every week"*).
2. It is to be personal (*"each one of you…"*).
3. It is to be planned (*"…you should set aside…"*).
4. It should be proportionate (*"a sum of money in keeping with your income"*).

Note also 2ⁿᵈ Corinthians 8:11, 12:

Now finish the work, so that you may complete it just as eagerly as you began, according to your means. For if the eagerness is there, the gift is acceptable according to what one has, not according to what he does not have.

Before leaving this section on what belongs to God, note Malachi's words from God concerning His desire to have His people contribute to His kingdom:

"Test Me in this," says the LORD of Hosts. "See if I will not open the windows of heaven and pour out for you blessing without measure." (Malachi 3:10)

From personal experience, my wife and I have seen these words ring true in spades. We have tested God in our giving (our returning to Him what is His), and He has poured out blessings upon us without measure.

39

What We've Learned

We have almost reached the end of our journey—at least our journey through the Old Testament. Each lesson has ended with a small section listing key points on what we learn about God from that portion of the Bible being reviewed. Let's summarize this, and then add some of the conclusions we can draw from the Old Testament in general. This should provide a good overview of the lessons we've covered, plus get us ready for our journey through portions of the New Testament in volume 2.

What we learn about God:

- God has revealed Himself to us in a number of ways.
- The Bible is God's revealed word to us.
- The Bible is mostly God's story—not ours.
- God gave special powers and a special assignment to the Apostles of Jesus.
- God's revelation to us includes the Apostolic witness of who Jesus is. This is the Christian New Testament.
- God's creation is in rebellion against God, but God will provide His Anointed (the Messiah or Christ). From the New Testament, we learn that the Messiah is Jesus of Nazareth.

- From Psalm 2, we learn of three titles: Messiah (Christ), Son of God, and King (2:2, 5, 7). Concerning the Messiah, we also learn,
  - Political and religious leaders will conspire against him (2:1–3).
  - He will ask God for his inheritance (2:8).
  - He will have authority over all things (2:8, 9).
  - He will destroy those who do not honor him (2:12).
  - We are to seek refuge in him (2:12).
- God is the Creator. By implication:
  - God is all powerful
  - God is the Owner over His creation.
- God establishes the value system and makes the rules for His creation.
- What God has made is good. This places value in the world around us and in each one of us.
- God wants us to reflect who He is to each other and to the world around us.
- God gave Adam, and gives to us, instructions (commands).
- But God has also given us free will. Adam chose to disobey God and go against God's will. This disobedience brings death.
- Death is separation. Physical death is separation from the body. Spiritual death is separation from God.
- We also learn that Satan is an antagonist against God's created order, and Adam and Eve both became obedient to Satan.
- God affirms that Satan will be destroyed.
- God's plan of redemption and forgiveness will be through one born of a woman (the seed of woman of Genesis 3:15).
- Up to this point in the Story, though, we are told very little about him. We know he will defeat Satan, but this will involve his suffering and death.
- While we are told God will destroy Satan and Satan's "seed" through the offspring of woman, we see hints that man's predicament will be solved by God Himself coming to earth.

- God is a God who provides.
- God is a God of judgment and wrath.
- God is a God of mercy—not giving us the punishment that we deserve.
- But God is also a God of grace—giving us the blessings that we don't deserve.
- God enacts an unconditional covenant with a man named Abraham. Abraham has done nothing to merit God's favor. God chooses Abraham simply because God wanted to. This shows God's sovereign will.
- Through Abraham, God will establish a nation and all the nations on earth will be blessed. The Genesis 3:15 seed of woman will be a descendant of Abraham.
- God performs a covenant oath ceremony with Abraham. It significantly differs from what was normally done by the ancients, in that God declares He, Himself will guarantee the covenant and pay the price if the covenant is broken. He fulfills this promise at Calvary, the place of Jesus' crucifixion.
- God is a God who provides (we said this in the context of God providing the covering for Adam and Eve's nakedness). The Good News of God's story is that He will seek out his fallen image-bearers, and He will provide the pathway that will repair the four broken relationships associated with humankind's disobedience. God provides the way that opens His kingdom plans for humankind and allows us to return into His presence and to spend eternity with Him.
- In the story of Abraham's willingness to offer Isaac, we once again learn of "Jehovah Jireh" ("The LORD Will Provide"). Of course, the pinnacle of God's provision is the cross: God taking on the penalty we deserve to allow our forgiveness and reconciliation.
- As God orchestrates His plan of redemption, the descendants of Abraham become central to the Biblical Story. These are the Jewish people—the children of promise.

- God reveals that the Messiah will come from the line (tribe) of Judah, one of Jacob's sons.
- As we read about another of Jacob's sons, Joseph, we learn that God remains with His people, regardless of the circumstances.
- We also learn that "God works all things together for the good of those who love Him, who are called according to His purpose" (as we see in the Old Testament, and as Paul tells us in Romans 8:28 of the New Testament).
- God orchestrates historical events to accomplish His purposes and to fulfill His promises.
- In the story of Moses, we see God's commitment to His chosen people and His selection of Moses as the deliverer to bring salvation (freedom from Egyptian bondage and oppression).
- God tells Moses His name: I AM. Jesus will use this term to authenticate his Messiahship and Deity.
- There is only one God, yet throughout the history of humankind, people have worshipped other gods. This was true of the Egyptians at the time of Moses, and God uses a series of plagues to readily show the futility of worshipping anything or anyone other than God.
- The last plague at the time of Moses involves death. Salvation is offered to the Israelites and they can escape death by obeying God's instruction. This requires the placing of the blood of a lamb upon their doorposts. All of this prefigures the Lamb of God whose spilled blood offers salvation to those who trust him.
- God remains faithful to His people and His promises.
- Through Moses, God establishes a covenant with His chosen people and includes instructions as to how He wants them to live.
- We refer to this as the Mosaic Covenant, which includes the Ten Commandments and the rest of the Mosaic Law.

- The Mosaic Covenant is conditional and temporary. If the people obey, they will be blessed, if they disobey, they will be subject to a loss of blessings and punishment.
- The people enter the Promised Land. The victory in conquering the land is due to God—His sovereign will and His power—and not due to the people and their abilities (see Exodus 23:30, for example).
- God blesses the people when they uphold the covenant and obey His instructions, an example being their victory over Jericho. But His blessings are removed when they are disobedient, as seen in the initial defeat at Ai and the punishment given to Achan and his family.
- God expects obedience, but we can choose not to obey.
- God provides, but we must take possession of that which He is providing.
- After the time of Joshua, despite repeated cycles of disobedience, including the sin of idolatry and the worshipping of other gods, God delivers the people by raising up a series of judges (military leaders).
- There is a consistent theme in the Biblical Story of God providing salvation to His chosen people despite their on-going rebellion, unfaithfulness, and unworthiness.
- A review of two of God's provisions, the Law of Gleaning and the Law of Redemption, shows God's desire to provide for those in need.
- Jesus is our kinsman-redeemer, redeeming us and delivering us from the penalty of sin.
- God has a sovereign will and also a permissive will. He allows the people of Israel to reject Him and to go their own way in establishing their first king, an example of God's permissive will.
- But God will also intervene and do what is ultimately best for the people, God's sovereign will.
- God establishes a covenant with King David.
  - The Messiah will come from the line of David.

- The Messiah will reign with authority—and his rule will be unending.
    - The Messiah will be the Son of God.
- A righteous God cannot and will not let sin go unpunished.
- But God is a God of patience. During the time of the divided kingdom, ruler after ruler turns from the Mosaic Covenant and brings idolatry into the land, but God withholds His wrath.
- This has been said before: God is a God of grace—giving us the blessings that we do not deserve to get. And God is a God of mercy—holding back the punishment we do deserve to get.
- Throughout the Biblical Story, we see the repeated failure of God's chosen people—continually violating the first and greatest commandment as they worship pagan gods and engage in idolatry. But God is a God of patience.
- The forgiveness of one of Judah's most corrupt kings, Manasseh, provides a good example where we see God's grace and mercy.
- God warns the people on numerous occasions of their impending disaster unless they turn from their wicked ways.
- God uses the pagan nation of Assyria to punish Israel and Judah. But for a time, He spares Jerusalem.
- The punishment was deserved and predicted. It should not have come as a surprise.
- God's use of pagans to punish His people does not mean pagan nations escape God's wrath.
- Though we have only reviewed small sections of the Bible, we repeatedly see the accuracy of God's word. Foretold events (prophecy) become reality.
- We also see the conditions of the Mosaic Covenant played out. When the people obey God, they are blessed. When they disobey, the people face punishment. But we see examples of God's grace and mercy as he delays judgment and as he promises restoration.

- God speaks through prophets and prophetesses.
- Through His prophets, God points out the sins of the people. God also communicates His wishes. God's words are those of warning and future punishment as well as words of hope and encouragement.
- God's desire is that we seek Him.
- God will always protect a remnant and provide restoration.
- God works providentially by all means, including working through pagan rulers to bring about His greater purposes.
- Though the people doing God's work face obstacles, opposition, hostility, and even threats of annihilation, God never leaves them.
- God's glory, the Shekinah, appears in the wilderness tabernacle and Solomon's temple. But His glory does not appear in the second temple. This remains the case until the Light of the World—Jesus of Nazareth—appears in the temple during the feast of Tabernacles.
- The word of God is not just the words spoken by the prophets. The entire Bible is the word of God—and the Psalms, as part of the Bible, speak God's words.
- The Psalms contain additional revelations from God about Jesus—the Messiah, Son of God, and King. These include startling descriptions of Jesus' suffering and death, and also his glorification.
- God uses His word through the psalmists to encourage and to inform—and also to prepare the world for the Messiah.
- God's words through the prophet Isaiah include many references to the Messiah, who, among other titles, will be "Emmanuel"—God with us.
- Through Isaiah, we are given the announcement of his coming (Isaiah 40:3–5), his virgin birth (Isaiah 7:14), his ministry and proclamation of the good news (Isaiah 61:1, 2), his sacrificial death for our forgiveness (Isaiah 52:13–53:12), and his future return to establish his earthly kingdom (Isaiah 60:2, 3).

- Concerning God's plans for humankind's redemption, seven hundred years before Jesus of Nazareth died on the cross, through the prophet Isaiah God clearly explains why this will happen and what this will mean.
- Ezekiel's vision is that of God leaving the temple. But God does not abandon His people. He is with them throughout the exile and will bring them back into the land. A third vision shows God returning to a new temple.
- God must judge the sins of the people, but he remains faithful to His people—promising to return them to the land where they will prosper.
- Through the prophet Daniel, God reveals a progression of world empires: that of Babylon, the Medo-Persian empire, the Greek rule, and the final empire—the Roman empire.
- It will be during the Roman empire that the Messiah comes. The Messiah will die and will be cut off from the people. But after a delay and time of tribulation, he will return in glory.
- It will be during the church age that the Messiah will return.
- There is a four-hundred-year period where the voice of God through His prophets falls silent.
- After this a new prophet appears, saying, "Look, the Lamb of God who takes away the sins of the world."

As we have journeyed through the Biblical Story, we recognize the following:

1. The Old Testament is God's story.
2. The Old Testament shows us the prevalence of sin.
3. The Old Testament teaches that sin must be punished.
4. The Old Testament shows that it is God who makes the provisions for dealing with sin and the salvation of His people.

Let's briefly look at each of these.

1. The Old Testament is God's story.

   From the opening pages of the Bible, God reveals who He is. He is Creator. He is God and we are not. As our Creator, He knows what is best for us. He provides instructions and expectations. He does this for our benefit because he loves us.

   But we want to be our own gods and to decide for ourselves how we will go through life. We refuse God's Lordship. We replace God's value system with our own.

   We are plagued with continual sin and rebellion against God. The punishment for sin is death. Death is separation. Physical death is separation from the body; spiritual death is separation from God. All of us enter this world spiritually dead—and all must eventually face physical death.

   But God can bring us to new life. He has orchestrated His plan for our redemption. And that is the Biblical Story—all that God has done and continues to do to redeem humankind.

   God's mighty acts in history confirm His presence and reveal His plans. From the opening pages of the Bible, we learn of sin and rebellion, and a promised seed of woman that will destroy Satan and his followers. God's plan unfolds as we learn of God's selection and covenant with Abraham. Through Abraham's descendants all of the peoples of the world will be blessed. The story continues as God chooses Moses to deliver Abraham's descendants from Egyptian bondage and into the Promised Land. Through the Mosaic Law and God's covenant with Moses, we learn that God's chosen people will be blessed if they live up to God's requirements—but will be punished if they violate the covenant agreement.

Virtually all of the Old Testament from Genesis 12 on (up until Acts 2 of the New Testament) focuses on these chosen people of God. And all of the Old Testament prepares us for the arrival of the Messiah.

2. The Old Testament shows us the prevalence of sin.

In Ernest **Hemingway's** *The Sun Also Rises,* the character Mike Campbell is asked about his money troubles:

"How did you go bankrupt?"

"Two ways," Mike responds. "Gradually and then suddenly."

God's chosen people are spiritually bankrupt. This did not happen gradually, and then suddenly. The Old Testament shows this was continual. Throughout the recorded history of God's people, we see their repeated failures to be faithful to God and His covenants.

In their wilderness journey upon leaving Egypt, we witness repetitions where the Israelites do not place their trust in God. Throughout the period of the Judges, the Israelites continually show indifference to God and repeat a pattern of syncretism, corrupt worship, and injustice toward others. As that period ends, the people clamor for a king. But when given a king, their spiritual state does not change. Their idolatry and injustice continue—not just limited to the people but practiced by the kings themselves. This remains true throughout both the time of the monarchy as well as the period of the divided kingdom. The history of God's chosen people shows us the persistence and prevalence of sin. Sin is something that is ingrained.

No one is able to live up to the standards and requirements of the Mosaic Covenant.

3. The Old Testament teaches that sin must be punished.

   The people's sin must be punished and would be punished. This was the repeated message of the prophets—God's spokesmen. They continually point out the sins of the people and persistently warn of God's impending divine judgment— His approaching wrath. But these warnings fall on deaf ears.

   The conditional nature of the Mosaic covenant meant that the people would be blessed if they kept its requirements— but would suffer punishment should they fail to do so. Time after time we witness God's patience. We see He is both a God of grace, giving the people the good things that they don't deserve, and a God of mercy, holding off his righteous judgment.

   History shows how God's chosen people failed repeatedly to obey the covenant, resulting in God's eventual punishment of Israel. The nation becomes divided. The Assyrians conquer the Northern Kingdom and much of the Southern Kingdom. While Jerusalem escapes the Assyrians, the people's sinfulness continues, resulting in the complete destruction of Jerusalem through famine, plague, and sword. The temple suffers destruction as well.

4. But the Old Testament points us toward a savior who will accept our sin and be punished in our place.

   - Humankind is incapable of living up to God's instructions. And God, in His grace and mercy, knows He will provide the solution. In the Bible's earliest pages, we learn that Satan will eventually be destroyed through the seed of woman—but the Redeemer will suffer and die (Genesis 3:15).

- We saw this in Deuteronomy 18:15. Moses predicts an eventual Greater Prophet—we are to listen to him.
- We reviewed Psalm 2 and other Messianic Psalms pointing toward the Messiah. They describe what he will be like and what he will do. He will be God's Messiah, the King, and the Son of God.
- Through Isaiah we learn that he will also be Emmanuel— God with us. The One who is to come will also be called Wonderful Counselor, Mighty God, Everlasting Father, and Prince of Peace.
- And our review included looking at Isaiah 53, a description of what the Messiah, as Suffering Servant, will endure and why he accepts this affliction and death. God lays the sins of the people upon His Suffering Servant, who takes on the punishment we deserve.

The Old Testament is all about Jesus and prepares us for Jesus.

The Old Testament shows us God's people cannot keep the Mosaic Covenant. It is not the covenant that is flawed. It is the people. The prophet Jeremiah spent forty years warning the people of God's impending judgment of Jerusalem. He predicted that their exile would last seventy years. And he also foresaw a new covenant.

> "Behold, the days are coming, declares the LORD,
>   when I will make a new covenant
> with the house of Israel
>   and with the house of Judah.
> It will not be like the covenant
>   I made with their fathers
> when I took them by the hand
>   to lead them out of the land of Egypt—
> a covenant they broke,
>   though I was a husband to them,"
>   declares the LORD.

"But this is the covenant I will make with the house of Israel
    after those days, declares the LORD.
I will put My law in their minds
    and inscribe it on their hearts.
And I will be their God,
    and they will be My people.
No longer will each man teach his neighbor or his brother,
    saying, 'Know the LORD,'
because they will all know Me,
    from the least of them to the greatest, declares
    the LORD.
For I will forgive their iniquities
    and will remember their sins no more." (Jeremiah
    31:31–34)

The new covenant will involve the forgiveness of sins.

The prophet Ezekiel had visions of God leaving the temple. But he also foresaw a time when God would return to Jerusalem, and a time of a new covenant between God and His people:

> I will give you a new heart and put a new spirit within
> you; I will remove your heart of stone and give you
> a heart of flesh. And I will put My Spirit within you
> and cause you to walk in My statutes and to carefully
> observe My ordinances. (Ezekiel 36:26, 27)

The New Covenant will involve transformed hearts.

Forgiveness of sins and transformed hearts do not happen because of the people, or their strength, or their desires—or anything to do with what they want to do, hope to do, or promise to do. This is something that God does. The forgiveness of sins required the cross. God transforms hearts by putting His Spirit within those chosen for participation in His kingdom.

Jesus came to fulfill the Law of Moses. And he came to die. And at the Last Supper before his death, Jesus turns to his disciples and says,

> "This cup is the new covenant in My blood, which is poured out for you." (Luke 22:20)

Jesus—the Messiah, King, and Son of God—inaugurates the New Covenant.

The New Testament is the New Covenant, the focus of our next volume.

Hemingway: Ernest Hemingway, *The Sun Also Rises* (New York: Charles Scribner's Sons, 1954), 136.

40

A Message

We have come to the completion of our review of the Old Testament. What on earth are we going to do about all of this?

Can we truly believe that the Bible is the word of God?

It seems reasonable, and rational, that the universe didn't just magically appear. Scientific discoveries have confirmed that the universe had a beginning. We are compelled to ask: What, or better yet, *who* caused the universe to come about?

Einstein recognized that not only all matter had a beginning, time itself, had a beginning.

This suggests the "who" that created all of this is both immaterial and outside of time. We call the immaterial "spirit"—this Creator must be spirit. And we call entities outside the dimension of time as being eternally existent. The Creator must be eternal.

Of course, whoever did this must also be all powerful (omnipotent) and all knowing (omniscient).

All of these traits reflect the God of the Bible.

But let's continue.

If the entity that caused this to happen created us, shouldn't we assume He created us for a reason? And wouldn't He want to communicate with us and teach us something about who He is and what the purpose for His creation is (I'll use the pronoun "He" to refer to this Creator)?

If we look at events in history, don't we see a very unusual and special importance involving a man named Abraham and a group of people called the Jews? Why do we see this? What, or perhaps a better question would be, who made Abraham so special? And why?

We find out about Abraham through the words of the Bible and the events surrounding Abraham and his descendants. Doesn't this suggest the Bible, and this history, is one way the Creator has communicated with His creation? Why else would these words have been written down and exquisitely preserved century after century?

And some of the Jewish writers provide numerous details of events long before the events actually happen. How could mere humans do this? Doesn't the prophetic word coming true help authenticate the divine nature of what these people have written down?

All of this suggests the God of the Bible is the Creator. And it also suggests the Bible is God's Word to us.

And it is reasonable to assume that the Creator made all that there is, including you and me, having both a plan and a purpose.

So, what is God telling us?

Scripture, God's Word, is clear. We are to know about God and to live according to His desires and plans for us. We are to honor God properly in our worship of Him and in our dealings with others. The

Bible tells us we were created in God's image—and we are to reflect who He is as we go through life and as we relate to those around us.

But our rebellion against God is also clear. Each one of us is spiritually dead and, barring the rapture, we will all face physical death. The Old Testament clearly shows that sin must be punished. Israel's destruction by the Assyrians and Babylonians are historic fact. All sin requires punishment.

The Bible teaches that Satan, and sin, will eventually be conquered by the seed of woman—the Messiah, Son of God, and King.

Isaiah tells us our sins will be placed upon this Anointed One of God—and it is this Son of God who will accept the punishment we deserve.

The Psalmist tells us we are to seek refuge in the Messiah. The New Testament is going to tell us the only way for the forgiveness of our sins—the *only* way—is by accepting Jesus, God's Messiah, and the blood sacrifice he made on the cross.

If you have placed your faith in Jesus, you have escaped God's wrath. This word "faith" includes the elements of belief, trust, and obedience.

Those accepting what Christ has done on the cross and his resurrection do not and cannot face condemnation (Roman 8:1). They stand innocent before God with all sins forgiven—not because of what they have done, or will do, or promise to do, but because of what God has done. In God's eyes, the person placing their trust in the blood of Christ is without sin or blemish (Romans 3:22, 23).

But perhaps you are reading this, and, for you there is no God. Maybe you know a bit more about the Bible and about the historic Jesus, but from your perspective, Jesus is simply a moral man and a great teacher. Maybe you believe there is no such thing as hell or the concept of punishment from God.

God allows this.

This is His permissive will.

You can certainly hold to these beliefs. But regardless of their presence or how strong they might be, these beliefs are not relevant. If there is a God, and I believe the facts for this are indisputable, and if He has communicated with us, and I believe the facts for this are also indisputable, and if He has made provisions for an eternity with Him, and I believe the facts for this, too, are indisputable, then we should listen to Him. We should seek Him.

If you continue this study with volume 2, you will learn that, while we may not seek God, God seeks us. He loves us. He loves us so much that He died for us. And not only does He seek us, He finds us. And when He reaches out to us, He takes those who are spiritually dead and awakens them through the power and presence of the Holy Spirit.

Is God seeking you?

Right now?

Is He calling you to become part of His family and become a participant in the plans He has for His eternal kingdom?

If God is reaching out to you, you might be asking, "What do I do about it?"

It is here that I could share a short prayer. Or I could send you to the internet. You can discover quite a number of relevant prayers if you Google something along the lines of "The Sinner's Prayer," or words that are similar. There are an abundance of prayers, carefully structured and expertly written.

But Googling a prayer and selecting one from various options is a bit mechanical.

You can do this if you'd like.

But approaching God does not have to be that complicated, and none other than Jesus, himself, provides an excellent example on how to approach God.

Jesus tells the story of a very religious man belonging to a group of highly religious people in Judea. They were called the Pharisees. Pharisees were experts when it came to God's laws and instructions. They were very proud of how religious they were. In Jesus' story, a Pharisee goes to the temple and prays to God. He recites how pleasing he must be in God's eyes because of his good behavior.

But, standing apart from the Pharisee is a sinful man whose occupation is that of collecting taxes. Tax collectors in Jesus' day and in that part of the world were despised. Most collected taxes for Judea's enemy— Rome. And many, if not most, overcharged the people and pocketed some of the collected taxes for themselves.

This tax collector, off in a corner and too guilty to raise his eyes toward heaven, quietly speaks to God. He utters just five words in the Greek. We translate these:

"God, have mercy upon me, a sinner." (Luke 18:13)

This man presents himself to God—with an exceedingly short prayer. He recognizes he is a sinner, and that all he can rely upon is God's mercy.

And God hears this simple prayer. God fully forgives this sinful man.

How do we know this?

Because that's what Jesus tells us:

> "I tell you, this man, rather than the Pharisee, went home justified." (Luke 18:14)

To be "justified" means one's sins have been forgiven. To be "justified" means to be declared "not guilty" by God. In telling us that this man went home justified, Jesus is affirming that this man has been forgiven. No man can come to the Father except through Jesus—so if Jesus tells us this man is not guilty before God, I'm willing to take Jesus at his word.

Won't you take Jesus at his word?

Will you humbly come to God and ask for His mercy?

Admit that you are a sinner and desire God's justification—the desire to be declared not guilty. Seek God's mercy. Only God has the power to forgive your sins, because your sins are against God. And only God has paid the required price for those sins. He has taken upon Himself the punishment for your sins.

Place your trust in the blood of Christ and what he has done for you.

If God is seeking you, the prayer I'd recommend is,

> *"God, have mercy upon me, a sinner."*

If you have uttered this simple petition to God in a heartfelt way, I rejoice as you have entered into the family of God. You are now a participant in God's kingdom. He has wonderful plans for you.

May God bless you richly.

I look forward to continuing our journey together in volume 2.

APPENDIX A

Group Bible Study

The format of this series of lessons on the Biblical Story facilitates its use for group Bible study. If your group meets weekly, it is recommended that you cover this material in eight weeks. Have those in your group do five lessons each week on their own—and then, as you meet together, discuss the content covered by these lessons.

As you meet, the following are suggested activities and questions for discussion. For those familiar with learning methods, these follow Bloom's taxonomy. The easiest questions are the ones labeled "remembering." The "highest" level of this method involves the category "creating." I have found the "creating" assignments to require much more time and effort than what can be handled during a normal Bible study. Accordingly, I assign these as "special projects" for those interested and wanting to meet separately to do these or wanting to spend additional time on these. They can then report their results back to the group.

There are several ways to handle these activities and discussion questions.

- One method is to simply go down the list together and do the activities or discuss the questions as a group.

- Depending upon the size of your Bible study group, another method is to have different individuals or pairs of individuals select which of the categories they want to work on. Allow ten minutes for this activity. Regather and have each share what they have come up with—with the entire gathering discussing what gets presented.
- If possible, alternate between the two suggested methods above.

Session 1: Lessons 1-5

- **Remembering:**

  Fill in the blanks: God is God and _____.

- **Understanding:**

  How did Satan reverse God's desired order?

- **Applying:**

  Adam and Eve lost sight of all they had been given and focused on the one thing that was forbidden. How are we like that? Why do you think this is the case?

- **Analyzing:**

  How did Satan try to make God out to be unreasonable and unfair? Why do you think he took this approach?

- **Evaluating:**

  Is God's value system better than ours? Why or why not? Do we rely upon God's value system? Why or why not? Provide examples.

- **Creating:**

  List some of the ways we try to become our own God. Why do you think each of us wants to be our own God? Is this a good thing or a bad thing, or both? Why?

Session 2: Lessons 6-10

- **Remembering:**

  What are the four broken relationships that occur due to Adam and Eve's sin?

- **Understanding:**

  What are the key lessons we learn from Genesis 3:15?

- **Applying:**

  What are the implications to you, today, of the Abrahamic Covenant (God's covenant with Abraham)?

- **Analyzing:**

  According to the author, what is the difference between Christianity and religion? Give examples.

- **Evaluating:**

  What are the implications of Satan being the prince of this world? Include in your discussion 1st John 4:4.

- **Creating:**

  In what ways can a Christian be a "minister of reconciliation"? Put this into the context of the four broken relationships.

Session 3: Lessons 11-15

- **Remembering:**

  What is the name of God from God's discourse with Moses (the burning bush)?

- **Understanding:**

  John records Jesus' frequent use of the "I AM"? Why did Jesus do this? Why do you think these became a key part of John's focus in writing his Gospel? Put this into context of John 20:30, 31.

- **Analyzing:**

  What might some of the reasons be for anti-Semitism?

- **Evaluating:**

  What are at least three reasons God might have had when He tells Abraham to sacrifice Isaac?

- **Creating:**

  One key lesson of Abraham's willingness to sacrifice Isaac is the truth that "God will provide" (Jehovah-Jireh). Later we'll learn in detail why and how this is true regarding our salvation. But for now, what do you think the benefits are concerning God as the instrument of provision versus humankind?

Session 4: Lessons 16-20

- **Remembering:**

  What biblical books make up the Pentateuch (in order)?

- **Understanding:**

  What are four things we learn about Christ from God's covenant with David? Why is it important for this to be an unconditional covenant?

- **Applying:**

  Ruth is in the lineage of David and Christ. Would you want a person of Ruth's character in your lineage? What are some of the traits that shape your answer?

- **Analyzing:**

  The entire Israelite community was held accountable for the sins of Achan. Is that fair? Why or why not? Put this into the context of the Mosaic Covenant and the sovereignty of God.

- **Evaluating:**

  When we read the story of God's chosen people, the authors continually point out the sins and unfaithfulness of the people. Why do you think they do this? Why not show the people in the most favorable light?

- **Creating:**

  Deuteronomy 18:15 is discussed in lesson 16, which provides a partial list of how Jesus is greater than Moses. See if you can add to this list (one of my classes came up with a list of 21 comparisons).

Session 5: Lessons 21-25

- **Remembering:**

  What terms are used for the two kingdoms that result when the nation of Israel splits into two?

- **Understanding:**

  Why do you think King Hezekiah showed the visitors from Babylon his personal wealth and that of the temple? What does this teach us about human nature?

- **Applying:**

  Is there idolatry in America today? Discuss this from the perspective of the first two commandments.

- **Analyzing:**

  Discuss what you know about the period of the divided kingdom (also from the perspective of the first two commandments).

- **Evaluating:**

  Which do you think is more evil, the Israelites during the period of the divided kingdom, or America today? Explain.

- **Creating:**

  The Bible teaches those whom God loves, He disciplines (Revelation 3:19). Read all of that passage (Revelation 3:14-22).

In what ways is today's America like the church of Laodicea? Do you think our country should expect God's discipline? Why or why not?

Session 6: Lessons 26-30

- **Remembering:**

  What is the difference between "minor prophet" and "major prophet"?

- **Understanding:**

  In what ways is every Christian a prophet? Note: a *prophet* brings God's word to the people, a *priest* represents the people before God and offers sacrifices to God. You might add to this question, in what ways is every Christian considered a priest? Bring in Romans 12:1 as part of the discussion.

- **Applying:**

  In the Old Testament, God's people are continually warned through prophets. Do you think God provide warnings today? If so, are the warnings heeded? Why or why not?

- **Analyzing:**

  What is the sign of Jonah? Read Matthew 12, with a focus on verses 38-42, and explain the importance of this sign.

- **Evaluating:**

  Nowhere in the book of Esther is God mentioned. Why, then, is it included in the Hebrew Scriptures (our Old Testament)?

- **Creating:**

    Up to this point in our lessons, we've been reviewing some of the minor prophets. Read Hebrews 1:1, 2. Discuss what this implies.

Session 7: Lessons 31-35

- **Remembering:**

    What chapter(s) in Isaiah describes "the Suffering Servant"?

- **Understanding:**

    Briefly explain the curse God places upon Jeconiah and how it is fulfilled.

- **Applying:**

    Why do you think the people choose to listen to the false prophets instead of God's spokesmen like Jeremiah? Do we have "false prophets" in the church today? Explain.

- **Analyzing:**

    Jerusalem was demolished. The temple was destroyed. Do you think this was "fair" on the part of God? Why or why not? How do you think Marcion would have viewed this?

- **Evaluating:**

    What are your thoughts concerning whether or not Jesus will still have the scars associated with his death when he returns? Provide reasons for your answer.

- **Creating:**

  Go through Isaiah 52:13 – 53:12, but instead of analyzing the text from the perspective of it being a description of the Messiah, analyze it from the perspective of the text describing Israel. Thoughts? Where are some of the weaknesses of this approach (or conversely, the strengths when one views this as referring to the Messiah)?

Session 8: Lessons 36-40

- **Remembering:**

  Recite Ezekiel's three visions concerning where God is.

- **Understanding:**

  The people return to the devastated land for a new start—but the sins that led to the devastation continue. Why do you think this is the case?

- **Applying:**

  John in his Gospel tells us that Jesus came to his own, but they didn't recognize him. Why do people today fail to recognize who Jesus is? Do you think it is due to ignorance? Apathy? Is this intentional? Explain

- **Analyzing:**

  In the list "What we learn about God" (lesson 39), what do you think are the five most important items in this list? Discuss.

- **Evaluating:**

  What are the implications of Jesus telling the people that he is the light of the world—but also telling his followers that they are the light of the world? Put this in the context of John 15:1–8.

- **Creating:**

  From where we are in our study of the Bible, why do you think the New Covenant must include the presence of God's Spirit within the individual, and God's total forgiveness of sins? Compare this with the Mosaic Covenant and the history of God's people.

APPENDIX B

Biblical Timeline

(some dates are approximate)

1046 BC   Saul becomes king of Israel, as the tribes are united against common enemies such as the Ammonites, Moabites, Amalekites, and the Philistines.

1010 BC   David becomes king and will reign over a united Israel until 960 BC.

930 BC   After the reign of David's son, Solomon, the monarchy is split into two.

~780 BC   Amos begins his prophecies concerning the Northern Kingdom. Sometime during this period Jonah is sent to warn the Assyrians concerning their need for repentance.

~750 BC   Hosea begins his prophecies concerning the Northern Kingdom.

740 BC   Assyria begins invading the Northern Kingdom. Israelites begin to be deported, but also Assyrians begin to migrate into the land and intermarry (2nd Kings 17:5, 6).

Around this time Isaiah begins his prophecies. Micah begins his prophecies. Both foresee the destruction of Samaria and the eventual destruction of Jerusalem.

722 BC   Samaria, the capital of the Northern Kingdom (Israel), is taken by Assyria under Sargon II. This was after a three-year siege started by Shalmaneser V. The Assyrians are the world power from 880 BC until 612 BC.

705 BC   Sargon dies in battle.

703 BC   Sargon's death provides the opportunity for states under Assyrian domination to revolt, including Judah (2nd Kings 18:7).

701 BC   The fortified cities of the Southern Kingdom (Judah) are attacked by the Assyrian king Sennacherib. Judah is a vassal of Assyria during this time, paying annual tributes to the Assyrian king.

626 BC   Jeremiah begins his long prophetic ministry. He was born in 650 BC and dies in 570 BC. He lives to see the destruction of Jerusalem and dies in Egypt.

612 BC   In the 620s, Assyria undergoes a series of civil wars which weaken their empire. Finally, the Assyrian capital of Nineveh falls to the Babylonians (foretold by the prophet Nahum). Note: the actual fall of Nineveh was orchestrated by the Medes, who had formed an alliance with Babylon.

605 BC   The Egyptians, along with a small number of remaining Assyrian soldiers, are defeated (Battle of Carchemish) and Judah is invaded by Nebuchadnezzar, king of Babylon. Daniel is taken to Babylon.

601 BC	Jehoiakim, king of Judah who had previously allied the Southern Kingdom with Egypt, revolts against Babylon.
598-7 BC	Nebuchadnezzar lays siege on Jerusalem. Jehoiakim is killed and is succeeded by his son, Jehoiachin (also called Jeconiah). When Jerusalem falls, Jeconiah and officials within his administration, along with prominent citizens of Jerusalem, are taken to Babylon. The prophet Ezekiel is among those exiled.
	To replace Jeconiah, Nebuchadnezzar appoints Jeconiah's uncle, Zedekiah, as king. Jeremiah warns Zedekiah not to go against the Babylonians—that what Jerusalem has suffered was God's rightful punishment.
589 BC	Zedekiah forms an alliance with Egypt—resulting in a second attack on Jerusalem by Nebuchadnezzar. This leads to Jerusalem's complete destruction. Zedekiah is blinded and taken to Babylon, where he remains until his death. Zedekiah would be Israel's last king.
539 BC	The Persian king Cyrus captures Babylon.
538 BC	Cyrus authorizes Jews from Babylon to rebuild the temple.
520 BC	The prophets Haggai and Zechariah encourage the people of Jerusalem concerning the building of the temple.
516 BC	The returned exiles under the leadership of their governor, Zerubbabel, finish the temple. King Darius of Persia is in power.
483 BC	Events in Persia associated with Esther (the book covers a ten-year period).

458 BC   The community in Jerusalem is strengthened, both
           in numbers and also spiritually, with the arrival of
           the priest Ezra and several thousand more Jews from
           Babylon. The king of Persia, Artaxerxes encourages Ezra
           to reconstitute temple worship and the following of the
           Mosaic law (Ezra 7:17, 25, 26).

445-4 BC   Artaxerxes (this same Persian king) permits his cupbearer,
           Nehemiah, to return to Jerusalem to rebuild its walls
           (Nehemiah 6:15). Nehemiah becomes the new governor
           and introduces reforms to help the poor (Nehemiah
           5:2-13). He admonishes the people to discontinue the
           practice of mixed marriages, to keep the Sabbath, and
           to meet their tithing obligations (Nehemiah 10:30-39).

433 BC   Nehemiah returns to the service of the Persian king.
           Later he once again returns to Jerusalem, only to find
           that the Sabbath was being broken, tithes were ignored,
           priests had become corrupt, and there was widespread
           intermarriage with foreigners (Nehemiah 3:7-31).

334 BC   Alexander the Great begins his conquest of Persia, as
           Greece becomes the world power.

323 BC   Alexander the Great dies, and four generals divide
           the territory under Grecian control and establish their
           rulership. One of the kings is Seleucus I—who establishes
           the Seleucid empire (312 BC – 64 BC). The Seleucids rule
           Judea and are associated with Syria.

167 BC   The Seleucid king, Antiochus IV desecrates the temple
           in Jerusalem. This leads to the Maccabean revolt, which
           lasts for seven years.

146 BC	The Grecian empire comes to an end through the defeat at the Battle of Corinth by Rome. During this time period the Hasmoneans rule Judea semi-autonomously from the Seleucids. The Hasmoneans (also spelled Hasmonaeans) are descendants of the Maccabean family.
64 BC	Rome wrests control of Judea from Syria.
37 BC	Herod is appointed as king of Judea.
6 - 1 BC	Sometime between 6 BC and 1 BC Jesus is born. Many scholars place the birth at 3 BC or 2 BC.

INDEX OF SCRIPTURE

CPSIA information can be obtained
at www.ICGtesting.com
Printed in the USA
BVHW080959060820
585686BV00001B/7